THE COMMON THINGS:
ESSAYS ON THOMISM AND EDUCATION

American Maritain Association Publications

General Editor: Anthony O. Simon

Jacques Maritain: The Man and His Metaphysics
Edited by John F.X. Knasas, 1988
★ ISBN 0-268-01205-9 (out of print)

Freedom in the Modern World: Jacques Maritain, Yves R. Simon, Mortimer J. Adler
Edited by Michael D. Torre, 1989, Second Printing 1990
★ ISBN 0-268-00978-3

From Twilight to Dawn: The Cultural Vision of Jacques Maritain
Edited by Peter A. Redpath, 1990
★ ISBN 0-268-00979-1

The Future of Thomism
Edited by Deal W. Hudson and Dennis Wm. Moran, 1992
★ ISBN 0-268-00986-4

Jacques Maritain and the Jews
Edited by Robert Royal, 1994
★ ISBN 0-268-01193-1

Freedom, Virtue, and the Common Good
Edited by Curtis L. Hancock and Anthony O. Simon, 1995
★ ISBN 0-268-00991-0

Postmodernism and Christian Philosophy
Edited by Roman T. Ciapolo, 1997
◆ ISBN 0-8132-0881-5

The Common Things: Essays on Thomism and Education
Edited by Daniel McInerny, 1999
◆ ISBN 0-9669226-0-3

The Failure of Modernism: The Cartesian Legacy and Contemporary Pluralism
Edited by Brendan Sweetman, 1999
◆ ISBN 0-9669226-1-1

★ Distributed by the University of Notre Dame Press
◆ Distributed by The Catholic University of America Press

THE COMMON THINGS: ESSAYS ON THOMISM AND EDUCATION

Edited by

Daniel McInerny

With an Introduction by

Benedict M. Ashley, O.P.

American Maritain Association

Library of Congress Cataloging-in-Publication Data

The common things : essays on Thomism and education / edited by Daniel
McInerny : with an introduction by Benedict M. Ashley.
     p. cm.—(American Maritain Association publications)
    Includes bibliographical references and index.
    ISBN 0-9669226-0-3
    1. Thomas, Aquinas, Saint. 1225?–1274. 2. Maritain, Jacques,
1882–1973. 3. Education—Philosophy. 4. Education, Higher—
Philosophy. 5. Catholic universities and colleges—Philosophy.
I. McInerny, Daniel. II. Series.
LB125.T52C66   1999
370′.1—dc21   99-18576
                                             CIP

Manufactured in the
United States of America

American Maritain Association
Anthony O. Simon, Secretary
508 Travers Circle
Mishawaka, Indiana 46545

Distributed by The Catholic University of America Press
Washington, D.C. 20064

Contents

The Private Life of the Modern Academy

Manifesting the Common

Political Aspects

Editor's Note

τοῦ λόγου δ ἐόντος ξυνοῦ ζώουσιν οἱ πολλοὶ ὡς ἰδίαν ἔχοντες
φρόνησιν.

—Heraclitus

It would be more than generous today, after the manner of Jacques Maritain in 1943, to characterize education as at a crossroads. In the fifty-five years since Maritain published his Yale University Terry Lectures as *Education at the Crossroads*, the better part of educational institutions at all levels, both in the United States and abroad, has clearly made its choice of roads to take. That road, to put it quite bluntly, leads away from truth and toward the privacies of custom, technique and contingent desire. It leads away from the common things available to human beings simply insofar as they are human.

The essays in this volume were inspired by reflection upon the positive nature of Maritain's contributions to the philosophy of education, and so at least in that regard, if not always in a more explicit commitment, they represent a further Thomistic contribution to the modern debate on education at all levels, public and private, but with an emphasis on post-secondary education and Catholic higher education in particular. In a rich variety of ways these essays not only point the way back to the crossroads; they go on to indicate something of the landscape along the road not taken by contemporary education.

The essays are arranged in three sections. The essays in the first section, "The Private Life of the Modern Academy," constitute a trenchant critique of the contemporary malaise in education, while those in the second section, "Manifesting the Common," provide various perspectives on what the alternative to the current situation might look like. The volume closes with a section entitled, "Political Aspects," a group of essays which expand the discussion to include broader political, even global concerns. There is no better way to introduce the reader more fully to the themes of the volume than to direct him to Fr. Benedict Ashley's inspired introduction, which not only makes for an excellent introduction to the specific essays in the volume, but also serves as a masterful introduction to educational theory from a Thomistic point of view. I would like to thank Fr. Ashley for so graciously responding to the invitation to write this introduction.

I would also like to thank the Executive Committee of the American Maritain Association for inviting me to edit this volume, and a trio of past editors, Anthony O. Simon, Curtis L. Hancock, and Roman Ciapolo, who lent me their good counsel. In addition, I would like to thank the Jacques Maritain Center at the University of Notre Dame, and the St. Gerard Foundation, for their material assistance in the production of this volume. The Department of Philosophy at the University of St. Thomas, Houston, and the Center for Thomistic Studies, also provided me with many forms of assistance and encouragement during the preparation of the volume. Also deserving of special thanks is Miss Dolores Daly who created the artwork for the cover, Miss Sarah Houser who provided indispensable editorial help of various kinds, and Miss Maribel Lopez who aided me in the early stages of the project as part of the University of St. Thomas Faculty-Student Research Program. Many heartfelt thanks, too, go out to my wife Amy, who helped me all along the way but most of all during the final sprint of proofreading and revisions.

Not least, of course, I would like to thank the contributors for their important and stimulating work in helping bring Aquinas to the fore of the contemporary debate on education.

Introduction

Benedict M. Ashley, O.P.

In my sophomore and junior years at the University of Chicago, 1934–36, I participated in the Great Books Seminar led by the President of the University, Robert Maynard Hutchins, and by Mortimer J. Adler.[1] What brought me there was Adler's shocking public lecture, "Have There Been Any New Ideas In Modern Times?" Just to ask so heretical a question opened the door for me to the Catholic faith. Not long after, Hutchins invited Jacques Maritain to campus and I began to see how new, ever new, is the Christian wisdom of St. Thomas Aquinas. Now I, for over 50 years a member of the same Order of Preachers in which Aquinas lived and taught, still think of Thomas as my brother and myself as his awe-struck student.

Hutchins and Adler hoped to reform American higher education which they considered corrupted by over specialization, scientism, and the pragmatic instrumentalism of John Dewey. The essays in this volume make clear that Hutchins and Adler did not check the fatal progress of modernity in our schools into the irrationalism of post-modernity.[2] For Catholic schools, also, this has meant a secularization which is erasing their *raison d'etre*.

Yet the hopes of Hutchins and Adler, noble as they were, were not grounded, as were Maritain's, in the Good News of the Gospel, which not only says to us, "Be perfect,"[3] but promises that,

---

[1] See William H. McNeill, *Hutchins' University: A Memoir of the University of Chicago 1929–1950* (Chicago: University of Chicago Press, 1991) for an account of this fascinating chapter in the history of American education. McNeill and I were classmates and fraternity brothers.

[2] On this see John Deely, *"Quid Sit Postmodernismus?"* in Roman T. Ciapolo, ed., *Postmodernism and Christian Philosophy* (American Maritain Association, 1997), pp. 68–96,

[3] Matthew 5:48.

> Everyone who listens to these words of mine and acts on them will be
> like a wise man who built his house on rock. The rain fell, the floods
> came, and the winds blew and buffeted the house. But it did not col-
> lapse, it had been set solidly on rock.[4]

Because the Gospel wisdom on human perfection and the powers of grace
and nature by which virtue and wisdom can alone be attained are rock
solid, Catholic education, whether in a university or outside it, has survived
and will survive every deluge of irrationality.

Viewing the rainbow in the skies of the Third Millenium of the Gospel,
it is essential to remain hopeful, as Pope John Paul II has encouraged us,[5]
because the self-deconstruction of Enlightenment modernity concurs with
the opening up, for the first time since Babel, of the entire globe and the
whole human race to free communication.

Several of the essays in this volume join with Allan Bloom's lament in
his *The Closing of the American Mind*[6] over the ways multiculturalism is
used to justify the trashing of our "western heritage." Only an ignorance of
the classical texts, and above all of the Scriptures of Judaism and Christianity can lead us to think of these religions as merely "western" or of the
western culture derived from them and the Greeks as tightly closed to
world cultures. There has always been an osmotic intercommunication between the great cultures, between Greece, Egypt, and India for example. In
the Third Millenium this will become a busy global internet. Christians
have always longed to proclaim the Good News plainly to all nations, and
the Third Millenium is our opened door.

These essays display various aspects of what St. Thomas Aquinas,[7] and
Maritain as one of his greatest modern interpreters, had to say about education and specifically Catholic education. Many of the essayists stress what
St. Thomas called the "interconnection of the virtues," and what today is
called a "holistic" approach to education, or by others "the formation of the

---

[4] Ibid., 7:24–25

[5] Pope John Paul II, *As the Third Millenium Draws Near (Tertio Millenio Adve-
niente), Origins* 24 (24 November 1994): pp. 401–416, n. 45.

[6] For all its eloquence, Bloom's book (New York: Simon and Schuster, 1987)
falls very much short of the Hutchins-Adler view of education; but all three authors
too much emphasize "great books" and "contact with great minds," rather than the
systematic disciplines as such. Aristotle's *Organon* can present unnecessary difficulties for a student who simply wants to know logic.

[7] For an extensive collection of St. Thomas' texts relevant to education see
Pierre H. Conway, O.P., *Principles of Education: A Thomistic Approach* (Washington, D.C.: The Thomist Press, 1960; see also my reprinted article, *St.Thomas and
the Liberal Arts* (Washington, D.C.: The Thomist Press, 1959).

person." This contrasts with the impermeable walls in our universities between different "fields" and their rigid dichotomies between "theory vs. praxis," "facts vs. values," "objectivity vs. subjectivity," "sciences vs. humanities," "information vs. interpretation," etc. Indeed, genuine education does draw out the potentialities of the whole person.

Yet it must not be forgotten that Aquinas's view of human perfection is frankly "intellectualist." For him truth is the highest of values,[8] the indispensable source of authentic love and moral virtue which can flow only from a true knowledge of self, world, and God. Consequently, Aquinas's epistemology is fundamental to his conception of the person and its total perfecting. Thus the body-soul unity of the person, which Professor Redpath well explains in his essay, rests on Aquinas' understanding of how we arrive at truth. This implies, therefore, that a holistic education must aim at *wisdom* in the sense of a unified vision of reality.

Yet how can education provide us with this unified vision of reality necessary for the holistic development of the human person if it leaves us with nothing but a data base of random information lacking sapiential unification? Just as our human body is a complex of many differentiated organs, so the human soul has many differentiated powers, and human wisdom is a complex of many different sciences and arts.[9] Yet in their diversity these disciplines must somehow be organically unified in such a way as to leave them differentiated yet coordinated, avoiding the Platonic-Cartesian error of trying to reduce all knowledge to a single mode.[10] If there are many distinct virtues, moral and intellectual, and many sciences and arts, the perfection of the whole person requires these first to be distinguished and then somehow also to be unified. This is why Maritain wrote his *magnum opus* with the subtitle *Distinguish to Unite*.[11]

This problem of unity-in-diversity from which the very name of "university" is taken, was keenly felt by Aristotle in opposition to his teacher Plato who sought to reduce all knowledge to a single principle. It requires us to discover what discipline can serve as a "first philosophy" capable of unify-

[8] See *Summa Contra Gentiles* (ed. Marietti), I, chap.1: "Oportet igitur ultimum finem universi esse bonum intellectus. Hoc autem est veritas." ("Therefore it is necessary that the ultimate end of the universe is the good of the intellect; this, however, is truth.")

[9] *Summa Theologiae*, Ia, q. 77, aa.1–4; IaIIae, qq. 60–62; 65.

[10] Aristotle, *Metaphysics* II.3 994b32ff.

[11] Jacques Maritain, *Distinguish to Unite or The Degrees of Knowledge*, trans. under the supervision of Gerald B. Phelan (New York: Charles Scribner's Sons, 1959).

ing the other disciplines. Aristotle, therefore, first reviewed the existing disciplines to see if any might fulfill this demanding role.

Influenced by Kant, who at the beginning of the Enlightenment rejected the possibility of proving God's existence in a theoretical way but accepted it as a postulate of ethics, thus making ethics the supreme science, many moderns, including Marx, the pragmatists, and some liberation theologians have subordinated theory to praxis. Aristotle could not accept such a reduction, since he was convinced that all practical truth although irreducible to theoretical truth, must be grounded in it.[12] Good human living must be "according to nature," and nature must be known by a theoretical science. First philosophy, therefore, must be theoretical not practical.

The great theoretical sciences are logic, mathematics, and natural science, and some moderns believe that human knowledge is unified by the analysis of language or more profoundly by logic. For Aristotle, however, logic and grammar are not sciences of reality, but only arts of how to think and talk about reality.[13] A better candidate, therefore, was mathematics. The Pythagoreans and Platonists had reduced natural science to mathematics and all philosophy to a hypermathematics since the ideal forms were in some sense "numbers." While some today reduce mathematics to logic, Aristotle maintained that mathematics is a science of the real, since its subject is quantity and quantity is a fundamental aspect of material reality. Yet the mathematician deals with quantity only as idealized by the imagination,[14] hence mathematics presupposes natural science which deals with quantity in its concrete physical existence. It cannot, therefore, serve as a first philosophy.

Thus Aristotle came close to the conclusion which today actually prevails in our universities, namely, that "first philosophy" is natural science to which all other disciplines must submit if they are to claim truth value. Since Aristotle was convinced that all valid human knowledge (except perhaps that received by divine inspiration[15]) had to be critically reduced to

---

[12] *Metaphysics* I.2 982b10ff.; II 1 993b19–30.

[13] Thus logic should be learned before any of the sciences of the real, see *Metaphysics* IV.2 1005a5.

[14] On Aristotle's view of mathematics see Hippocrates G. Apostle, *Mathematics as a Science of Quantities*, A. Madelberg and E.A. Dobbs, eds. (Grinnell, Iowa: The Peripatetic Press, 1991).

[15] An important recent study in Italian, Abraham P. Bos, *Teologia cosmica e metacosmica* (Milan: Vita e Pensiero, 1991) shows that in his own exoteric dialogues Aristotle, like Plato, recognized our need of divine revelation for complete wisdom.

sense knowledge, and ultimately to the sense of touch.[16] Thus natural science had epistemological primacy.

Nevertheless, in the last book of his *Physics* in which he establishes the basic principles of natural science and again in the *De Anima* where he reaches the study of the human person as the goal of natural science, Aristotle arrived at conclusions which make evident that natural science cannot be "first philosophy." In the *Physics*[17] he shows that, since the sensible universe is a system of bodies acting on each other, ultimately this system of causes which act only if they are themselves caused to act must depend for their action on realities which are non-material, and which therefore fall outside the scope of natural science. In the *De Anima*[18] he shows the human intelligence by which we know the science of nature, must itself be one such immaterial first cause.

This means obviously that reality, "being as such" is not merely material, but includes both material and immaterial beings, the latter known by us only by analogy with material beings and hence known not in themselves but as causes or principles of material effects.[19] Thus we cannot, as Plato hoped, attain to a natural wisdom by which all reality is known in the vision of a single principle, the One,[20] since we know that One only through the conclusions of the special sciences, not directly in itself. Nevertheless we can and should develop a first philosophy, which is also a "theology," since it treats of reality in relation to its principles or first causes, and by which all the other sciences are coordinated by analogy in relation to the absolutely First Cause. This still leaves each special science its relative independence based on its own proper principles.

---

[16] *De Anima* III.13 435l1ff.; Aquinas, *Summa Theologiae*, Ia, q. 91, a. 3; *Quaestio Disputata De Anima*, a. 8.

[17] "It is clear, therefore, that the first movent is indivisible and is without parts and without magnitude," *Physics* VIII.10 267b25.

[18] *De Anima* III.5 430a14–25.

[19] See Aquinas, *In Metaphysicam Aristotelis Commentaria* (ed. Marietti), proemium: "Nam praedictae substantiae separatae sunt universales et primae causae essendi. Eiusdem autem scientiae est considerare causas proprias alicuius generis et genus ipsum. . . . Unde oportet quod ad eamdem scientiam pertineat considerare substantias separatas, et ens commune quod est genus cuius sunt praedictae substantiae communes et universales causae." ("For the aforesaid separated substances [God and the intelligences] are the universal and first causes of existence. For it pertains to the same science to consider its subject genus and the proper causes of that genus . . . Hence it is necessary that it should pertain to the same science to consider separated substances and being as such which is the [subject] genus whose universal and common causes are the aforesaid [separated] substances.")

[20] *Republic* VII 517a.

Does it follow that this transcendent first philosophy is dependent on natural science? Since the shock of the "scientific revolutions" of modern science it appears that since natural science consists in ever shifting hypotheses, any first philosophy dependent upon it also must be tentative. It is this fear that has led Thomists to desert Aquinas's defense of Aristotle's metaphysics, too intimately linked, it seems, with his obsolete natural science. Hence they have been forced to seek a new basis for metaphysics which they claim to find in Aquinas' writings other than his commentary Aristotle's *Physics*. Thus Neo-Thomists have hoped to isolate the permanent truths of "being as such" from the shifting hypotheses of modern natural science.

One way to do this is simply to deny all certitude to modern science and to seek certitude for metaphysics not on an empirical basis, but in a Kantian *a priori*, a surrender to the "turn to the subject" by which Descartes initiated modern philosophy and took sides with Plato against Aristotle. This strategy was adopted by Joseph Maréchal and the Transcendental Thomists. A university based on this view would seek to correlate all human knowledge by reference to the human knower, the self-conscious subject of knowledge. Another strategy has been taken by determined opponents of transcendentalism, the Existential Thomists, led by Etienne Gilson and Jacques Maritain. They have claimed that the basis of metaphysics is the judgment that *esse* or existential act is "the most profound principle in the sensible existents before them."[21] Consequently for most Existential Thomists a philosophy of nature becomes unnecessary since its traditional problems can be absorbed by metaphysics. Metaphysics itself stands alone, receiving nothing essential from natural science.[22]

---

[21] The quotation is from a summary by an ardent defender of Gilson, John F. X. Knasas, *The Preface to Thomistic Metaphysics: A Contribution to the Neo-Thomist Debate on the Start of Metaphysics*, American University Series (New York: Peter Lang, 1990), p. 186. Knasas collects the principal texts relevant to the debate. An appendix, pp. 177–186, details the difference with Maritain. Gilson's view seems to have won out among Existential Thomists.

[22] Disagreement among interpreters of Aquinas is understandable, since many reconstruct his metaphysics largely mainly from the very early opusculum *De Ente et Essentia* and the *Summa Theologiae*, not a philosophical work, but neglect his commentary on Aristotle's *Metaphysics*, Aquinas' only mature, systematic work on metaphysics. Aristotle's work is a puzzling collection of unedited essays (see Alan Code, "[G.E.L.] Owens on the Development of Aristotle's Metaphysics" in William Wians, ed., *Aristotle's Philosophical Development* (Lanham, MD: Rowman & Littlefield, 1996), pp. 303–326, but Aquinas presents it as a coherent treatise, disagreeing only on a few points which he explicitly criticizes.

Maritain agreed in part with Gilson, although he based metaphysics not so much on the existential judgment as on a "metaphysical intuition at the third degree of abstraction" by which we see that "being as such" is not merely material beings (first degree of abstraction) nor idealized quantity (second degree of abstraction) nor even logical beings (third degree of abstraction but purely mental), but "common being" including all these.[23] He was the exception among the Existential Thomists, however, in his reluctance to abandon Aquinas' philosophy of nature or reduce it to metaphysics. Instead he attempted to save it by claiming a formal distinction between it as *dianoetic*, that is, able to penetrate to the essences of material things and therefore enjoying certitude, in contrast to modern science which is merely *perinoetic*, able to go no further than to describe the properties of things and fit these into merely probable models, whether these be *empiriometric* (mathematicized) or *empirioschematic* (non-mathematicized).[24]

A university that followed Maritain would not reduce a philosophy of nature to metaphysics and would make room for both mathematicized science and the humanities, but it would still permit metaphysicians and philosophers of nature to claim a superior certitude unattainable by the other disciplines. To meet skepticism as to its claims of superiority on the part of the experts in the modern disciplines it would have to rest its case on "intuitions" either without empirical verification or at the most with commonsense plausibility. In my opinion, well before Vatican II these claims by Thomists to arrive at metaphysical certitude by an end run around modern science began to discredit official Thomism. After the Council's relaxation of insistence on Thomism in education this implausible claim led to its rapid decline in prestige in our Catholic universities.[25]

Maritain's attempt to save a philosophy of nature, outside metaphysics, by distinguishing it *formally* from modern science, and his empiriometric-empirioschematic distinction were not consistent with Aquinas' doctrine on the specification of sciences, since a discipline restricted to mere probabil-

---

[23] His views on the philosophy of nature are argued both in *The Degrees of Knowledge* and in *Philosophy of Nature* (New York: Philosophy Library, 1951).

[24] Matthew S. Pugh, "Maritain and Postmodern Science," in *Postmodernism and Christian Philosophy*, pp. 168–182, defends Maritain's views but without the benefit of the recent criticism of William A. Wallace, O.P., *The Modeling of Nature: Philosophy of Science and Philosophy of Nature in Synthesis* (Washington, D.C.: The Catholic University of America Press, 1996), especially pp. 224–237.

[25] For a fuller account of this decline of Thomism see my analysis, "The Loss of Theological Unity: Pluralism, Thomism, and Catholic Morality," in Mary Jo Weaver and R. Scott Appleby, eds., *Being Right: Conservative Catholics in America* (Bloomington-Indianapolis: Indiana University Press, 1995), pp. 63–87.

ity would have been characterized by Aquinas not as a *scientia*, but a *dialectic* in the service of some true science. Also for Aquinas the mathematization of natural science did not necessarily render it incapable of certitude. Aristotle's works in natural science show that he proposed much as merely a probable dialectic preparatory to establish a principle or definition or as complementary speculation.[26] It is true that much of modern science has the same dialectical character and hence is merely probable, but it is not true, as William A. Wallace has shown,[27] that modern science never attains certitudes nor that it is merely perinoetic.

Maritain was deceived by the fact that many scientists and philosophers of science as a result of Kantian presuppositions *heuristically* claim nothing but probability for their science, that is, as a strategy for avoiding premature claims of certitude. While much of Ptolemaic astronomy was merely probable, its conclusion that our earth is a sphere, and that an eclipse of the sun is due to interposition of the moon are not probable but certain, not indeed in the mode of a mathematical conclusion, but in the less "clear and distinct" mode proper to our physical knowledge.

What then would a university unified by an authentically Thomistic metaphysics be like? The metaphysicians would not claim to have any data other than that supplied by the special sciences nor to be independent of these sciences in its own conclusions. Hence Kant was wrong to think that metaphysics is an empty mental projection exceeding our empirical knowledge. In fact, a sound metaphysics derives its empirical content from the special sciences and exceeds this content only by legitimate inferences from empirical effects to spiritual first causes of these effects. This Kantian, idealist error has dominated modernity even to the analytic philosophy of our days and has distorted the self-understanding of scientists themselves in regard to their own scientific methodology and achievement.

For Aquinas the first question to be asked in every science is whether and how its proposed special subject really exists.[28] Speculation about mere possibilities in the manner of Leibnitz or Kant is not *scientia*. Hence, if there is to be a metaphysics, its subject, "being as such," an analogical *ens commune* extending to all the subjects of the special sciences and their causes, must first be shown to exist. Aristotle and Aquinas did not answer

[26] See Wallace, *The Modeling of Nature*, pp. 266–275.
[27] Ibid., pp. 377ff.
[28] The subject of logic "exists" only as mental relations, but logic deserves to be called a science only because the logical principle of non-contradiction on which it is based can be shown to be grounded in the real as this is studied by natural science and reflectively by metaphysics.

this question by appealing to a special metaphysical "intuition" as Maritain did, nor to an existential judgment of the primacy of existence as Etienne Gilson and others have done, or to a merely commonsense apprehension that there must be a God and a human soul, but by appealing to the fact that natural science (*physica*) establishes critically the existence of the subjects of the other sciences, because *physica* alone reduces its data directly to sense knowledge. In the case of metaphysics, therefore, it is the proofs established by *natural science* of the existence of the "unmoved movers" of the things of our sense experience, namely, the First Cause, the purely spiritual intelligences, and the human intelligence, which require and make possible a discipline of metaphysics.[29]

Such a Thomistic interdisciplinary concept of metaphysics concedes to Kant that metaphysics has no data of its own, but is a reflection on the data of the special sciences and hence would be unnecessary and empty without their diversity, but it firmly rejects Kant's agnosticism about our ability to know the beings that really are. Hence it also rejects all those philosophical systems, whether Hegelianism, Transcendental Thomism, or Heideggerianism, based on the supposition that true thinking begins within some "horizon of Being" in whose light all "beings" must be understood.[30] For Aquinas's thought begins and ends with "beings" since nothing else exists. "Being" signifies either (1) the beings that are compared with each other, of which material beings are the proper object of the human intellect, or (2) the Absolute Being, God, knowable only through the beings he causes but infinitely different from them they by the fact that He is the Necessary Existent who has freely given them their finite being.

Unfortunately modern Thomists have for the most part abandoned this conception of metaphysics, attributing it to Aristotle but denying it to Aquinas. They have been frightened by the Kantian attack on the traditional proofs of God's existence and awed by the success of modern science and

---

[29] For a fuller development of this thesis see my article, "The End of Philosophy and the End of Physics: A Dead End," in *Postmodernism and Christian Philosophy*, pp. 12–22; also "The River Forest School of Natural Philosophy", in R. James Long, ed., *Philosophy and the God of Abraham, Essays in Memory of James A. Weisheipl* (Toronto: Pontifical Institute of Mediaeval Philosophy), pp. 1–16; and "Thomism and the Transition from the Classical World-View to Historical-Mindedness," in Deal W. Hudson and Dennis Wm. Moran, eds., *The Future of Thomism* (American Maritain Association, 1992), pp. 109–122.

[30] For the widely different understandings of the term "metaphysics" today see Takatura Ando, *Metaphysics: A Critical Survey of its Meaning*, 2nd enlarged edition (The Hague: Martinus Nijhoff, 1974).

technology. Moreover, they have mistakenly accepted Kant's interpretation of modern science according to which science merely imposes innate mental categories (or, for post-Kantians, mentally constructed models) on empirical data without any hope of reaching any concrete *ding an sich*. Hence, neo-Thomists have tried to save our knowledge of God and the spiritual human soul by inventing a metaphysics standing on its own feet in mid-air.

The true task of metaphysics in a university, therefore, is to provide a critical, interdisciplinary coordination of the various independent disciplines within the diversity of disciplines. It would also provide a systematic reflection on what these disciplines contribute to our understanding of ourselves, the world, and God and our application of this to the guidance of human behavior and our good use of the resources of our environment.

As these essays make clear, the modern university is dominated by modern science and the technologies based on it. The other disciplines are marginalized as little more than the histories of subjective opinions. This is so because modern science suffers from the distortions introduced by Descartes, Hume, and Kant which deprive natural science of the fundamental analysis of our experience of the changing, empirical reality which Aristotle supplied in his *Physics* and which underlies all of Aquinas's philosophy and its service of theology. One has only to read any current exposition of the achievements of modern science such as *The Quark and the Jaguar* by the leading physicist Murray Gell-Mann,[31] to see that the very questions about time, place, causality, chance, complexity which Aristotle explored as the foundation of an empirical study of the changing world of the senses are still debated in our modern science but obscured by Kantian idealism.[32] Only when Thomists face up to this central fact of our times can they root their metaphysics in modern science and thus help our universities find unity in the rich diversity of knowledge. Natural science itself has nothing to fear from this self-criticism, in that its results would not be dictated by metaphysics, though the self-criticism itself would be prompted by the critical interdisciplinary questions metaphysics would raise. Fidelity to the empirical method of natural science, which Aristotle and Aquinas ardently defended, does not require that natural scientists claim to exhaust the possibilities of objective knowledge nor that what they know about the secondary causes of the material universe and human behavior may not cast light on the existence and character of immaterial reality.

---

[31] Murray Gell-Mann, *The Quark and the Jaguar* (New York: W.H. Freeman and Company, 1994).

[32] This is thoroughly documented by Wallace, *The Modeling of Nature*, see especially Chapter 6, pp. 197 ff.

Metaphysics, however, would not raise critical questions only to the natural scientists. In the case of the humanities it would ask about the truth value of these disciplines. Are they founded in merely subjective opinion and custom? All the questions now being raised by deconstructionism and hermeneutic philosophy would be asked of the liberal arts. No matter how "creative" human thinking may be, it must ultimately face questions of the true, the good, the beautiful, the theoretical, productive, or ethical. Hence a metaphysician will ask the humanities faculty whether they are leading their students to see the relevance of these disciplines to fundamental questions about reality, about truth, goodness and beauty, as several of our essayists urge. As for the disciplines of human behavior, the moral virtues,[33] and their relation to human nature individual and social cannot be neglected if education is to perfect the whole person. Finally, the ecological questions about the use of technology in relation to the moral ends of human life will be raised by the metaphysician facilitating an interchange between moralists, political theorists, natural scientists, and technologists.

For the Christian the immaterial world, known only to the metaphysician through its empirical effects, has been revealed through the Church in something of its splendor. The other world religions claim in some way also to experience transcendent reality. Consequently, beyond metaphysics, a Catholic university, open to ecumenical discussion with other religions and even with secularists not totally closed to transcendence, will seek a still higher unification of knowledge in the wisdom of theology. In his *Summa Theologiae* Aquinas himself supplies so successful a unification of the whole scope of sacred theology that we scarcely need a better to organize a university theologically, though of course there are other ways of doing this. For example, St. Bonaventure in his *Breviloqium* furnishes another excellent model, perhaps less critical but more contemplative.

According to Aquinas, theology goes even further than metaphysics toward unity in that it is able to unite both the theoretical and the practical realms in a single discipline,[34] as Plato supposed possible in a philosopher-king, but which are in fact difficult to reconcile. As an acquired science, theology does not absolutely need metaphysics or the special disciplines,

---

[33] The present popularity of "virtue ethics" has often led to confused accounts of what Aquinas' understood by this term. For a penetrating analysis see Romanus Cessario, O.P., *The Moral Virtues and Theological Ethics* (Notre Dame, Indiana: University of Notre Dame Press, 1991). On the relation of the Greek virtues to Bible teaching see my, *Living the Truth in Love: A Biblical Introduction to Moral Theology* (Staten Island, New York: Alba House, 1996), pp. 34–40; 77.

[34] *Summa Theologiae*, Ia, q. 1, aa. 4 and 5.

but it is well served by them.[35] Hence, Catholic students need a systematic knowledge of their faith commensurate with the modern culture in which they live, and integrated with their other studies.

St. Thomas also maintains that theology as a *scientia*, although truly sapiential, is inferior to the infused gift of wisdom from the Holy Spirit, which is mystical, co-natural knowledge.[36] I congratulate my confrère Fr. Romanus Cessario for his lucid exposition in this volume on the Gift of Counsel according to Jean Poinsot (John of St.Thomas). Poinsot was the great Thomistic commentator on whom Maritain especially depended and who showed how the spirituality of Aquinas centers on the gifts of the Holy Spirit. Only through these gifts can the theological virtues of faith, hope, and love be perfected so as to achieve the ultimate unification and deification of the human person in the contemplation of the Triune God. Catholic students possess these gifts through baptism and confirmation and, if education is to be truly holistic, their cultivation should be at the heart of education. Therefore, in a Christian university, also, there ought to be the opportunities for liturgical prayer and contemplation in which Jesus Christ, Eternal Wisdom, is the "only Teacher" (Mt 23:10).

Aquinas's understanding of theology as well as the metaphysics in its service as interdisciplinary, however, is not merely static but dynamic, since in his *Commentary on Boethius' De Trinitate*[37] he shows how metaphysics proposes an order of learning by which the human intelligence progresses from one formally independent discipline to another, preparatory to theology. In this order the liberal arts: grammar (linguistics), poetics, rhetoric, dialectics, logic, and mathematics pure and applied provide the student with the tools of learning and communication. Then with the aid of these tools, especially of mathematics, natural science can be studied, culminating in an anthropology, and followed by ethics and politics. All these disciplines are thus unified analogically by metaphysics, and for Christians still more perfectly by sacred theology.

This is a pedagogical, educational order of learning but it is rooted in epistemological necessity. Undoubtedly there is what Réginald Garrigou-Lagrange[38] called "a commonsense metaphysics" by which even the un-

[35] Ibid., Ia, q. 1, a. 5, ad 2.

[36] Ibid., Ia, q. 1, a. 6, c. and ad 3.

[37] The relevant part is translated by A. A. Mauer as *Divisions and Methods of the Sciences,* (Toronto: Pontifical Institute of Mediaeval Studies, 1953). For Aquinas's texts on the order of learning see note 5 above.

[38] *La Sens commun, la Philosophie de l'Etre et les formules dogmatiques* (Paris: Beauchesne, 1909); 3rd ed. (Paris: Nouvelle Librairie Nationale, 1922).

trained mind can grasp that there is a God, a human spiritual soul, and many other truths treated in a disciplined way by metaphysics, just as it can also get some idea of what quantum physics is all about from a popular book on modern physics. Nevertheless, to understand these truths in a critical manner, the learner must pass through a necessary epistemological order of learning. This order exists not only within a single science, so that one needs to understand modern physics to be able really to understand modern chemistry, or chemistry to understand biology; but also between independent disciplines, so one must know logic before one studies mathematics, and at least the fundamentals of natural science before one attempts ethics or metaphysics. No wonder then that our universities, lacking an interdisciplinary discipline, supply a mere flea market of information rather than a systematic education!

The greatest problem of metaphysics is that of the One and the Many which extends even into sacred theology in the doctrine of the Trinity. The Pseudo-Dionysius, whom Aquinas so often quotes, saw in Neo-Platonic fashion all reality as a hierarchy descending from the One such that at each point of the order the lower member received *all* its perfections from the next higher member but in a less unified and thus inferior condition. Aquinas, however, held that a higher member of the hierarchy of being contains the lower only *generically*, so that each species and indeed each individual in the hierarchy has at least some perfection unique to itself alone.[39] Thus a human being possesses the generic perfections of minerals, plants, and animals, but we cannot naturally sparkle like a diamond, hibernate like a tree, or swim like a whale. Nor is even one grain of sand a mere duplicate of any other. The Creator is no Xerox machine.

Moreover, in a Thomistic hierarchy the differences in perfection increase in ascending order. Two atoms of hydrogen are hard to distinguish except by position, but a man is very different from an ape and within the human species two men are highly individualized by their genomes. Aquinas says that in the angelic hierarchy this spread of perfection increases so dramatically that each angel is a species in itself and the lowliest seraph vastly different from the loftiest cherub.

Only in the infinite perfection of God, the One, is every perfection of actual and possible creatures contained in total unity. Hence Aquinas's God is not "onto-theo-logical" in Heidegger's sense but infinitely other than the

---

[39] For documentation on this point see my article "Cosmic Community in Plotinus, Aquinas, and Whitehead," *Cultura y Vida* (Buenos Aires: Sociedad Tomista Argentina, 1995), Appendix A, p. 33.

hierarchy of creatures by his absolute infinity and simplicity. Yet the marvelous hierarchy of the creation does reflect, to a degree freely chosen by the Creator, something of God's infinite perfection. We each image God, but each mirrors God in a unique way. In the Trinity the persons are absolutely equal because the Father communicates his total being to Son and to the Holy Spirit through the Son. Their distinction is found purely in relations of origin so that in the One God there are Many (Three) Persons. This totality of communication, therefore, becomes the model which the Church, the human political community, and the family imitate. The university in its hierarchy of unity-in-diversity ought to reflect something of the same sublimely beautiful order.

Unfortunately this dynamic progression of the Thomistic theory of the order of learning is often passed over, even by those who know Aquinas well. For example, to cite an example from an otherwise excellent work, Germain Grisez, after correctly arguing that the first principles of ethics, since they are practical, cannot be reduced to the theoretical science of anthropology, concludes that ethics does not presuppose an anthropology.[40] For Aquinas, however, while it is true that as first principles of a special science the axioms of ethics are indemonstrable and therefore *formally* independent of any other discipline, nevertheless in the order of disciplined learning ethics *materially* presupposes anthropology, the ultimate topic of natural science, since without at least some basic but disciplined understanding of human nature as studied by natural science the first practical principles of ethics cannot be seen in a critical way as immediately evident. Thus the study of ethics by one who has only a commonsense knowledge of anthropology as a part of natural science can never rise above a commonsense understanding. Similarly, to attempt to construct a metaphysics without a basic disciplined understanding of natural science is bound to fail, since only when natural science has shown that the material world cannot exist without immaterial causes is it evident that natural science is not "first philosophy," and that therefore a distinct discipline of metaphysics is possible and necessary.

Although Maritain did not stress Aquinas's theory of the order of learning, he did make an original and important contribution to our understanding

---

[40] See Germain Grisez, "The First Principle of Practical Reason: A Commentary on the *Summa Theologiae* 1–2 Question 94, Article 2," *Natural Law Forum* 10 (1965): pp. 168–201 and *The Way of the Lord Jesus,* vol. 1, *Christian Moral Principles*, Chapter 4, Question G, pp. 105–106. Grisez is quite right to stress against Suarez that first practical principles are not speculative principles, but a disciplined understanding of practical principles presupposes disciplined speculative knowledge. A physician without biological science is an ill-trained practitioner.

of *intellectus*, the fundamental power of intelligence to grasp certain general truths directly from experience, as distinguished from *ratio*, the other power of intelligence to reason from these truths as first principles. Differing sets of first principles are the axioms by which one discipline is distinguished from another, e.g. the axioms of arithmetic are quite different from the axioms of ethics (*pace* Spinoza and his attempt to construct ethics on the model of geometry). Though such axioms are often said by Platonizing Thomist manuals, to be "self-evident," for Aquinas himself they are not such, but evident from sense experience. Maritain wrote extensively on "connatural" and "preconceptual" knowledge and "creative intuition."[41] The term "preconceptual" is not the happiest, since for Aquinas every actualization of the intellect is a concept.[42] In his terminology Maritain seems to retain the Cartesian understanding of the concept as a "clear, and distinct idea." What Maritain really meant by a "preconcept" was an "unformulated" or "unverbalized" concept. When such concepts are fully actualized and combined into judgements based on direct experience they become the first principles of reasoning. Maritain showed that in the case of the first principles of the arts these concepts are commonly not fully actualized prior to the actual process of production which they nevertheless guide. They are "formative ideas" which become clear to artists themselves as they "create" their works. While angelic knowledge is wholly intuitive, human intellection is so dependent on the senses and so rudimentarily intuitive that it must actualize its intuitions through discursive ratiocination, by what we call "research," "analysis," "theory construction," and "verification." Even the artist has to exercise a degree of self-criticism of ratiocinative kind. While Thomist epistemology is often presented as a kind of rationalism, a process of discursive argument, Maritain deserves great credit for insisting that the first principles of every science and art are known, not by reason, but by intuition, and that this intuition rests on sense experience and imagination, i.e. is aesthetic.

[41] See his *Creative Intuition in Art and Poetry* (New York: Pantheon, 1953) and discussion in my *Theologies of the Body: Humanist and Christian* , 2nd ed. (Braintree, Massachusetts: Pope John Center, 1996), pp. 312–319; and Maritain, "The Natural Mystical Experience and the Void," in *Redeeming the Time* (London: Geoffrey Bles, The Centenary Press, 1943), pp. 225–255.

[42] "In intellectu nostro utimur nomine conceptionis, secundum quod in verbo nostri intellectus invenitur similitudo rei intellectae." ("In our intellect we use the term "conception" because in our intellectual word is found a similitude of the thing known intellectually.") *Summa Theologiae*, Ia, q., 27, a. 2, ad 2. Thus if Maritain's "preconceptual knowledge" implies some similitude to its object, which it certainly must, it is already "conceived" albeit imperfectly. By *verbum* here Aquinas means the concept, not the verbal sign by which it is formulated.

Though, in my opinion, Maritain's aesthetics, due to its relative neglect of the teachings of Aristotle's *Poetics*, is not developed enough to provide a satisfactory basis for a critical theory of the fine arts, it does very much help us to understand the role of imagination and of affectivity in the activity of *intellectus* or "intuition." This doctrine is vital to any theory of education, since it helps us to understand why one student can immediately grasp the viewpoint of a particular discipline and another cannot and hence what a teacher must strive to awaken in the latter kind of student. No one can really enter into mathematics without an awakened mathematical imagination or into ethics without a sensitive ethical imagination. Moreover, Maritain's related studies of mysticism, and especially of the natural mysticism which seems to be the aim of yoga and other religious disciplines, are invaluable in the study of comparative religion, an ecumenical aspect of both natural and sacred theology especially relevant for the Third Millenium.

Maritain also understood that just as a university needs to cultivate the whole person if the minds of students are to enter into the special disciplines with a healthy sensitivity to the basic truths of experience, so also the university needs to be a human *community of learning*. Learning goes on not just in the classroom but through the daily life of study and exchange of ideas, not to mention the communal worship of students and teachers. James V. Schall, S.J., tells us how Maritain created "Thomist Circles," friendly intellectual groups which were formative of both moral and intellectual virtue. Joseph W. Koterski, S.J., in his account of the model "Queen's Court Residence" at Fordham, shows us how such communities of learning can still be created.

Such communities, however, in turn can flourish best in a healthy political order to which a holistic education of its citizens ought to contribute. Maritain knew only too well what had happened to the excellent European universities with the rise of fascism and national socialism. Many of the present essays emphasize the close relation of Maritain's educational views to his political writings on "integral humanism" and democracy. My revered teacher Yves R. Simon, a disciple of Maritain and himself a brilliant political theorist, once said to me that he felt Maritain's temperament and experience did not make politics his *forte*.[43] Hence it must be admitted

---

[43] Perhaps, I must admit, the same criticism might be made of St. Thomas as a political philosopher compared with Aristotle. The argument for monarchy in the incomplete *De Regno ad Rehem Cypri* (*De regimine principum*) is very abstract and conditioned by the status of its addressee (see Jean-Pierre Torrell, O.P., *St. Thomas Aquinas,* vol 1, *The Person and His Work*, trans. Robert Royal (Washington, D.C.: The Catholic University of America Press, 1996), pp. 169–171); the *Sententia Libri*

that Maritain's political writing was too much influenced by the tragic crisis of World War II. With great courage and prophetic insight he rejected the totalitarianism of both Communism and the Fascism of Franco and his allies. Hence he became an advocate of "democracy" as a government for the common good based on subsidiarity, a position which, through Maritain's influence as well as that of John Courtney Murray, was adopted by Vatican II and the papal magisterium.

But Maritain gave little attention to the problems of rule by majority vote, popular non-participation, and demagogic manipulation which, as Aristotle observed, make democracy no less ambiguous and fallible as a means to achieve the true common good than are monarchy and aristocracy. St. Thomas's advocacy, following Aristotle, of a "mixed" or republican form of government is more realistic, as the Founding Fathers of our own Republic realized. Perhaps it was this too unqualified defense of democracy that trapped Maritain into the controversy with Charles De Koninck over the "primacy of the common good." Maritain's debatable distinction between "individual" and "person" in relation to the common good has, contrary to his intentions, been used to support the individualistic personalism of our democratic culture which so many of these essayists criticize.[44]

To sum up, in a contemporary theory of education, to which this volume makes an important critical contribution, I would want to stress five points: (1) To be holistic education should take place in a Christian learning community; (2) It should inculcate a participatory type of learning which will prepare our students for living in a participatory republic; (3) It should follow the natural order of learning which proceeds from the liberal arts through natural science and the ethical sciences to unification by metaphysics and theology; (4) With these theoretical subjects it should integrate the practical arts through which most students make their living; (5) All the disciplines should be rooted in a natural science freed from the distortions

---

Politicorum Aristotelis only gets to III.6 (see Torrell, pp. 233–34*)*; and of the misnamed *Epistula ad ducissam Brabantiae* (*De regimine Judaeorum*), (Torell, pp. 218–220). Torrell writes, "The eight concrete questions to which Thomas had to respond hardly lend themselves to great developments" (p. 219). Much the most important contribution of St. Thomas is his argument for the republic or "mixed government" he attributes to Moses, *Summa Theologiae*, IaIIae, q. 105, a. 1. Aristotle's *Politics* is one of his very greatest works in its analysis of concrete data while Aquinas makes very little use of such data from his own times.

[44] For bibliography on this controversy see my *Theologies of the Body*, p. 480, n. 105.

both of Platonic dualism and of Enlightenment idealism so as to be solidly rooted in our empirical knowledge of ourselves and our world.

Is this utopian? Well, I believe our post-modern collapse into irrationality makes such a reform of education a necessity for our survival and Christian hope urges us to strive for it.

The Public University
and the Common Good

John M. Palms

When Jacques Maritain focuses on education, he reminds those of us in the university of our wider obligations to our society. Like centrifugal forces, tremendous revolutions in our times are pulling apart the most elemental fabric binding together our society, which is a shared sense of the common good. These centrifugal forces in the various realms of human interaction, whether they be political, economic, ethnic, religious or cultural, increasingly threaten any shared value system that might supersede individual interests. To suggest the most obvious examples, we see this in the conflicts between liberal and conservative, rich and poor, the majority race and the minority races. These tensions have persisted in this country from the beginning.

Today the debate has changed. The question no longer seems, Can we agree on how to pursue the common good? Now it seems to be, Is there a common good? But are there not ideals, ethical purposes, and values that are intrinsic to a good society? If so, can we agree on how to define the common good that will lead toward this type of society? From the perspective of those of us in the university, the question is, Can the university help define and shape the common good and contribute to building a good society? If certain conflicts are *centrifugal* forces pulling at the fabric of our society, perhaps the public university can help provide a counteracting *centripetal* force by its earnest attention to the civic and ethical responsibilities this question implies.

What I want to reflect upon today is Maritain's relevance to these questions I have mentioned, especially in regard to an institution at the pinnacle of our educational system, the public university. The public university should be a crossroad of the intellect. It provides a concentration of sophisticated thinkers from many disciplines. It is trusted with academic freedom so that it can provide a forum for the free exploration of ideas. It provides a public square that brings together the knowledge and wisdom of the elders and the idealism and energy of the young. It provides a setting in which understanding and truth can be pursued with civility, reason, deliberateness, and broad, even holistic, rational perspectives, in a manner that is not dogmatic or doctrinaire.

We do still believe in the pursuit of truth in the university—which is to say we also believe that truth can be obtained. Further, we believe we best pursue truth through the combined contributions of the many types of thought and analysis available—from anthropology to zoology, from English to engineering, from theology to biology, from physics to philosophy.

In *Education at the Crossroads*, Maritain alludes to the holistic conception of the human intellect and imagination that prompts the university's various intellectual endeavors. As he writes: "Due to the very fact that he is endowed with a knowing power which is unlimited and which nonetheless only advances step by step, man cannot progress in his own specific life, both intellectually and morally, without being helped by collective experience previously accumulated and preserved, and by a regular transmission of acquired knowledge."[1]

We should be particularly mindful of Maritain's phrase, "a knowing power . . . which . . . advances step by step." With this phrase, he suggests why the university can both seek understanding and truth and yet avoid dogmatism. In indicating the gradual movement of our knowing, this phrase affirms how the university can be both confident in its knowledge and yet humble before the limited light that this knowledge casts on ultimate questions. But though the questions remain, the understanding grows. The understanding grows because of the careful application of reason.

The surety of this understanding increases further because the university's methods, facts, and ideas receive constant scrutiny in and out of the academy. We remember Thomas Jefferson's powerful observation: "[T]ruth is great and will prevail if left to itself; that she is the proper and sufficient antagonist to error, and has nothing to fear from the conflict unless by human interposition disarmed of her natural weapons, free argument and debate, errors ceasing to be dangerous when it is permitted freely to contradict them."[2]

---

[1] Jacques Maritain, *Education at the Crossroads* (New Haven, Connecticut: Yale University Press, 1943), p. 2.

[2] Julian P. Boyd, ed., *The Papers of Thomas Jefferson*, vol. 2 (Princeton: Princeton University Press, 1950), p. 303.

Tempering its knowledge with skepticism—but with a skepticism that does not degrade into cynicism—the university maintains its integrity as it proposes what is sound and wise. This balance between the continued search for truth and legitimate skepticism about what it teaches and discovers gives the university the credibility and moral authority that allow it to presume, as has been said, "to set the standards of truth for a society, to stipulate the rules that distinguish good sense from nonsense, truth from error, excellence from mediocrity . . . [and] . . . to attempt to *shape* thought and conscience."[3] I write this essay as someone new to the philosophy of Jacques Maritain. But reading *Education at the Crossroads*, I was struck most of all by his holistic view of learning to which I alluded a moment ago. I believe it is a view consistent with the holistic responsibilities of the university. His title is in fact wonderfully resonant with meaning for the role of the university in our culture. He sees the human being as a crossroad of two forces: materialistic desires—the physical desires, the expressions of our incarnate condition and of our individuality—and something deeper, more profound, if unquantifiable—the human spirit, or personality for Maritain, grounded in the *"act of existence."*

Most importantly for the role of the university, Maritain says that we possess this dual nature not alone but in relation to wider societal responsibilities. He writes, "[O]ne does not make a man except in the bosom of the social ties where there is an awakening of civic understanding and civic virtues."[4]

With such ideas, Maritain reminds us of a critical question before higher education: Is our sole mission with our students making them technically skilled graduates? Or should we also strive to bring issues of mutual respect, character, virtue, civic obligation, conscience, and the common good once again into their educational experiences?

These questions have their own crossroad in the history and ideas of the public university. The idea that education has a vital civic role has been central to the public university in America since the first ones were founded.

The University of South Carolina is one of these universities. It enjoys the distinction of being the first public university to be fully funded by *its* state. In 1801, the South Carolina General Assembly created South Carolina College, as it was then known. The state fully allocated for its needs

---

[3] Charles W. Anderson, *Prescribing the Life of the Mind* (Madison, Wisconsin: University of Wisconsin Press, 1993), p. ix.

[4] Maritain, *Education at the Crossroads*, p. 19.

with $50,000, a great sum back then. During this same time, three other public universities were created: the University of Georgia, the University of North Carolina, and the University of Virginia. They were given varying sums of public money and expected to raise the rest from private sources.

Whether fully or partially funded by their states, all four of these universities were expected to perform the civic role that Maritain asked of the educational system some 150 years later—and which is still needed and expected of the public university today. Further, while Maritain's ideas reflect his own religious convictions, they also describe a role of public universities that were not founded for religious purposes. In fact, the religious fervor that swept the South in the antebellum period and which still affects today's South did not arrive until after these universities were created. In 1800, only ten percent of white Southerners belonged to a church.[5]

When the citizens founded these universities, then, they made the investment and the commitment for civic rather than sectarian reasons. These institutions were seen not merely as *intellectual* crossroads, but also as *civic* crossroads. They were seen as crossroads in which the next generation of leaders would learn together how to bring the newly created American republic safely out of the tensions and burdens of independence. They were seen as *civic* crossroads in which the next generation of leaders could share together the experience of higher learning based upon principles of citizenship and civic responsibility. That is, they were crossroads of education where people could together seek, define, and advance the common good.

Consider the University of South Carolina. The Preamble to an Act to Establish South Carolina College calls upon the institution "to promote the instruction, the good order and the harmony of the entire community," the entire state. Its motto, established at USC's beginning, is one of the great mottos in higher education. It is taken from a poem by Ovid in which he appeals to the noblest nature of a young, well-educated king. The Latin that appears on the University's official seal reads, *"Emollit Mores Nec Sinit Esse Feros."*

Translated, this motto says, "Learning humanizes character and does not permit it to be cruel." Not practical purposes, but higher moral obligations bind us one to another and should serve as the University's guiding hand.

Similar ideals helped found the University of Georgia. The words of one early patron emphasize the presumption of a common good that this public

[5] William J. Cooper, Jr. and Thomas E. Terrill, *The American South: A History* (New York: Knopf, 1990), p. 263.

university was expected to foster, "As it is the distinguishing happiness of free government that civil order should be the result of choice and not necessity, and the common wishes of the people become the law of the land, their public prosperity and even existence very much depends upon suitably forming the minds and the morals of their citizens."[6]

The University of North Carolina was also called upon to promote virtues that would advance the common good. It was created in part to help form "citizens capable of comprehending, improving and defending the principles of government; citizens who, from the highest impulse and a just sense of their own and the general happiness, would be induced to practice the duties of social morality."[7]

Finally, we know that a sense of the common good was the very reason Thomas Jefferson worked to create the University of Virginia. He believed that well-educated citizens would provide ultimate security for the flourishing of true democracy—that the quality of their educated judgment and the society's common good were bound together.

How archaic, how anachronistic do such ideals of virtue and the common good sound today! Yet these idealistic missions were part of the reason, if not the primary reason, that the public university in America found public support and came into existence. Such missions may even help explain why people then were comfortable supporting public universities with their tax dollars. These universities were expected not simply to "skill" their students, but also to advance noble qualities in them, qualities which were seen as being intrinsically valuable, as well as essential to the common good. This meant, of course, that there *actually was* a sense of higher values and the common good, that everything was not of equal merit. Best practices and principles could be discerned from among competing ideologies and interests.

These founders would have agreed with an opinion expressed by Charles Anderson in his excellent book about the contemporary university entitled *Prescribing the Life of the Mind*: "If we were to insist that all we could say in the end was that there were many diverse points of view and that we had no way of telling the better from the worse, the general opinion would be

---

[6] Abraham Baldwin as quoted in E. Merton Coulter, *A Short History of Georgia* (Chapel Hill, North Carolina: University of North Carolina Press, 1933), p. 267.

[7] Hugh T. Lefler and Louis R. Wilson, eds., *A Documentary History of the University of North Carolina: 1776–1799*, vol. 2 (Chapel Hill, North Carolina: University of North Carolina Press, 1953), p. 35.

that we might as well close our doors and disband. In the public mind, we are *expected* to seek the truth and to teach our best approximations of it."[8]

We know that today it is hardly implicitly trusted that universities contribute to the examination, definition, and advancement of a common good. Individual families support the educational costs of their children. Taxes provide a portion of the university's expenses. State and federal funds contribute to the development of particular programs or research. But is there a *communal* sense that providing higher learning is something worthy of broad public investment? Is there a sense that the *society as a whole* should support public higher education? Instead, we face a cynicism about the public university's mission and performance that helps explain why state funding has decreased so much.

None of the four public universities I have named get even fifty percent of their budget from the state. The University of Virginia gets 14 percent. My own university gets just 38 percent of its budget from direct state appropriations. I suspect those of you from public universities can cite a similar problem.

Of course, a variety of national and state economic factors have helped reduce state financial support. But don't people also seem to feel that universities aren't contributing anymore to the common good—or that universities are in fact a cause for cultural demise? Isn't there a perception that the principal benefactor of our excellent public higher education system is the one getting the degree, not the community? Isn't it true that the people don't see our graduates developing qualities that will encourage them to postpone their self-aggrandizement and to consider the larger needs of their society, their communities, and their families?

Ironically, universities themselves share responsibility for this cynicism to which we are subject. We have gone too far toward a concept of education that justifies itself based only upon practical performance in the areas that can be measured. We brag about our students' SAT scores, the number of graduates we produce, how many get jobs, their starting salaries, the dollar amounts of research we do, the contributions we make to economic development. We love to quantify things. We know how our students hate essay tests and papers where we make subjective judgments. Tenure and promotion decisions reflect the same aversions. We want to know how many articles our colleagues publish, how many students they teach, how many graduate students they advise, how many research dollars they attract.

---

[8] Anderson, *Prescribing the Life of the Mind*, p. xi.

These are all viable and valuable aspects of evaluating universities. But do we *only* want to evaluate a university or a person by what can be measured? In Raphael's famous painting, "The School of Athens," Aristotle and Plato walk side by side. Plato points to the sky, Aristotle to the earth. They are debating two different philosophies of education: Plato's idealism, his sense of ultimate forms, and Aristotle's realism, his sense of particular, substantial forms. Don't both views of reality belong in the modern university, that place where we apply our minds in best practice to the fullness of human experience? After the Industrial Revolution, we changed our universities based upon the German model. In the hundred years since then, we seem to have forgotten that a broader civic and ethical role—*beyond* what could be measured—helped produce the public university in the first place.

For Maritain, this problem belongs to a wider symptom of a moral illness affecting humanity. As Joseph Pappin, Dean of the University of South Carolina's Lancaster campus, has put it: "Maritain's assessment of the human condition . . . hinges upon the false deification of man, a secularized world view, an exaltation of the autonomy of the individual will, a narrowing of reason to the quantifiable and the rise of the nominalistic perspective, a reversion to primitive instincts and experience as a realm of authentic human experience."[9]

This passage indicates that Maritain recognized the positivist view that contributes to the public university's current problems. This passage also indicates that Maritain saw a wider societal and ontological dilemma. In terms of the university, this crisis that Maritain diagnoses is revealed in society's cynicism about the university's role in matters of civic virtue, responsibility, character and conscience. But if Maritain is right about this larger problem, can we in the university even hope to bring such issues back to bear on our work?

Before I answer that question, I would observe that in the day when the first public universities were founded, there were also profound societal fractures and tensions. There were heated debates over federal versus state control, individual rights versus public responsibilities, slavery versus emancipation, and secular versus religious authority.

In fact, these tensions were part of the reason public universities were

---

[9] Joseph Pappin, III, "Maritain's Ethics for an Age in Crisis," in Deal W. Hudson and Matthew J. Mancini, eds., *Understanding Maritain: Philosopher and Friend*, (Macon, Georgia: Mercer University Press, 1987), p. 292.

brought into existence. In late eighteenth-century South Carolina, for example, the Upstate and the Lowcountry were engaged in a struggle for political and economic power. The General Assembly decided to build South Carolina College in the center of the state in order to provide a central place where young men from both areas could come together.

I have already described the words of the Latin motto on our seal. It is worth noting as well that beneath those words on the seal appear two figures, one representing Liberty, and the other the Goddess of Learning, Minerva. On the seal, they are shaking hands, their weapons and shields at rest. As the founders of the university believed, learning, liberty and peace stand together. Diverse interests can come together for the common good. Freedom does not necessarily mean strife, relativism, or anarchy; it can also mean peaceful agreement and understanding.

I wonder: If *Maritain's sense* of our dilemma inspires him to a renewed, holistic vision of the university, does *our* contemporary crisis likewise call us to a higher moral purpose and responsibility? As Maritain wrote in words that echo the ideals of the first public universities, ideals that seem needed today, "To the very extent that it is entrusted with an all-important function in the common good, [education] is bound in conscience to feel responsible toward the entire community, and to take into consideration the requirements of the general welfare."[10]

Today, what does such a responsibility entail? I believe it entails that we admit two things:

One, that because the university will shape its culture and society whatever it does, it must *recognize outright* and *advance formally* the notion that certain forms of knowing and behavior are more legitimate to society than others. Every competing interest and ideology does not have equal weight. There *are* methods of reason and debate that provide a way to make sound intellectual, ethical, and responsible choices. More than recognizing this fact, the university should bring such issues to the foreground of its attention—rather than pretend it can do its work responsibly without engaging them directly.

Second, the university should admit that if it is going to shape its students' lives and inevitably its society, it must incorporate within the students' experiences those realms of knowing that are not necessarily quantifiable. Matters of values and ideals require us to engage aspects of human experience *beyond* the realm of measurement. They require the application

---

[10] Maritain, *Education at the Crossroads*, p. 99.

of theology, philosophy and other humanities that deal with matters of conscience and spirit.

My point here is not to suggest at all that we should diminish attention to science or the quantifiable. I know better, having spent the better part of my life as a physicist. On this note, I have been pleased to learn that Maritain took a close look at the "new physics" of his day with admiration. He observed, "Few spectacles are as beautiful and moving for the mind as that of physics thus advancing toward its destiny like a huge throbbing ship."[11] Thus engaged by physics, Maritain also sought to evaluate its implications for his theories of knowing. He wrote, "It is fitting that our reflection should linger a moment over the New Physics, not to indulge in any rash prophecies on the future of its theories, but to see whether its scientific progress confirms or invalidates the epistemological principles we have been trying to establish up to this point."[12]

The relevance of Maritain's example is not so much that he explored physics with empathy and interest. It is that he, the philosopher, explored a field that depends upon quite different methods than his own, methods based in quantification.

As I have noted, the university needs various approaches and disciplines for its credibility and for the quality of its contributions to society. Maritain's example suggests that it also needs scholars crossing the hard lines of their specialty—and bringing back into their work a *holistic* conception of human experience.

The questions arise: Are we just federations of independent disciplines split into two ways of thinking? Or can we admit that the way of the scientific method and the quantitative, and the way of the humanistic and the spiritual, can not only co-exist but can *co*-contribute to human understanding? Are we ready to insist that faculty make this happen? Are we ready to insist that our own universities make this happen?

We might think of the crossroad of the university as resting upon two tectonic plates. One is the rational and quantitative, the other the humanistic and spiritual. Firmly interlocked, the foundation is strong. Too great a rift between them, and collapse must follow. As Lincoln reminds us in his allusion to Scripture, "A house divided against itself cannot stand."[13]

We know the scientific method has proven its place in the university.

[11] Jacques Maritain, *Distinguish to Unite or The Degrees of Knowledge*, trans. under the supervision of Gerald B. Phelan (New York: Charles Scribners' Sons, 1959), p. 154.

[12] Ibid., 155.

[13] Abraham Lincoln, *Great Speeches* (New York: Dover, 1991), p. 25.

However, the university cannot deny that unquantifiable forces of human nature also have a place in the understanding we seek. Aren't there other realms of experience that belong— as they have been expected to belong since the beginning—in the work of the public university?

I have noted how the contributions of the university build slowly but steadily, through the gauntlet of skepticism. Whatever fields seek to be a part of this dialogue must also justify themselves upon the highest standards of reason, scholarship, and integrity. But if they *do* justify themselves accordingly, if they apply the methods and practical reason that undergird the university's moral authority, they can help us choose best practices from worst, right ideas from wrong.

We must seek to benefit from their wisdom. Otherwise, we have stunted the conversation from the beginning. Otherwise, the university no longer serves as a crossroad, but as a one-way street which leads to dogma. I fear that is the pathway to placing justice in the hands of those with the most power, rather than in the minds of those with the soundest reasoning and principles. Where down that road lies the common good?

Maritain's vision of our society provokes these kinds of issues for the public university. These institutions must re-assume the entire responsibility with which our citizens first entrusted us. The university's work should rest not simply upon practicality and measurability, but also upon a noble and holistic conception of human beings and their education. Such idealism, grounded in reason, can perhaps offer us the *centripetal* force of ethics and civility needed in our age of *centrifugal* fragmentation.

In closing, I would point again to that image of the crossroad. As I have suggested, the public university was intended to be a crossroad in which the next generation of leaders could come together around the idea of civic virtue and the common good. Today, do we admit that the public university should do more than skill its students? Do we admit that matters of conscience, civic obligation, and virtue also have a role in the educational process? Do we accept that there are *many* forms of legitimate understanding that can contribute to this higher ethical and civil responsibility?

Finally, if we believe that the future of our society requires a shared conception of what, in particular, constitutes a *"good society,"* do we also believe that the public university should help *define*, *build* and *advance* this common good?

I propose these as questions worthy of direct debate within the public university. More than that, I propose that our society expects us to confront such questions. I do not propose to know the answers. I do propose that the university should.

The State of the Academy and the Hope for the Future

Herbert I. London

This paper is divided into two distinct themes which in themselves mimic Jacques Maritain's belief in degeneration and revitalization. In the traditional vision, the university perpetuated the idea of Western civilization in two separate but related ways. First, it imparted a sense of intellectual method which rejected dogmatic, orthodox, and conspiratorial formulations in favor of a broad-minded empiricism and a regard for the world's complexity. Second, it conveyed an underlying appreciation for the values of free society's respect for the individual and for the ideals of personal liberty and constitutional democracy which emanated from it. As a result, the university experience had a dual character, in part a process of intellectual training and in part a process of socialization.

This view of the academy, however, is alien to the spirit of what aspires to become the new, activist vision, protected by the same institution of tenure and academic freedom as the traditional version, yet fundamentally at odds with it methodologically and substantively. Armed with a variety of totalistic visions and millennial expectations, its partisans have little sympathy for open discourse or analytic procedures that fail to guarantee desired conclusions. As Howard Zinn, erstwhile professor of history at Boston University, once put it, "In a world where justice is maldistributed, there is no such thing as "neutral" or representative recapitulation of the facts." In such a view, objective truth is only what the present dictates or the future requires.

The organizing principle of the new scholarship inheres in its purpose rather than in its methods or theories. And its purpose is unremitting attack on cultural institutions, as well as political and economic institutions. This is a scholarship which sets out to prove what is already known—in short, the direct antithesis of what scholarship is.

29

Yet the ally in this systematic campaign to "capture the culture" (to borrow a phrase from Antonio Gramsci) is tenure and academic freedom. The classroom is now frequently employed as the setting for ethnic and class antagonism. Until recently the university served as an important means of assimilating the upwardly mobile and integrating future leaders of American society. A significant portion of the professorate now strives to do the reverse, fostering political estrangement and cultural segmentation. Tenure and academic freedom in the febrile minds of would-be revolutionaries have been transformed from institutions that militate against external pressure and manipulation into institutions that promote them.

The agitation organized by students during the overheated period from 1967 to 1973 was prompted, in my judgment, by rootlessness. The combination of war, the draft, a desire for social experimentation, spiraling divorce rates, promoted activism instead of thought, problem-solving instead of evidence gathering, doing instead of reflecting. The university as a center of learning was converted into the Paris Commune.

As I look back to that period, the high-school education that students received did not help matters. It was an era of curriculum experimentation producing a generation out of touch with basic cultural cues and unfamiliar with even the rudimentary facts about government and history. As Chester Finn Jr. and Diane Ravitch have pointed out in *What Do Seventeen Year Olds Know?* the answer, after much testing, is not very much. Thrust into a college setting, in thralldom to a utopian vision, these naive seventeen-year-olds, who do not know that the American Revolution came before the French Revolution, turned into right-thinking revolutionaries. Rather than arriving at opinion through a process of learning, reasoning and concluding, these products of American high schools made judgments *parti pris*, as if they were in the air they breathed or the coaxial cable that brought them visual images.

The prototypical student radical of the late sixties has been replaced by a different, complacent prototype today, albeit rootlessness is a feature common to both generations. In the past, rootlessness manifested itself as rebellion, now it is manifest as a search for orthodoxy, whether that takes the form of symbols, deconstruction or the emergence of an obsession with Third World authors. Students, as befits their age and idealism, have been in search of facile answers to complex questions, but it is—or should I say was—the responsibility of faculty members to lead them to a path which truth is sought rather than slogans.

It is, of course, customary for university presidents to proclaim that graduates are being prepared to face the demands of modern life. Yet the meaning of these words "prepare for life" is ambiguous. Recently a colleague tried to address this problem by proposing that students should learn problem-solving techniques as undergraduates. When pressed, he had to admit that problem-solving without knowledge was impossible. On another occasion I heard a distinguished scholar refer to the need for student "experience." Again the claim had a spurious ring to it. If experience is the essence of education, then my grandfather quite obviously deserved a Ph.D. in experience.

Professor Jacques Barzun advances the notion of *preposterism* to make the point that since knowledge is valuable, every intending college teacher shall produce research. The resultant knowledge explosion has had its fallout in every sector of society. There is more published to little purpose than was ever the case before. And the more that is published, the less we understand about our nation, our individual roles, our principles, our beliefs, and ourselves. So much of this so-called research is produced at the expense of teaching. Professor Barzun contends that the best liberal arts colleges have "a strong grip on solid subject matter and trust to its broadening, deepening and thickening effect." If this claim was once true, it is most certainly less true now. Universities compete for scholars judged mainly by reputation. Despite lip service given to teaching, it is much less valued than research, as both the allocation of chairs and salary determination amply show.

The explosion of research has also trivialized the curriculum through the proliferation of courses which pay obeisance to what is fashionable; one critic of higher education refers to the course guidebook as the "Chinese menu for dilettantes." What the extensive listing of courses actually represents is the abdication of faculty responsibility. In an atmosphere in which the purpose of higher education has been obscured by a reformist agenda and the curriculum has been turned into a battleground for departmental scrimmage, the number of courses grows in proportion to designated self-interest and the effort to accommodate "new" disciplines. The by-product of this change is an undergraduate program often devoid of commitment to teaching and often lacking an coherent purpose.

The ambiguity in the curriculum of most colleges is deeply embedded in the general ambiguity of what a university should be. There are two oft repeated contradictory messages in higher education: this is a public institution capable of participating in the affairs of state (At New York University we say "a private university in the public service"), and this is an elite institution, an ivory tower, if you will, whose majesty should not be compromised by the affairs of state. Retaining the dignity of the university, specifically its devotion to research, is increasingly difficult when the desire to merge and blur all roles and all purposes dominates university life.

It is instructive, I believe, that as demands are imposed on universities which they cannot fulfill and do not resist, the rhetoric associated with higher education has changed. Literature describing the institution invariably refers to saving neighborhoods and even saving nations, having world-class athletic programs and world-class laboratories; rarely do these descriptions mention the value of simple exchange between mentor and student that may inspire a thirst for knowledge, that may enrich the soul.

A. N. Whitehead maintains in *Science and the Modern World* that the twentieth-century research university is constructed according to principles of seventeenth-century physics. He argues that the revolutionary physics of our century, with its reconceiving self and world and its integration of fields of study, came too late to be incorporated into a Newtonian structure of mechanical parts separated by function. The "new" university is in fact old at heart, fracturing science and the humanities and reducing truth, goodness and beauty to mere expressions of subjective judgment. Moral virtue, which was an essential component of education before the Enlightenment, has been relegated to the archaic as professional and technical study are in the ascendancy.

William James's discussion of this "scientific nightmare" did not deter the evolution of the modern university, nor did the emergence of revolutionary ideas in physics and philosophy that defy narrow disciplinary boundaries. These ideas offered a conception of an integrated world of freedom, responsibility, and moral vitality. But the university was already well on its way to a Cartesian world of departments and bureaucracy. Although I may be daydreaming, I'm persuaded that many people outside the academy believe that the university has failed to address the common concern for meaning, for the humane and for the ethical.

In the present form of the university each department guards jealously a domain of expert knowledge, a subject-matter base underwritten by professional associations. Hence, will-nilly, the university has become a gatekeeper for professional power and academic identity. The combination of narrowly defined areas of interest combined with the pathology of the late sixties and beyond has produced courses that verge on the absurd, such as "Clitoral Hermeneutics" which I saw listed under Feminist Studies at a west coast college. Moreover, as technology is increasingly focused and as professionals are increasingly specialized, judgments about the world that emerge from the study of disciplines are construed solely in technical terms, often imperiling a sense of broadly defined human significance, the common *humanities* that inspired the liberal arts in the first place. Of course in some instances, the "new" disciplines such as semiotics challenge human significance.

It is hardly surprising that a new breed of humanities professor has similarly relegated all subject-matter to the realm of ideology, on the principle that truth is transitory. Universals are repudiated by this new-age professor, nurtured by an environment that is narrowly specialized. Professionalizing the humanities should be seen as an essential contradiction. It is worth recalling in this context the subtitle of Allan Bloom's *The Closing of the American Mind*. It is *How Higher Education Has Failed Democracy and Impoverished the Soul's of Today's Students*.

The failure of the modern university is, in my opinion, its unwillingness to consider "holistic" thinking that cuts across disciplinary barriers and the trivialization of knowledge with courses that foster a political ideology. To conceive of a mind separate from a body is to misunderstand the interdependence of all the elements within the self. At the same time, an obsessive concern with the self, with the ego's interests, has converted much learning into the pursuit of "I." I have lost patience with colleagues who start every discussion with the words, "How do you feel about . . . ?" The question is ultimately foolish unless clearly related to a reasoned conception of life.

When Wittgenstein engaged Freud in a conversation about psychotherapy, the would-be master of the mind replied that through protracted and undirected talk one can ultimately decipher the mystery of the unconscious. Wittgenstein, however, remained unpersuaded. "Sigmund," he reportedly said, "the reason I believe your assumption is wrong is that talk without limit or purpose ends in futility." It seems to me that Wittgenstein was not only making a point about psychotherapy, but also about education. Pedagogy demands limits and purpose. We cannot study everything or know anything without some idea of what is to be learned.

With cynicism about higher education increasing at a rate slower only than the increase in tuition, it is time to consider the end of the university as we have known it. I should hastily note that I do not welcome this outcome; my observation is little more than a logical extrapolation from what I have seen and experienced in the last quarter of a century.

In her book *The Case Against College*, Caroline Bird maintains that in calculating the costs and benefits of a college education, middle-class parents should not automatically rule in favor of college for their children. Whether a degree provides the economic rewards widely promised relative to the investment is, however, less significant than the fact that the university is a likely casualty in a changing climate of opinion.

How will the university change? Although presently impervious to market conditions because of regulations, retrenchment of public funds for public institutions and student aid will lead inexorably to new ways of delivering education. The Internet is in fact a potential worldwide university. Parents are already rebelling at the expenditure of $30,000 for an education in what Veblen once called "trained incapacity." Conceive of middle class folks who scrimp and save to send Mary or Johnny to a prestigious college where students learn to speak a form of psychobabble, do not understand the polity in which they reside and call their folks bourgeois pigs. Consider the search for orthodoxy that has emerged *pari passu* with the rootlessness of the young. And consider as well a spiritual awakening, and the contours of a "new" university became apparent.

Higher education will change, and from the point of view of someone who has observed standards vitiated in the zeitgeist, the change cannot come soon enough.

The Enlightened Mentality and Academic Freedom

Alice Ramos

I. Introduction

To be in a crisis is to be at a decisive moment, a turning point. In the medical field a crisis indicates a change in a disease the result of which will be either recovery or death. We might diagnose, as others have done, American Catholics as suffering from an identity crisis, at a moment when our country and culture stand in the greatest need of the kind of witness which we ought to have been uniquely equipped to offer.[1] Yet rather than think that this situation of crisis will lead to the demise of American Catholicism, or to put it in another way, the separation of American Catholics from Rome, I prefer to think that this crisis will result in a recovery, since we are becoming more and more aware of the problem and the need for a solution.

Awareness of the problem, although late in the day, has begun to penetrate colleges and universities which call themselves Catholic and which have gradually become little more than "shadowy imitations of secular institutions."[2] What it means for a university to be Catholic is for many not at all clear, given that in the name of pluralism so many Catholic colleges and universities have simply become like their liberal counterparts and thus lost their distinctiveness. However, it is true that "our colleges and universities are beginning to analyze and deliberate about and agonize over the threat to their Catholic character."[3] It is this analysis and deliberation which will

---

[1] Marvin R. O'Connell, "A Catholic University, Whatever That May Mean," in Theodore M. Hesburgh, C.S.C., ed. *The Challenge and Promise of a Catholic University* (Notre Dame, Indiana: University of Notre Dame Press, 1994), p. 236.

[2] Ibid., p. 240.

[3] Ibid., p. 241.

hopefully lead to a recovery; in addition, the present leadership in the Catholic Church is certainly working to foster such a recovery: one has only to think of the pope's document on Catholic universities, *Ex Corde Ecclesiae*, which so clearly states the identity and mission of a Catholic university, or the writings of Cardinal Ratzinger on the nature and mission of theology and his reflections on the theologian's academic freedom in relation to the institutional Church.

In his book *The Catholic Moment*, Richard J. Neuhaus refers to Ratzinger as a "crisis theologian," a term associated with certain European theologians of the 1930s. "Crisis theology" is distinguished from a theology of cultural synthesis and accommodation. The latter assumes that the world is well-disposed and receptive to the Christian message, that the world is in effect a friendly place. For crisis theologians, however, the "principalities and powers of the present age are in unremitting rage against the truth."[4] Although these theologians would agree that Christ is the beginning and the end of the whole of history's yearning, "this is asserted now by hope, only to be empirically vindicated in the End Time."[5] And what is very much on Ratzinger's mind is whether or not as we approach the End Time faith will be found on earth, for Ratzinger, like the pope, believes in the possibility of apostasy.[6]

It would seem then that what "crisis theology" is stressing, with its vision of the present age as waging battle against the truth, is reminiscent of the Augustinian conception of human history as a struggle between two implacably opposed spiritual forces: Augustine spoke of the City of God and the Earthly City or City of the World. The first is dedicated to God and to His will and to His glory, whereas the second is dedicated to something wholly different. According to Alvin Plantinga, the Augustinian struggle is present in the areas of scholarship and science, for we are not to think that these are religiously and metaphysically neutral, since they too are deeply involved in a three-way struggle or contest, the main protagonists of which are Christian theism, perennial naturalism, and creative anti-realism.[7] As Plantinga sees it: "the contemporary western intellectual world, like the world of [Augustine's] times, is a battleground or arena in which rages a

---

[4] Richard J. Neuhaus, *The Catholic Moment* (San Francisco: Harper & Row, Publishers, 1987), p. 189.

[5] Ibid.

[6] Ibid.

[7] Alvin Plantinga, "On Christian Scholarship," in Hesburgh, ed., *The Challenge and Promise*, pp. 268–270.

battle for our souls."[8] In addition, Plantinga, following Alasdair MacIntyre, notes that there are many contemporary academics and intellectuals who think of themselves as having no commitments at all: they are committed neither to perennial naturalism nor to any form of antirealism, and they are of course far from Christian theism.[9] But as Plantinga sees it, this lack of commitment is rooted in the thought that there is no such thing as truth as such; as he puts it: "Commitment goes with the idea that there is really such a thing as truth; to be committed to something is to hold that it is true, not just in some version, but *simpliciter* or absolutely—i.e., not merely true with respect to some other discourse or version, or with respect to what one or another group of human beings think or do."[10] To desire the truth, to be committed to the truth, should then engage one's freedom, in such a way that we may speak of exercising one's freedom *for* the truth. However, "The postmodern spirit, with its relativist, subjectivist, deconstructionist tendencies, seems to have abandoned any traditional quest for truth and to have turned its energies instead in the direction of power."[11] The purpose of this paper will be to show how commitment to the truth, to a community of faith and to tradition, is imperative for the Catholic theologian so that his work does not degenerate into an individualistic, liberal enterprise. We will also see how the issue of academic freedom among contemporary Catholic theologians in colleges and in universities which are themselves Catholic is reminiscent of Kant's treatment of the uses which a clergyman-scholar may make of his reason. Let us begin with the enlightened mentality of Kant which so permeates the intellectual world of today.

II. The Enlightenment and the Clergyman-Scholar

In his essay "What is Enlightenment?," Kant distinguishes between the private and public uses of the clergyman-scholar's reason. A contemporary reader of Kant cannot help but see in the distinction a foreshadowing of the problem of academic freedom among present-day theologians. While some thinkers in the eighteenth century had defined enlightenment with reference to the goal it fostered, that is, the destiny of man, Kant defined enlightenment not in terms of what it achieved, but rather in terms of what it es-

---

[8] Ibid., p. 269.
[9] Ibid., p. 277.
[10] Ibid., p. 278.
[11] Thomas V. Morris, "A Baptist View of the Catholic University," in Hesburgh, ed., *The Challenge and Promise*, p. 228.

caped.[12] For Kant, enlightenment meant a release from that immaturity which arises not from a "lack of understanding," but rather as a consequence of a moral failure, that is, a "lack of resolution and courage" to use one's understanding "without the guidance of another."[13] If man is to live in an "enlightened age," he must release himself from "self–incurred tutelage"; in other words, he must dare to make use of his reason "without direction from another."[14] According to Kant, for enlightenment to prosper, "all that is needed is freedom," and the freedom Kant had in mind is "the most innocuous form of all—freedom to make *public use* of one's reason in all matters."[15]

By the "public" use of reason Kant meant that "use which anyone may make of it as a man of learning addressing the entire reading public." This use of reason is contrasted to the "private" use which a person may make of his reason in a particular *civil* post or office with which he is entrusted.[16] In man's private use of reason he behaves "passively," bound by an "artificial accord" to advance or to defend certain "public ends." He functions as "part of a machine," and as such he cannot argue. By contrast, in his public use of reason man acts as "a member of the complete commonwealth or even of a cosmopolitan society"; within such a framework, an individual "may indeed argue without harming the affairs in which he is employed in a private capacity." Restrictions on the private use of reason in no way contradict the goal of enlightenment, but the public use of reason must remain free, since "it alone can bring about enlightenment among men."[17]

To illustrate the difference between the public and private uses of reason, Kant makes reference to soldiers, citizens, and clergymen. Of these three cases, Kant devotes particular attention to the responsibilities of a scholarly clergy. A clergyman may write whatever he pleases in books and articles addressed to the reading public, but when he is addressing his pupils or his congregation, he is bound to adhere to his church's "symbols"—those basic doctrines of the faith to which clergymen and teachers

---

[12] James Schmidt, "What Enlightenment Was: How Moses Mendelssohn and Immanuel Kant Answered the *Berlinische Monatsschrift*," p. 11, unpublished manuscript.

[13] Immanuel Kant, "Beantwortung der Frage: Was ist Aufklärung?," trans. H.B. Nisbet in H. Reiss, ed., *Kant's Political Writings* (Cambridge University Press, 1970), p. 54

[14] Ibid., p. 54.

[15] Ibid., p. 55.

[16] Ibid.

[17] Ibid., p. 56.

were required to swear allegiance before taking up their posts.[18] At the center of Kant's discussion is the question of the limits of those duties which bound an official of a church. Kant argued that, insofar as they were fulfilling their responsibilities to the church as an institution, clergymen must adhere to the teachings of the church, even in those cases in which they might have reservations as to their truth. According to Kant, "[t]here is nothing in this which need trouble the conscience."[19] What a man taught as an officer of the church "is presented by him as something which he is not empowered to teach at his own discretion, but which he is employed to expound in a prescribed manner and in someone else's name."[20] "He will say: Our church teaches this or that, and these are the arguments it uses. He then extracts as much practical value as possible for his congregation from precepts to which he would not himself subscribe with full conviction, but which he can nevertheless undertake to expound, since it is not entirely impossible that they may contain truth."[21] The interest of Kant's clergyman here is in the practical, not in the dogmatic, dimension of religion. For Kant, it is "not entirely impossible" that the doctrines of the church be true, but in any case, religion is a matter of practical faith, not of theoretical certainty. However, there is a limit to how far a clergyman can go in maintaining this separation between official dogma and personal conviction: "nothing contrary to the essence of religion" must be present in the teachings of the church, for if this were the case the clergyman "would not be able to carry out his official duties in good conscience, and would have to resign."[22]

According to Kant then, the use which the clergyman employed as a teacher makes of his reason in the presence of his congregation is purely *private*, since the congregation constitutes no more than a domestic gathering. In such a situation, Kant considers that the priest "is not and cannot be free, since he is acting on a commission imposed from outside."[23] As a scholar, however, addressing the world at large through his writings, the clergyman makes public use of his reason and "enjoys unlimited freedom to use his own reason and to speak in his own person."[24] It is evident from

---

[18] Ibid.
[19] Ibid.
[20] Ibid.
[21] Ibid.
[22] Ibid., pp. 56–57.
[23] Ibid., p. 57.
[24] Ibid.

what has been said that Kant saw nothing objectionable in a church requiring its representatives to teach the doctrines of their religion according to certain established conventions. But for Kant, no church was free "to commit itself by oath to an unalterable set of doctrines."[25] To do so would impede the progress of knowledge and thus create a barrier for enlightenment. As Kant put it: "One age cannot enter into alliance on oath to put the next age in a position where it would be impossible for it to extend and correct its knowledge . . . or to make any progress whatsoever in enlightenment. This would be a crime against human nature, whose original destiny lies in precisely such progress."[26]

In order to determine whether any particular measure could be adopted as a law, "we need only ask whether a people could impose such a law upon itself."[27] While for short periods of time it might be necessary to impose a particular set of political and social arrangements, pending a better solution, even during such periods Kant insists that "each citizen, particularly the clergyman, would be given a free hand as a scholar to comment publicly, i.e., in his writings, on the inadequacies of current institutions." However to agree, "even for a single lifetime," on a permanent, unquestionable religious constitution, would be to adopt a law which would "virtually nullify a phase of man's progress." The renunciation of enlightenment, whether by a people, a monarch, or even an individual, "means violating and trampling underfoot the sacred rights of mankind."[28]

In the name of the spirit of freedom then, Kant holds that "ecclesiastical dignitaries, notwithstanding their official duties, may in their capacity as scholars freely and publicly submit to the judgment of the world their verdicts and opinions, even if these deviate here and there from orthodox doctrine."[29] Because of the particular attention paid to the clergyman-scholar, Kant's essay portrays *matters of religion* as the focal point of enlightenment, i.e., of man's emergence from his self-incurred immaturity."[30] According to Kant, religious immaturity is the most dangerous type of servility; as he puts it: "Dogmas and formulas, those mechanical instruments for rational use (or rather misuse) of [man's] natural endowments, are the ball and chain of his permanent immaturity. And if anyone did throw them off,

[25] Ibid.
[26] Ibid.
[27] Ibid.
[28] Ibid., p. 58.
[29] Ibid., p. 59.
[30] Ibid.

he would still be uncertain about jumping over even the narrowest of trenches, for he would be unaccustomed to free movement of this kind."[31] In order to make enlightenment possible, the guardians of the people in spiritual matters must therefore be allowed unlimited freedom to make public use of their reason. If this were not the case, we would have, according to Kant, a permanently absurd situation.[32] But because the guardians of the people in religious matters have in effect been able to throw off "the yoke of immaturity," they will "disseminate the spirit of rational respect for personal value and for the duty of all men to think for themselves."[33] In an age of enlightenment, then, intellectual freedom is to be fostered so that man be able not only to think freely but also to act freely.[34]

III. The Church and the Theologian

Although the case of Kant's clergyman-scholar may be slightly different from that of today's Catholic theologian, if only because not all Catholic theologians are clergymen, there are nonetheless some striking similarities. Kant's appeal to the clergyman's public use of reason is an appeal to reason on one's own without regard to the community of faith to which the clergyman belongs. This particular use of reason relies on its own authority, thus disconnecting itself from church authority viewed as something externally imposed. The freedom which the public use of reason requires in the case of the clergyman-scholar is therefore a freedom *from* authority, *from* permanent and unquestionable truths, rather than a freedom *for* the truth. And this, all in the name of progress towards greater enlightenment, an enlightenment which is not necessarily a movement toward truth.[35] It is evident therefore that in the public use of his reason the clergyman-scholar is acting as an individual, apart from the tradition and the community to which he belongs. He is therefore writing and speaking as man, as a lone individual, and not as a "cog in a machine"—to use an "enlightened" phrase—who has a function to fulfill within a given group.

This enlightened mentality as portrayed in Kant's essay and as found in contemporary scholarship and theology is, I believe, subject matter for many of Cardinal Ratzinger's essays. Let us begin first of all with

---

[31] Ibid., p. 55.
[32] Ibid., p. 57.
[33] Ibid., p. 55.
[34] Ibid., p. 59.
[35] Alasdair MacIntyre, *First Principles, Final Ends, and Contemporary Philosophical Issues* (Milwaukee, Wisconsin: Marquette University Press, 1990), p. 66.

Ratzinger's characterization of freedom within the academy. In an essay titled "On the Essence of the Academy and Its Freedom," Cardinal Ratzinger says: "academic" freedom is freedom for the *truth*, and its justification is simply to exist for the sake of the truth, without having to look back toward the objectives it has reached."[36] In this essay Ratzinger speaks of the Christian option which considers truth as prior to making, and we might also add, prior to doing. There is no doubt that in the modern age, truth has been manipulated to such an extent that we might say the following: "If you can't do what you want to do with the truth, then you change it, so that it suits you and your actions." One has only to think of the area of moral theology, in which a false compassion at times takes precedence over the truth. The promotion of people's happiness, a short-lived happiness at that, also seems of more importance than truth-orientation. But if man's capacity for action, if man's freedom, is unchecked by truth, then sooner or later while appearing to be free, man will find himself enslaved because he has closed himself off from the transcendent. As Ratzinger puts it: "anarchic pseudo-freedom is at work behind every refusal of the bond to the truth and of the demands it makes. Those counterfeit freedoms, which predominate today, are the real menace to true freedom."[37] To open oneself to the truth is in effect to journey toward the divine. It is for this reason that Ratzinger says:

> To think through the essence of truth is to arrive at the notion of God. In the long run, it is impossible to maintain the unique identity of the truth, in other words, its dignity (which in turn is the basis of the dignity both of man and of the world), without learning to perceive in it the unique identity and dignity of the living God. Ultimately, therefore, reverence for the truth is inseparable from that disposition of veneration which we call adoration. Truth and worship stand in an indissociable relationship to each other; one cannot really flourish without the other, however often they have gone their separate ways in the course of history.[38]

According to Ratzinger, therefore, freedom for the truth cannot exist without the acknowledgment and worship of the divine.[39]

Now what Ratzinger says here is of utmost importance for the contemporary theologian, for the true theologian does not produce or make the

---

[36] Joseph Cardinal Ratzinger, "On The Essence of the Academy and Its Freedom," in *The Nature and Mission of Theology*, trans. Adrian Walker (San Francisco: Ignatius Press, 1995), p. 37 (hereafter *NMT*).

[37] Ibid., p. 41.

[38] Ibid., p. 40.

[39] Ibid., p. 41.

truth. Theology is for Ratzinger a specifically Christian phenomenon which follows from the structure of faith: faith is not separable from truth, it has to do with truth, for what faith initially reveals is, "In the beginning was the Word." It is because of this Word that eternal reason penetrates all of creation; faith reveals to us that eternal reason is the ground, the foundation, for all things. It is only natural therefore that faith should seek understanding. "Understanding, hence, rational engagement with the priorly given Word, is a constitutive principle of the Christian faith, which of necessity spawns theology."[40] The theological enterprise is therefore a pondering about what God has said and thought before us. If theology abandons this secure ground, then it becomes a private project; as Ratzinger puts it: "The truth of faith . . . is not bestowed upon the isolated individual, for God has willed instead to build history and community with it. It has its place in a common subject: the people of God, the Church."[41] Theology must therefore be understood within the context of the community of faith which is the Church. Among certain theologians, present-day so-called academic freedom is resistant to this close bond between the theological enterprise and the believing community. But without church teaching, theology renders itself sterile. If the authority of the church is considered a foreign element for the science of theology, then both theology and the church are harmed in their integrity: "For a church without theology is impoverished and blind. A theology without a church, however, soon dissolves into arbitrary theory."[42] Essential to the theologian is not only methodology but also a deep participation within the community of faith. For this reason, Ratzinger stresses the priority of faith, the priority of the Word which is the measure of theology, and which requires its own organ, that is, the Magisterium, the teaching authority of the Church. Ratzinger does not think that Catholic theologians reject church authority in principle, though it does seem that they regard church authority as alien and extrinsic to their thought. This is especially the case of theologians in a university setting, who consider themselves to be part of a world of science in which "nothing counts except the "reasonable" and "objective" argument."[43] Authority for

---

[40] Ratzinger, "On The 'Instruction Concerning the Ecclesial Vocation of the Theologian,'" in *NMT*, p. 103.

[41] Ibid., p. 104.

[42] Neuhaus, *The Catholic Moment*, p. 140.

[43] Ratzinger, "The Spiritual Basis and Ecclesial Identity of Theology," in *NMT*, p. 47.

such theologians is viewed as a power play. And yet, theology will only be historically relevant in its presence within the church, so that it does not dissolve into ideology whose interest is centered on the acquisition of power.

Since the Council, the Magisterium has often been portrayed as "the last holdover of a failed authoritarianism."[44] According to Ratzinger, "The impression [given] was that the insistent claim to competence on the part of a nonacademic authority threatened to keep thought under tutelage, whereas in reality the path to knowledge could not be prescribed by authority but rather depended solely upon the force of argument."[45] These words are no doubt reminiscent of the enlightened mentality. The orientation of theology toward a strictly "scientific" status according to the standards of the modern university tends to divorce theology from the life of the Church.[46] It is for this reason that it has become imperative to reflect on the relationship of theology to the Magisterium. In an essay titled "The Spiritual Basis and Ecclesial Identity of Theology," Ratzinger begins by referring to the words of Heinrich Schlier: "It is unlikely that any sensible Christian would contest that the care for the Word of God among men is entrusted to the church alone."[47] Schlier's words came at a time in history in which there was an attempt to convert Lutheran Christianity into a German Christianity; however, for our purposes here what is important is Schlier's emphasis on the fact that theology exists in and from the church, that it is bound to the creed and thus to the teaching Church. The teaching office of the Church is not, as some contemporary theologians seem to think, primarily "jurisdictional," that is, concerned with discipline and order, it is rather concerned with truth, with the truths of both faith and morals, because the Magisterium is charged with the care of souls.[48] When the theologian accepts as "the voice and the way of the truth the greater understanding which is already present as a prior given in the church's faith,"[49] then he accepts the church's proclamation of the Word as the measure for theology, and recognizes that theology is not the measure for the proclamation.[50] When the the-

---

[44] Ratzinger, "On The 'Instruction . . . ,'" in *NMT*, p. 102.
[45] Ibid.
[46] Ibid., p. 116.
[47] Ratzinger, "The Spiritual Basis . . . ," in *NMT*, p. 45.
[48] William E. May, "Catholic Moral Teaching and the Limits of Dissent," in William W. May, ed., *Vatican Authority and American Catholic Dissent* (New York: Crossroad, 1987), p. 90. May emphasizes, along with Aquinas, that the teaching office of the Church is primarily pastoral in nature, charged with the *cura animarum*.
[49] Ratzinger, "Pluralism as a Problem for Church and Theology," in *NMT*, p. 97.
[50] Ibid. See also Neuhaus, *The Catholic Moment*, p. 143.

ologian thus accepts church authority in his work, he participates in the church's task of instructing souls in the faith and thus caring for souls. As Ratzinger puts it: "When one teaches, not on his own authority, but in the name of the common subject, the church, the assumption is that he recognizes this fundamental role [caring for the faith of the faithful] and freely obliges himself to it."[51] Ratzinger emphasizes the free commitment on the part of the theologian for the truth, for the unadulterated proclamation of the faith to souls. Thus it would seem that the theologian who separates himself from church teaching in the name of scholarship is not rightfully caring for souls. For some contemporary theologians, critical method is incompatible with confessional faith since they feel that the latter requires the theology scholar to accept specific conclusions on dogmatic grounds.[52] Such dogmatism would be for them a hindrance to their free use of reason. Not to recognize church authority, *auctoritas*, is really to separate oneself from the believing community, and therefore to carry out the theological enterprise in private, as the lone individual of Kant's clergyman-scholar, for *auctoritas* is the basic presupposition of community life.[53]

On a number of occasions, Ratzinger notes how theology is rooted in the church:

> Insofar as the Church is a corporate subject which transcends the narrowness of individuals, she is the condition which makes theological activity possible . . . .[T]wo things are essential for the theologian. First, the methodological rigor which is part and parcel of the business of scholarship; . . . philosophy, the historical disciplines and the human sciences as privileged partners of the theologian. But he also has need of inner participation in the organic structure of the church; he needs that faith which is prayer, contemplation and life.[54]

Ratzinger reminds us here of what the great theologians of the Middle Ages had already seen so clearly: that mere learning does not suffice for theological understanding, but that it must be complemented by a life of prayer, born of love. Theology is for Ratzinger a matter of conversion, of devotion to a community and to the truths it bears. The work of the theologian does not begin with unthinking submission to authority, which Ratzinger considers to be a juridical view of theology, but rather begins and always returns to the recognition of the ultimately authoritative Christ, that is, the Word

---

[51] Neuhaus, *The Catholic Moment*, p. 145.

[52] Plantinga, "On Christian Scholarship," in Hesburgh, ed., *The Challenge and Promise*, p. 290.

[53] Ratzinger, "On 'The Instruction . . . ,'" in *NMT*, p. 113.

[54] Ibid., p. 105.

that always precedes us, the I who becomes our I.[55] Thus, for Ratzinger, conversion, the losing of self to the other, the Pauline assertion, "I live, no longer I, but Christ lives in me" (Gal 2), is the presupposition of theology.[56] It is evident therefore that theology involves not only reasoning but a quest for perfection, for sanctity, which is in reality a commitment, an exercise of freedom for the truth.

IV. Conclusion

In closely linking theology and sanctity, Ratzinger is not indulging in sentimental or pietistic speech, for he is, as was noted above, following the tradition of the great medieval theologians. St. Thomas reminds us that learning must be joined to the experience of divine things in order to carry out the work of the theologian. And St. Bonaventure points not only to the desire for truth and understanding inherent in the faith, but also to the dynamism of love, which desires to know the beloved more intimately. As Richard of St. Victor puts it: "Love is the faculty of seeing."[57] And love for the Christian is nurtured in prayer, in dialogue with the divine. And it is this dialogue which enables seeing, that is, knowledge and understanding. Ratzinger reminds us that knowledge involves a similarity between the knower and the known, that like is known by like. Consequently, in order for theological understanding to take place, the theologian must enter into the reality of the divine and become one with it. In speaking for example of the theologian's study of Christ, Ratzinger says:

> Real advances in Christology, therefore, can never come merely as the result of the theology of the schools, and that includes the modern theology as we find it in critical exegesis, in the history of doctrine and in an anthropology oriented toward the human sciences, etc. All this is important, as important as schools are. But it is insufficient. It must be complemented by the theology of the saints, which is theology from experience. All real progress in theological understanding has its origin in the eye of love and in its faculty of beholding.[58]

It would seem, then, that together with learning the more the theologian surrenders his subjectivity, the more he finds himself within the unity of a

---

[55] Neuhaus, *The Catholic Moment*, p. 147.
[56] Ibid., pp. 140–142.
[57] Ratzinger, *Behold the Pierced One: An Approach to a Spiritual Christology*, trans. Graham Harrison (San Francisco: Ignatius Press, 1986), p. 27.
[58] Ibid.

new subject, which makes possible contact with the ground of all reality.[59] Theology thus involves a surrender of the autonomous subject in an acceptance of the Word which always precedes us. The greater the conversion of the theologian, the greater his penetration into the truth. Thus it may be said that the more the theologian is himself interiorly transformed, the more he will be able to transform the souls of those whom he teaches. The theologian in the university thus has a tremendous responsibility. The Catholic university, in particular, is called to this transformation of humanity; only thus does she and especially the theologian contribute to the progress of society.[60] We might end therefore by recalling that contemporary scholarship is not neutral and that the contemporary western intellectual world is indeed a battleground for souls.

[59] Ratzinger, "The Spiritual Basis and Ecclesial Identity of Theology," in *NMT*, p. 51.
[60] See John Paul II, *Apostolic Constitution on Catholic Universities* (Washington, D.C.: U.S. Catholic Conference, 1990).

Was Ist Aufklärung? Notes on Maritain, Rorty, and Bloom With Thanks But No Apologies to Immanuel Kant

Francis Slade

> Our crucial need and problem is to rediscover the natural faith of reason in truth.
>
> Jacques Maritain, *Education at the Crossroads*

I

Education at the Crossroads is Jacques Maritain speaking at Yale in 1943 as a philosopher and as a Catholic about education, doing then and there what he had always done and continued to do until his death: speaking as a philosopher and as a confessing Catholic. What strikes us as we look back at Maritain through the books that he has left us is his public loneliness. And in that light what must impress us is the love of truth and the aspiration towards wisdom out of which these books had to have been written.

Because Maritain's public voice was always that of a Catholic as well as a philosopher, he exemplified what Josef Pieper calls "existential honesty as a philosopher," refusing to "disregard the truths of divine revelation that you have accepted in faith."[1] Consequently as a philosopher he was largely ignored outside Catholic milieu. Being a Catholic and making no secret of its significance for his thinking as a philosopher, what he said was considered

[1] Josef Pieper, *In Defense of Philosophy* (San Francisco: Ignatius Press, 1992), p. 113.

beyond the permissible limits of what can be accepted as serious public discourse. As Richard Rorty puts it, "To be part of society is, in the relevant sense, to be taken as a possible conversational partner by those who shape the society's self-image."[2] Maritain spoke and wrote, and was accorded polite, even respectful receptions, but he had no conversational partners among the shapers of the society's self-image. He was not part of what Rorty calls "society." His presence is undetectable on the radar screens that catch what counts as instances of canonically-done twentieth-century philosophy.

Maritain's situation was hardly unique; it was, and it is, the situation of Christianity, and the Catholic Church in particular, in European modernity. Intellectual disestablishment of Christianity at the Enlightenment was followed by political disestablishment, which in time became social marginalization. Religious modernism is one of the responses to this. Modernism grasps that the Church is not a private sect, existing on the margins of society, excluded from the public space and accepting that exclusion. It understands that to be public again Christianity must become reestablished in some sense, and, that to do this, it must overcome the intellectual disestablishment effected by the Enlightenment. Modernism's response, both Protestant and Catholic, is "aggiornamento," i.e., the abandonment of everything in historical Christianity that does not conform to Enlightenment standards of rationality. Modernism's "aggiornamento" leaves us with what looks a lot like Enlightenment, but hardly resembles historical Christianity. Modernists successfully reestablish themselves as "conversational partners," but they have nothing to say which differs in substance from what can be said by anyone who is not a Christian; they become undetectable on the radar screens of orthodoxy. Richard Rorty's formulations again serve to delineate the situation of Catholic belief when Enlightenment modernity and postmodernity has become the public voice:

> To say that there is no place for the questions that Nietzsche or Loyola would raise is not to say that the views of either are unintelligible. . . . Nor is it just to say that our preferences conflict with theirs. It is to say that the conflict between these men and us is so great that "preferences" is the wrong word. . . . Rather we heirs of the Enlightenment think of . . . Nietzsche or Loyola as . . . "mad." We do so because there is no way to see them as fellow citizens . . . people whose life plans might, given ingenuity and good will, be fitted in with other citizens. . . . They are crazy because the limits of sanity are set by what we can take seriously. . . . We do not conclude that Nietzsche and Loyola

---

[2] "On Ethnocentrism," in *Philosophical Papers*, vol. 1 (New York: Cambridge University Press, 1991), p. 206.

are crazy because they hold unusual views on certain "fundamental" topics; rather we conclude this only after extensive attempts at exchange of . . . views have made us realize that we are not going to get anywhere.[3]

The "*we*" here is the Rortian *we*, the meaning of which is, in Rorty's words, "contrastive in the sense that it contrasts with a "they" which is also made up of human beings—the wrong sort of human beings."[4] Rorty is saying that *we*, the heirs of the Enlightenment, cannot converse with *you* who believe as Loyola did. And since *we* define the terms of public discourse, what *you* say must be private. No one of course wishes to be "the wrong sort of human being." Someone in this position finds himself pushed in the direction of a divorce between what he asserts privately to himself and what, as one of the *we*, he says is true. While in his heart he may know he's right, he's not allowed, and does not allow himself, to tell anyone, a theme upon which there are a number of variations depending upon the enthusiasm manifested for the suppression of private belief in favor of public utterance. What Sir Paul Rycaut, Secretary to the English Embassy at the Porte, noted in his *Memoirs* (1668) about the conduct of Christians living under Ottoman rule describes the behavior which tempts many Christians, and is adopted by some, living under, and accepting, the rule of the aggressively secular elites—the Rortian *we*—of our society:

> It is worth a wise man's observation how gladly the Greek and Armenian Christians imitate the Turkish habit, and come as near to it as they dare, and how proud they are when they are privileged upon some extraordinary occasion to appear without their Christian distinction.

We may take as an instance of this temptation the "seamless garment," a contribution to what has been called "the ideological vulgate, always in the process of being reworked,"[5] which imitates the habit of the secular elites

---

[3] Richard Rorty, "The Priority of Democracy to Philosophy," *Philosophical Papers* vol. 1, pp. 187–188; 191. One is reminded here of the opening of Auguste Comte's *Catechisme Positiviste*: "Au nom du passé et de l'avenir, les serviteurs théoriques et les serviteurs pratique de l'HUMANITE viennent prendre dignement la direction générale des affaires terrestres . . . en excluant irrévocablement de la suprématie politique tous les divers esclaves de Dieu, catholiques, protestants, ou déistes, comme étant à la fois arrières et pertubateurs." *Catechisme Positiviste* (Paris: Garnier), p. 1.

[4] *Contingency, Irony, and Solidarity* (New York: Cambridge University Press, 1989), p. 190. The Rortian "we"—the right sort of human beings—is variously described. It will mean something like we twentieth-century liberals or we heirs to the historical contingencies which have created more and more cosmopolitan, more and more democratic political institutions. But the core identity is "liberal intellectuals of the secular modern West." Rorty, *Philosophical Papers*, vol. 1, p. 29.

as closely as those who propose it dare. Repeated suppression of what one would like to think one believes in favor of what it is allowable to say as publicly acceptable—"self-censorship," to employ the current vogue term—shapes what one actually believes in conformity with what it is publicly acceptable to say. Is it possible that Mario Cuomo really believes that abortion is morally wrong? What he said he privately believed was never discernible beyond the sheer assertion of it. It never made any difference, it never possessed any visible *morphē*, shape, or form. The assertion was empty. What counts is what is visible, what is publicly said and done. In what he publicly said and did abortion does not appear as an immoral act. On the other hand, everyone knows that Governor Cuomo really believes that capital punishment is an immoral act. The old Roman liturgy in the Collect of the second Mass of Christmas Day prayed for the life lived in obedience to revealed truth:

> *Da nobis, quaesumus, omnipotens Deus: ut, qui nova incarnati Verbi tuo luce perfundimur; hoc in nostro resplendeat opere, quod per fidem fulget in mente.* (Grant, we beseech Thee, almighty God, that we, upon whom is poured the new light of Thy Word made flesh, may show forth in our actions that which by faith shineth in our minds.)[6]

[5] Alain Besançon, "The Confusion of Tongues," *Daedalus* (Spring 1979): p. 40. The "seamless garment" refers to the effort made by some American Catholics to soften the political impact of the Catholic stance against abortion by asserting that principled opposition to abortion should entail acceptance of those provisions of the liberal welfare state they denominate as "life issues." Being consistent on all life issues is "the seamless garment." The dominant liberal elites will tend to be morally inconsistent on one point, abortion, while conservatives who oppose abortion would tend to be inconsistent when it is a question of the other "life issues." Thus candidates of the secularized liberal elites could be considered to be morally superior, despite their aggressive position on abortion, and, the implication is, should be preferred at elections to conservative candidates. This also meant that Democrats who professed to be Catholics need not take issue with their party's identification with "abortion rights." In the "seamless garment" we have a mixture of the secular political agenda of social justice with a religious rhetoric intended to legitimate it and to justify the posture of the ecclesiastical bureaucracies whose members aspire "to be taken seriously"as conversational partners by the "liberal intellectuals of the secular modern West" (Rorty, *Philosophical Papers*, vol. 1, p. 29). Cf. James Hitchcock, "The Guilty Secret of Liberal Christianity," *New Oxford Review* (October 1996): pp. 10–17; and Peter Berger, "The Decline of Secularism," *The National Interest* (Winter 1996–97): p. 12.

[6] Romans 1:6 speaks of "the obedience of faith"; 1:7 that "the just man shall live by faith." On the etiolation of belief that occurs with the separation of life from faith, see Jacques Maritain, "The Substitute for Theology Among the Simple," in *The Collected Works of Jacques Maritain*, vol. 20 (Notre Dame, Indiana: University of Notre Dame Press, 1997), pp. 275; 284–88.

"I believed and so I spoke, we too believe, and so we speak," St. Paul says, citing Psalm 116.[7] Christianity cannot live in the privacy of the heart. It is the religion of publicness. To cease to profess it publicly is "to lose the Faith." This is because Christianity is the religion of truth. That is why Christianity is rightly known as "Catholic." The Catholic understanding of truth is that all truth is from God, given by Him and received by us, whether it be truth known by natural reason or by supernatural revelation. Its being from God does not cancel either human thought or human will. Knowledge of the truth presupposes both exercise of mind in the case of truths naturally knowable by us and the exercise of will in the case of supernatural truths. The Catholic understanding of truth is structurally the same as the Catholic understanding of nature and grace. Grace and salvation are entirely from God, but they are completely dependent upon human assent: "Be it done unto me according to Thy word."[8] The Catholic-Christian understanding of truth is presented by St. Augustine in *Confessions* XII.25:

> They are proud and have not known Moses's meaning, but love their own, not because it is true, but because it is their own. Otherwise they would have an equal love for another man's true opinion, just as I love what they say when they speak the truth, not because it is theirs but because it is true. Therefore, because it is true, it is by that very fact not theirs. Therefore, if they love it because it is true, then it is both theirs and mine, since it is the common property of all lovers of truth. But in that they contend that Moses did not mean what I say but what they say, I will have none of them, I do not love them, because even if what they say is so, yet their boldness is not the boldness of knowledge but of rashness, it is born not of vision but of pride.[9] Your judgments, O Lord, are to be feared with trembling. For Your truth is not mine, nor his, nor any other man's, but belongs to all of us whom You publicly call to its communion warning us most terribly that we must not will to keep it for ourselves lest we be deprived of it. Whoever arrogates completely to himself that which you propose for the enjoyment of all men, and desires that to be his own which belongs to all men, is driven from what is common to all men to what is really his own, that is from truth to a lie. For he who speaks a lie speaks his own.

[7] 2 Corinthians 4:13.

[8] Luke 1:48.

[9] Augustine is saying here that they hold it is their asserting it, that makes it true; it is because it is *theirs* that it is true. As has been well said, "Such is human vanity that we often prefer having any view, just so long as it is ours, to having the truth." John C. McCarthy, "Some Preliminary Remarks on 'Cognitive Interest' in Husserlian Phenomenology," *Husserl Studies* 11:146, 1994–95.

Those who love truth because it is *theirs* understand truth as originating from themselves; it is true because they made it true. They have made the truth and this is why they claim it is theirs. They love it as their creation. This is their boldness, the boldness of the rash, born of arrogance. And this is why Augustine does not love them and will have none of them. They appropriate for themselves what is God's. Truth does not originate in men. "Your truth is not mine, nor his, nor any other man's, but belongs to all of us whom You publicly call to its communion." *Your truth Not mine, nor his, nor any man's*: In making us capable of thinking, God has made us capable of truth. The public call to communion in the truth is thinking. Thinking is communion in the truth, not generation of the truth. Thinking as the disclosure of the truth is the essentially public act. That human beings do not originate truth by generating it from themselves is most emphatically confirmed by revelation in which God discloses the truth about Himself to us. Just to the extent that we understand truth as originating from ourselves—*willing to keep it for ourselves*, in Augustine's words—to that extent, Augustine says, *we are deprived of it*. Truth disappears from our vocabulary as an operative term defining human speech. What men say becomes unrecognizable in terms appropriate to truth; it is taken as self-creation, freedom. *Each turns aside into a world of his own*.[10] What men say becomes instruments of power. Rorty gets it exactly right here:

> Philosophical superficiality and lightmindedness helps along the disenchantment of the world. It helps make the world's inhabitants more pragmatic, . . . more receptive to the appeal of instrumental rationality.[11]

In a postmetaphysical culture thinking ceases to be access to the truth which God has manifested to all. Rorty remarks that a postmetaphysical culture is as possible and as desirable as a postreligious one.[12] But in this instance Rorty doesn't get it quite right. Whether or not a postreligious culture is desirable, a postmetaphysical culture is a necessary condition for a postreligious one, if the postreligious one is, as ours is, a post-Christian one. Recently, Cardinal Ratzinger has observed that

> the indigence of philosophy, the indigence to which paralyzed, positivist reason has led itself, has turned into the indigence of our faith. . . . If

---

[10] Cf. Heraclitus, DK B89.

[11] "The Priority of Democracy to Philosophy," *Philosophical Papers*, vol.1, p. 193.

[12] *Contingency, Irony, and Solidarity*, p. xvi.

the door to metaphysical cognition remains closed . . . faith is destined to atrophy: it simply lacks air to breathe.[13]

As St. Clement of Alexandria pointed in the second century when he described the role of Greek Philosophy as *praeparatio evangelii*[14]: the Gospel, addressed to the minds of men, presupposes reason in its full and reflective exercise. The exclusion of Christianity from reason is what the Enlightenment is all about. The Enlightenment attack on Christianity attacks not only the explicit symbols of belief, the articles of the Creed, but also the conceptions of reason and truth which Christianity presupposes, the *praeambula fidei*.[15]

II

Was ist Aufklarung? Enlightenment is reason understood as rule. Enlightenment is consubstantial with classic modern philosophy from Descartes to Hegel. Classic modern philosophy has two major components: on the one hand, as everyone recognizes, the determination of the boundaries of human knowledge and how the mind should conduct itself in acquiring knowledge[16], epistemological and methodological concerns, the establishment of what may be called "inner sovereignty,"[17] and, on the other, political philosophy. That political philosophy is a component of equal stature in the modern philosophical project is perhaps not quite so widely acknowledged as the ascendancy of the epistemological. As the nineteenth century progressed political philosophy ceased to be a thematic interest for philosophers—Hegel's *Philosophy of Right*, published in 1821, is the last great statement of modern political philosophy—and modern philosophy became for all intents and purposes equated with epistemology. The explicitly political phase of modern philosophy had passed. Between the seven-

---

[13] "The Current Situation of Faith and Theology," *L'Osservatore Romano*, English edition, 6 November 1996. This was an address given by Cardinal Ratzinger during the meeting of the Sacred Congregation for the Doctrine of the Faith with the presidents of the doctrinal commissions of the bishops' conferences of Latin America, Guadalajara, Mexico, May, 1996.

[14] *Stromata* I 28–29; VI 67; p. 117.

[15] St. Thomas Aquinas, *Summa Theologiae* Ia, q. 2, a. 2, ad 1.

[16] Thus *Novum Organum, Regulae ad Directionem Ingenii, Discourse on Method, Tractatus De Intellectus Emendatione, Essay* and *Treatise on Human Understanding, Critique of Pure Reason*.

[17] The term, but not the sense given to the term here, is appropriated from Gerhard Kruger, *Philosophie und Moral und der Kantischen Kritik*, 2nd ed. (Tubingen: J.C.B. Mohr, 1967), p. 9, n. 2.

teenth and the nineteenth centuries the political part of modern philosophy had done its work; it had created a new form of rule, the State. Its conclusions were palpably present in the modern political structures of Western European countries and the United States and their imitators. Regimes which did not conform to this pattern were regarded as regimes lacking moral legitimacy. The propositions of modern political philosophy were almost everywhere dominant. These propositions were regarded as self-evident, in no need of justification. The propositions of modern political philosophy as an actual political system and ideology were known, in Europe at least, as *Liberalism*. At the end of the nineteenth century and through the first half of the twentieth the only critical reflection on the principles of modern political philosophy, or on *Liberalism*, came from Reaction and Revolution, that is from positions outside the agreed-upon propositions. Since the propositions of modern political philosophy were considered the sentences of reason itself, their defense against the opposition to them was in essence simple. Reaction and Revolution were manifestations of the irrational. The fundamental issues had been settled. There was nothing to do here, nothing to question. Thus the political component of modern philosophy receded into the background.

I am not saying that there is no serious political thinking, great political thinking, being done in the nineteenth century. I am saying that it is not being done by modern philosophers. Great names in nineteenth-century political thinking, such as de Tocqueville, Burckhardt, and Acton, are historians prognosticating a future in terms of their understanding of what has happened in the past. Tocqueville, Burckhardt, and Acton are preoccupied with threats to liberty that have their source in modern political philosophy's great creation, the *State*. All were partisans of constitutional rule and fearful for its future. Tocqueville and Acton would have agreed with Burckhardt's statement, "The state's form becomes increasingly questionable and its radius of power even broader. . . . "[18]

What is distinctive about modern political philosophy? What makes modern political philosophy *modern*? The answer, of course, is that it is precisely what makes modern philosophy modern. Pre-modern political philosophy had dealt with the various claims men make to rule, or more exactly, with the claims that are endemic to the political association as such: the claims of the wealthy, the poor, the middle sort, the better sort. These

---

[18] *Force and Freedom: Reflections on History*, ed. James Hastings Nichols, (New York: Pantheon Books, Inc., 1943), p. 227.

competing claims are what politics is about because politics is about who will rule over the political association. Pre-modern political philosophy regarded all of the arguments that support these various claims to rule as *political* arguments, that is, arguments advanced by those who claim rule as their right, arguments which show why it is right that this kind of man, or these kinds of men, rule in the city. They are arguments for rule, and for rule of a certain kind. Of course it is not a difficult task for philosophers to take these arguments apart, to show their deficiencies as arguments.[19] But having done so, it must be recognized that nothing, nothing political at least, has been accomplished when this is done. For what would be put in their place? Philosophical arguments that justify some form of rule as yet unrecognized by human beings, a *novus ordo seculorum*?

Pre-modern political philosophy, as distinguished from modern political philosophy, is not political because it provides a philosophical, as distinguished from a political, basis for rule. The political bases for rule are present in the city and its citizens; they are not derived from philosophy. The "Philosopher-King" of the *Republic* does not exercise rule on the basis of philosophy, but on the basis of the kind of people present in the city who understand themselves in terms of a "noble," or "royal" falsehood, "an old Phoenician tale."[20] Pre-modern political philosophy is concerned principally with evaluating the claims men make why it is right that they should rule in the city in order to determine what kind of rule is best for the political association. Most of all it is concerned to point out that there is something better than ruling over human beings; that the best kind of activity is not ruling but contemplative knowing, and thus to show that rule has an intrinsic limit; and consequently that the attempt to derive from it fulfillment commensurate with what is the highest in man is endless and futile.[21] The existence of philosophy as contemplative fulfillment and perfection of man not only manifests the whole which contains the city as an articulated part,

---

[19] "All of these considerations appear to show that none of the principles on which men claim to rule and to hold other men in subjection to them are strictly right." Aristotle, *Politics* III.13 1283b27.

[20] He rules as a *king*. They are lucky he is a philosopher, because he lacks any desire to rule. *Republic* V 520d22–26; 520e31–521b10. This is what makes the city best.

[21] "I consider this mighty structure as a monument of the insufficiency of human enjoyments. A king whose power is unlimited, and whose treasures surmount all real and imaginary wants, is compelled to solace, by the erection of a Pyramid, the satiety of dominion and the tastelessness of pleasures, and to amuse the tediousness of declining life, by seeing thousands laboring without end, and one stone, for no purpose, laid upon another." Samuel Johnson, *Rasselas*, ed. George Birkbeck, (Oxford: Clarendon Press, 1949), p. 114.

but in doing so it places the city within the whole. By not ruling philosophy rules.

This is the greatest benefit which philosophy renders to the political association, not as the service of a servant, but as magnanimous gesture. It was in this sense, as Josef Pieper points out, that pre-modern political philosophy understood philosophical *theōria* to be "an indispensable constituent of the common good itself."[22] Beyond this, pre-modern political philosophy limits itself to recommending the rule of laws—what we call constitutional rule—as generally the best form of rule for men, and to warning against tyranny as the worst of all forms of rule, worst because in being rule over men as slaves by means of speech, tyranny is the perversion of that which distinguishes men among the animals. Thus pre-modern political philosophy exhibits moderation and restraint both in what it expects of politics and what it expects of itself with respect to politics, the moderation and restraint which classical philosophy recognizes as emblematic of reason.[23]

Yet this very restraint and moderation is the weakness of pre-modern political philosophy. It does not satisfy political men, those who do not wish to see, or cannot see, anything beyond ruling over human beings.[24] It is not going to satisfy Machiavelli, for instance. Modernity views this restraint and moderation as a form of excess.[25] But then so does Callicles in Plato's *Gorgias*. The components of modernity are not *modern*. They are coeval with the human mind and the possibilities in terms of which the mind enacts itself. Classical philosophy acknowledges this weakness, but it belongs also to its moderation and restraint to acknowledge that it cannot be overcome. Not everything is transparent to reason.

---

[22] Josef Pieper, *In Defense of Philosophy*, p. 59.

[23] "We always picture Plato and Aristotle wearing long acdemic gowns, but they were ordinary decent people like everyone else, who enjoyed a laugh with their friends. And when they amused themselves by composing their *Laws* and *Politics* they did it for fun. It was the least philosophical and least serious part of their lives: the most philosophical part was living simply and without fuss. If they wrote about politics it was to lay down rules for a madhouse. And if they pretended to treat it as something important it was because they knew that the madmen they were talking to believed themselves to be kings and emperors. They humored these beliefs in order to calm down their madness with as little harm as possible." Blaise Pascal, *Pensées*, trans. A.J. Krailsheimer (Baltimore, Maryland: Penguin Classics, 1996), no. 331, pp. 216–217.

[24] This is why classical political philosophy favors the rule of gentlemen.

[25] See Machiavelli, *Il Principe*, XV.

Modern political philosophy casts off the restraint and moderation characteristic of pre-modern philosophy. Of course it does not despise philosophy as Callicles did, but it is ashamed that philosophy was able to be despised. Therefore it despises the cause of its shame; it despises pre-modern philosophy. It despises the way philosophy had accepted its weakness vis-a-vis political men. It despises Socrates' inability to defend himself successfully before the Athenians. It despises Socrates wrapped in contemplation at the siege at Potidaea during the Peloponnesian War, described by Alcibiades in his speech in praise of Socrates in the *Symposium*.[26] Modern philosophy turns itself into political philosophy in the strong sense. It aims to rule. It will become a partisan among the parties who vie for supremacy in the city. It will take apart the arguments upon which political men base their claims to exercise rule and show the pretentiousness of these claims. It will advance, in opposition, the only claim worthy of respect, the claim to rule of reason itself, a claim which equalizes and cancels all the other claims. Reason ruling the political association is known as *Sovereignty*. *Sovereignty* transforms the political association into the *State*. Reason can make this claim because, according to modern philosophy, reason as such is rule. It is the essence of reason, as modern philosophy and the Enlightenment understand reason, to rule. It is because reason as such is rule, that the claims of reason to political supremacy are justified. Reason understood as rule is what makes modern philosophy *modern*. Political philosophy was not just an *ad hoc* issue for modern philosophers, a response to the political problems created by the religious divisions of Europe after the Reformation, for instance. It was a manifestation of modern philosophy's essential character.

This essential character can be expressed in a word, Kant's word. Enlightenment is *Kritik*, reason ruling over itself, giving itself the rules. *Kritik* is Kant's word, but what it names is not peculiarly Kantian. *Kritik* names what modern philosophy is. This is usually read as the priority of the epistemological, but to say that epistemology comes first is simply to say reason establishes itself as rule. *Kritik* means reason as the act of self-appropriation, *the act of establishing itself as reason*. The fundamental character of reason is not the *nous* of *theōria*. It does not mean self-discovery in the presence of intelligible objects. Reason creates itself as reason in ruling over itself because mind is not naturally, or spontaneously, given to itself in this mode. It has to be made over beyond its natural givenness, for this nat-

[26] *Symposium* 219e5 ff.

ural givenness is without direction. The first sentence of Aristotle's *Metaphysics*, "All men by nature desire to know," is just the problem. This natural desire for knowledge is a naive appropriation of the mind.[27] Left to itself, this natural desire carries us into the dreamland of purely speculative reason, or into the endless play of possibility that is skepticism.[28] Reason as rule emerges from the play of possibilities concerning what it could be. Creating itself as rule, reason suppresses skepticism. But in order to suppress skepticism and to take possession of itself as rule, any intimation that there is a teleology immanent in reason must be denied. The critique of knowing as fulfillment and perfection is at the root of the epistemology of modern philosophy. The contemplation of truth cannot constitute the fulfillment of man, if reason is to establish itself as rule. And unless reason establishes itself as rule, we cannot become autonomous. It is because reason can create itself as rule, that reason is free, not subject to anything outside itself. *Kritik* teaches us to use reason in order to establish ourselves as rulers, and in the act of establishing reason as rule, to emancipate ourselves from what, at the beginning of his *opusculum*, Kant calls "self-incurred immaturity."[29] Slightly amending what Gilles Deleuze says in *La Philosophie Critique de Kant*, "The first thing we learn from the Copernican Revolution [in Philosophy] is that we are giving the orders."[30] The Enlightenment asserts its superiority to what preceded it—classical philosophy and Christianity—not just insofar as *science*, but its *moral* superiority as well. As moral ideal autonomy supplants the fulfillment, perfection, completion of the *telos* being realized.

The problem with Enlightenment reason, reason as rule, is the initial situation out of which it understands itself to arise. Reason must make itself as rule; it is not given to itself as rule. Reason as rule emerges from the play of possibilities concerning what it could be. Reason is free because the initial situation is taken to be directionless. Reason's autonomy as rule is founded upon an act by which reason creates itself as rule. It is without any immanent *telos*. That is why it can be rule. Reason as rule arises out of a

---

[27] Descartes, *Discourse on Method*; *Meditations* I.

[28] "As to it [philosophy] belongs the universal survey [*consideratio*] of truth, so belongs to it the universal doubt of truth." St. Thomas Aquinas, *In III Metaphysicorum Aristotelis Expositio* lect.1, no. 343.

[29] The first sentence of *Was Ist Aufklärung?*: "Enlightenment is man's emergence from his self-incurred immaturity." Immanuel Kant, *What is Enlightenment?*, in Hans Reiss, ed., *Kant's Political Writings* (Cambridge University Press, 1970), p. 54.

[30] Gilles Deleuze, *La Philosophie Critique de Kant* (Paris: Presses Universitaire de France, 1963), p. 19.

condition understood to be indetermination. This suggests that the autonomy of Enlightenment reason presupposes a freedom of sheer spontaneity, and that reason as *Kritik* is groundless. This is the point at which what is called "postmodernity" kicks in.

III

"Postmodernity," or a certain version of it, is what has happened to higher education in this country according to Allan Bloom. "Reason," he says in *The Closing of the American Mind*, "has been knocked off its perch by the master lyricists of postmodernism, Nietzsche and Heidegger, and their followers." But it is not so much Nietzsche and Heidegger, both, according to Bloom, "genuine philosophers," who are responsible for the condition of American higher education, as it is the vulgarized versions of Nietzsche and Heidegger. Bloom calls the university the "home of reason." "The university as we know it, in its content and its aim, is the product of the Enlightenment. . . . The foundations of the university have become extremely doubtful to the highest intelligences . . . ; the essence of it all is not social, political, psychological, or economic, but philosophic. . . . Western rationalism has culminated in a rejection of reason."[31]

Bloom says that Socrates "was the founder of the tradition of rationalism . . . the essence of the university . . . [which] exists to preserve and further what he represents." Bloom identifies Socrates with the Enlightenment conception of reason, with the proposition that everything is questionable except reason itself. "Enlightenment is Socrates respected."[32] He gives no indication that there is anything problematic about this identification. We, however, can recognize that Bloom's Socrates is indistinguishable from the *ego cogitans* of Descartes. Bloom finds nothing problematic about this because the identity of ancient and modern philosophy *qua* philosophy is one of his essential theses.[33] When Bloom says that the American mind, the university, has become closed, he does not mean that it has abandoned Socrates in favor of Nietzsche and Heidegger, but that it has abandonned Socrates for vulgarized, or popular, versions of Nietzsche and Heidegger, what he calls "the Nietzscheanization of the Left or Vice Versa." For Bloom

---

[31] *The Closing of the American Mind* (New York: Simon & Schuster, 1987), pp. 260; 152; 377; 256; 262; 312; 240.

[32] Ibid., pp. 307; 272; 267. Socrates respected is Socrates as ruler.

[33] "The great modern philosophers were as much philosophers as were the ancients. They were perfectly conscious of what separates them from all other men, and they knew the gulf is unbridgeable. They knew that their connection with other men would always be mediated by unreason." Ibid., p. 290.

himself philosophy, the ultimate openness, embraces both Socrates and Nietzsche: "Reason itself is rejected by philosophy itself."[34] But such openness is accessible only to the genuinely philosophic souls and so must remain the prerogative of the few. What Bloom calls the "closing of the American mind" is the democratization of openness. It is "reason rejected," but not "by philosophy itself." It is here that Bloom locates the divergence between Socrates, who in this respect stands for all ancient philosophers, and modern philosophical enlightenment. The difference according to Bloom lies not within philosophy, but in the respective stances taken towards the non-philosophical many; it is a difference in how they address the non-philosophical many. The difference is rhetorical, not philosophical.

"The philosophers in their closets or their academies have entirely different ends than the rest of mankind." For Bloom all philosophers are finally indistinguishable, because all philosophers are identical as philosophers even if they teach very different things. Bloom says philosophy is a life; it is a life whose forms are protean. Being a philosopher does not depend on the content of what one teaches; it consists of being *open* to all the alternatives. Bloom calls this the contemplative life. According to Bloom openness is the capacity to entertain all questions, but to answer none of them. Answers are decisions, not knowledge. Openness is the prerogative of philosophers. And for this it is required that the majority of men remain closed, i.e., ignorant absolutists, who must give their souls completely to the societies of their place and time. "One has to have the experience of really believing before one can have the thrill of liberation." Democratization of openness is *closedness* because it shuts out the possibility of what Bloom considers to be the two "peak" human experiences: unconditional commitment to the horizons of a society and philosophy in its Bloomian version as endless, untrammeled questioning, the former being—but not for everyone—the condition of the latter. *Humanum paucis vivit genus.*[35]

There is an alternative to which Bloom is not open. It is that represented by philosophers such as Maritain. Consequently, Bloom in fact does distinguish among philosophers, between those who refuse as philosophers to disregard what they have accepted in faith and those whose claim to be philosophers excludes such thinkers from the ranks of philosophers. For Bloom philosophy is possible only in the light of the decision to reject divine revelation as impossible. Bloom thinks that modern and pre-modern

---

[34] Ibid., p. 311.
[35] Ibid., pp. 291; 43; 377; and Lucan *De bello civili*, V.343.

philosophy, insofar as it is not Christian, are continuous.[36] The essential agreement "among ancient and modern philosophers is lost sight of," Bloom says, "because scholasticism, the use of Aristotle by the Roman Catholic Church, was the phantom of philosophy . . . that was violently attacked by modern philosophers, more out of anti-theological ire than by dislike of ancient philosophy." Bloom insists that the difference between modern and pre-modern philosophy "was a dispute within philosophy and that there was an agreement among the parties to it about what philosophy is."[37] But Bloom is wrong about this. The differences between modern and pre-modern philosophy concern precisely what philosophy is. One way to state this difference is as a difference about how philosophy comes into existence. For modern philosophers philosophy is not just a possibility of human nature which is actualized in some human beings; rather, philosophy is the creation of the philosopher, something established by his own act. This is clearly visible in Descartes. For the ancients, however, philosophy is a discovery of a possibility inherent in the nature of man. Gerhard Kruger has described this difference in his essay, *The Origin of Philosophical Self-consciousness*, which defines modern philosophy's self-understanding of this difference:

> The freedom which always belongs to philosophy had a very different character for the Greeks than it has for us today. The Greeks made use of it naively; we take it explicitly into account. The freedom of philosophy is for us a self-conscious freedom. We understand ourselves as originating philosophy, while the Greeks encountered it as a possibility among other possibilities. The Greek knew the possibility of philosophy, but he did not know it as his own actual deed. The *nous* of Aristotle forgets itself in the contemplation of things, dwelling in *theōria* and absorbed into it. In this respect the Aristotelian position represents that of Greek philosophy generally. Even the Socratic-Platonic self-knowledge does not differ on this point. The problem of reflection, to be sure, is objectively latent in it, but there is no actual sense of it. . . . It

---

[36] "The great modern philosophers were as much philosophers as were the ancients. . . . The theoretical life remained as distinct from the practical life in their view as in the ancient one. . . . The modern philosophers knew that theory is pursued for its own sake. . . . " Bloom, *The Closing of the American Mind*, p. 290. On the contrary, it is just the denial that "theory is pursued for its own sake" that is constitutive of modern philosophy in its difference from ancient philosophy. Let note be made of the fact that Bloom can appear to give inconsistent accounts of this matter. See, for instance, p. 209.

[37] Ibid., p. 264.

is with the discovery of the free self as such that philosophy has left behind its classical *naiveté*.[38]

The philosopher (ancient) knew philosophy, but he did not know himself as the origin of philosophy ("his own actual deed"). The philosopher (modern) knows himself as the origin of philosophy. Philosophy is not something given with the givenness of man, but a manifestation of human freedom. Not to know this, not to know that it is we who "are giving the orders," is to be naive. This is the "self-incurred immaturity," emergence from which, Kant says, constitutes Enlightenment.[39] Thus *naiveté* is the characteristic accusation brought by modern philosophy against the ancient. Accusers such as Hume place ancient philosophers in the company of children and poets[40]; Descartes, indicting the ancients, says, "It is not enough to have a good mind; the main thing is to employ it well. The greatest souls are capable of the greatest vices as well as the greatest virtues."[41]

Naiveté means here accepting philosophy as given with the nature of man situated among the beings within the whole of that which is. "Leaving behind" that *naiveté* means recognizing that philosophy creates its own possibility, that it generates itself, and is self-constituted. On this point of difference Bloom does not distinguish Socrates from Descartes. Had he done so, he could have understood how there can be continuity between classical philosophy and the scholasticism he contemptuously dismisses and discontinuity between ancient and modern philosophy. It is because modern philosophy is discontinuous with pre-modern philosophy from the Greeks through the Middle Ages—a discontinuity for which the term *epistemology* serves nicely as a label—that it is continuous with postmodernism. It is modern philosophic rationalism, the Enlightenment, not philosophy, that ends in the rejection of reason. "Reason itself" can be "rejected by philosophy itself" because the reason that is rejected has been constituted by philosophy itself.

---

[38] *Die Herkunft des philosophischen Selbstbewusstseins* (Darmstadt: Wissenschaftliche Buchgesellschaft, 1962), pp. 1–3. Originally in *Logos* 22 (1933): pp. 225–227. The translation is my own.

[39] See note 28.

[40] *Treatise of Human Nature*, I iv 3. Unlike modern philosophers, children, poets and ancient philosophers do not understand themselves to be outside the whole about which they speak. Their speaking and their doing is given with the whole in which it occurs.

[41] *Discours de la méthode*, Etienne Gilson, ed., 3rd edition (Paris: Vrin, 1962), p. 2.

While modern philosophy is discontinuous with premodern philosophy, it is continuous with medieval theology. The contemptuous dismissal of scholasticism, i.e., medieval philosophy in so far as it is Christian[42], signals Bloom's failure to catch the significance of what he refers to as "the anti-theological ire" of modern philosophers, and to attend to its importance in understanding modern philosophy.[43] *Aufklärung* is "religion within the limits of reason alone," i.e., it is the denial that it is possible that the human mind could be addressed by divine revelation. Reason, as modernity construes it, must be closed to that possibility. Modern philosophy constitutes itself by rejecting the possibility of the truth of revelation. The rejection of this possibility is constitutive of what it means by reason. "Anti-theological ire" is not accidental to what modern philosophy is, it is its essence. To assure that the possibility of the truth of revelation is excluded from reason, reason must be self-constituted. Reason can be self-constituted and close off the possibility of revelation by constituting itself as rule. And it constitutes itself as rule by denying the immanent teleology of the mind towards truth.

Those ancient philosophers whom Bloom most admires[44], as well as me-

---

[42] Bloom does mention Thomas Aquinas favorably. "Professors of Greek forget or are unawares that Thomas Aquinas, who did not know Greek, was a better interpreter of Aristotle than any of them have proved to be." Bloom, *The Closing of the American Mind*, p. 376. This means that Aquinas was more of a philosopher than the professors of Greek. If so, then he was not completely a "phantom of philosophy." Perhaps Bloom meant to suggest that Saint Thomas Aquinas being more of a philosopher was less of a Christian. In his last book, *Love and Friendship* (New York: Simon & Schuster, 1993), p. 432, bracketing Aquinas with Aristotle and Kant, Bloom speaks of him as a philosopher.

[43] There is a certain irony here since Bloom himself is possessed of considerable "anti-theological ire." And to the extent that Bloom fails to acknowledge it as a formal element in his understanding of how philosophy is constituted, he is not clear about the requirements of his own position. This explains why Bloom's expression of his position displays inconsistency in the matter of ancient and modern philosophers. Bloom fails to appreciate that "the modern age does not have recourse to what went before it, so much as it opposes and takes a stand against the challenge constituted by what went before it." Hans Blumenburg, *The Legitimacy of the Modern Age* (Cambridge, Massachusetts: MIT Press, 1983), p. 75.

[44] When Bloom speaks of "the ancients" he almost always means Socrates/Plato or Aristotle. Moreover, Bloom's ancients are ancients assimilated to a romantic version of modernity for which the last word is "free creation." Right from the very beginning modernity meant liberation from the object, the successive versions of modernity being variations on this fundamental theme. Bloom's inclination to romanticism is clear in a statement such as the following from *Love and Friendship* (p. 510): "Human life is too ugly for anyone who thinks about it to rest content with it. This is the cause of the being of the gods, who underwrite the cosmic significance of human life. . . . [T]he poets . . . create gods for the consolation and uplifting of mankind. This longing impossible of fulfillment, culminates in the Olympian

dieval Christian philosophy, are in essential agreement concerning the immanent teleology of the mind and, therefore, about the highest act of mind which completes and perfects man's nature, *theōria*, contemplation.[45] For this to be the case we have to say that man is capable of truth, but that he does not generate it.[46] What Bloom calls "the peak," or end, exists, he believes, when "the best minds debate on the highest level."[47] Bloom applies the word *theōria* to this. But *theōria* means seeing; what Bloom calls *theōria* is *talking*. Bloom severs reason as the movement of discourse (*ratio* or *logos*) from the act of understanding (*intellectus* or *nous*) to which it is

---

gods, always young, always beautiful." Mind idealizes (and not least of all in the natural sciences). It is the power to go beyond what is given. Mind creates what is not given, what the given gives no inkling of. Mind does not disclose, but creates form. Mind is freedom. Form, irreducible to the given, manifests the creativity of mind. Contrast Bloom's statement above with Montaigne's: "There is nothing so beautiful and legitimate as to play the man well and properly . . . the most barbarous of our maladies is to despise our being." *Essays*, vol. 3, n. 13, trans. Donald M. Frame (Stanford, California: Stanford University Press, 1958), p. 852. The romantic flight from the world presented by the natural sciences, as well as that world itself, take their origin from the same source: the modern conception of mind. What makes decontsruction potent is this: form being understood as the way in which the mind has more or less arbitrarily decided to see itself. Deconstruction focuses on the arbitrary, dissolving form back into the materials out of which mind made it.

[45] The character of this agreement has been well expressed by Paul Ludwig Landsberg, "Kant als Sohn seiner Zeit," *Rhein-Mainische Volkszeitung*, nos. 94, 95 (1924). "Antikes und katholisches Europaertum hatte im Grunde dieselbe Art und denselben Begriff von Erkenntnis. Erkenntnis ist fur beide ein Vorgang, in dem das erkennende Bewusstsein eine *homoiosis*, eine *adaequatio*, eine seinsmassige Gleichwerdung mit dem erkannten Gegenstand erleidet. Erkenntnis ist ein *paschein*, ein *Erleiden*; der Gegenstand ist geichsam tatig, er strahlt hinein in das erkennende Bewusstsein." Cf. Erich Przywara, S.J., *Kantentfaltung und Kantverleugnung* in *Ringen der Gegenwart: Gesammelte Aufsatze 1922–1927*, vol. 2, p. 788.

[46] This is Pascal's point against Descartes when he says, "*Nous avons une impuissance de prouver, invincible à tout le dogmatisme. Nous avons une idée de la verité, invincible à tout le pyrrhonisme*" (#395). Truth is not founded upon our power of proof—*le dogmatisme*—as is the case with Descartes where the mind escapes skepticism because it generates truth about the world as long as it conducts itself according to the rules of method (*Pensées* #345). Bloom uses this same passage from Pascal's *Pensées* to describe his own position—see *Giants and Dwarfs: Essays 1960–1990* (New York: Simon & Schuster, 1990), p. 18. In doing this, however, Bloom does not recognize that Pascal is distinguishing himself from Descartes and so misconstrues its meaning.

[47] Bloom, *The Closing of the American Mind*, p. 347. Unlike the Latin Middle Ages as Bloom understands them, when, according to Bloom, "everyone except a few foolish and intrepid souls professed Christianity and the only discussion concerned what constituted orthodoxy" (p. 355).

ordered.[48] Bloom's *theōria* recalls Gadamer's description of what Schleiermacher calls "free dialogue":

> [in] which . . . the content of the thoughts 'plays almost no part.' Dialogue is the mutual stimulation of thought ('and has no other natural end than the gradual exhaustion of the process described'), a kind of artistic construction in the reciprocity of communication.[49]

No longer ordered to understanding, reason is movement without end.[50] Severed from understanding, reason does not move toward the disclosure of the intelligibilities whose presence is truth. Philosophy is endless talk about questions that cannot be resolved. The mind encounters itself as a multitude of voices. "Confusions within the philosophical enterprise create alternative voices, "I's" that are set in opposition, voices that can only at best quote one another's speeches while being unable to state them as their own."[51] This kind of encounter of the mind with itself is depicted by Milton near the beginning of *Paradise Lost*:

> Others apart sat on a Hill retir'd,
> In thoughts more elevate, and reasoned high
> Of Providence, Foreknowledge, Will, and Fate,
> Fixed Fate, free will, foreknowledge absolute,
> And found no end in wandering mazes lost.
> Of good and evil much they argued then,
> Of happiness and final misery,
> Passion and Apathy, and glory and shame:
> Vain wisdom all, and false Philosophie:
> Yet with a pleasing sorcery could charm
> Pain for a while or anguish, and excite
> Fallacious hope, or arm the obdured breast
> With stubborn patience as with triple steel.[52]

---

[48] St. Thomas Aquinas, *De Veritate*, q. 15, a. 1, c. A discussion, it may be remarked, which does not concern "orthodoxy."

[49] Hans-Georg Gadamer, *Truth and Method*, trans. (New York: Seabury Press, 1975), p. 165. The parenthesis and single quotes enclose material Gadamer is citing from Schleiermacher, *Dialektik* (ed. Odebrecht), p. 572.

[50] "Man by his reason apprehends movably, proceeding discursively from one thing to another, and having the way open by which hemay proceed to either of two opposites." St. Thomas Aquinas, *Summa Theologiae* Ia, q. 64 a. 2.

[51] Robert Sokolowski, *Moral Action: A Phenomenological Study* (Bloomington, Indiana: Indiana University Press, 1985), p. 185.

[52] *Paradise Lost* II, lines 555–569. What Milton describes here is the antithesis of that beatitude that constitutes the perfection, completion, perfection of the achieved *telos*. Mind so encountered he presents in these lines as a condition obtaining among fallen angels.

Bloom's account of the condition of the universities and colleges in *The Closing of the American Mind* won him applause, especially from those of more traditional inclinations who believed that in Bloom they had found someone who as a philosopher gave voice to those inclinations. However, I would suggest that what they had found—and here we return to Rorty—was an instance of philosophy as self-invention.[53] *The Closing of the American Mind* is a script which furnishes Bloom with many roles. Philosophy as self-invention, plus a considerable talent for histrionics, enables Bloom to play all the philosophers' parts: Socrates, Nietzsche, Plato, Rousseau, Max Weber, Heidegger, among others. They become for Bloom what Rorty calls "figures whom the rest of us can use as examples and as material in our own attempts to create a new self by writing a *bildungsroman* about our old self."[54] There is no difficulty understanding how, if philosophy is a form of self-invention, it can embrace both Socrates and Nietzsche. I conjoin them with me, Derrida says in a description of philosophy as the center of a self which invents itself.[55]

> Here Freud and Heidgegger, I conjoin them with me like the two great ghosts of the "great epoch." . . . They did not know each other, but according to me they form a couple, . . . They are bound to each other without reading each other and without corresponding. . . . [T]wo thinkers whose glances never crossed. . . . [56]

In effect Bloom says Socrates and Nietzsche can form a couple and in the conjoining I appear, I am that conjunction. Philosophy as self-invention is a cogito, which has relinquished its identity with reason, the very formula of postmodernity. So practiced it is, as Rorty points out, "a private project without public significance." But self-invention with the State as the guarantor of every form of self-identity is what late liberal society is all about, and in a society of this sort philosophy will be accorded recognition to the extent that it takes the form of "the uninhibited cultivation of individual-

---

[53] See Rorty, *Philosophical Papers*, vol. 2, pp. 195–196. In his review of *The Closing of the American Mind* ("That Old-Time Philosophy," *The New Republic*, 4 April, 1988, pp. 28–33) Rorty's tone is not unfriendly to Bloom.

[54] Rorty, *Contingency, Irony, and Solidarity*, p. 119. In this respect are not Rorty and Bloom instances of what has been called an "aesthetic metaphysics of individuality" characteristic of romanticism? Since "all individuality is a manifestation of universal life and hence everyone carries a little bit of everyone else within himself . . . the individuality of [an] author can be directly grasped "by, as it were, transforming oneself into the other." Cf. Gadamer, *Truth and Method*, pp. 167–68.

[55] This is the subtitle of Derrida's *The Post Card* (Chicago: University of Chicago Press, 1987).

[56] Ibid., p. 191.

ity."[57] Rorty describes as well as any of our contemporaries, and Bloom illustrates, what happens to philosophy when it loses what Maritain called "the natural faith of reason in truth," or, what comes the same thing, when its premise is "our inability to acquire any genuine knowledge of what is intrinsically good or right,"[58] and, in Rorty's words, "substitutes Freedom for Truth as the goal of thinking."[59]

As for philosophers who profess Christianity they are instructed by the First Epistle of Peter to "be ever ready to make a defense to anyone who calls you to account for the hope that is in you."[60] That we are called to account is the good news; it means "men by nature desire to know."

---

[57] The phrase is taken from Leo Strauss, *Natural Right and History* (Chicago: University of Chicago Press, 1953), p. 5.

[58] Ibid.

[59] Rorty, *Contingency, Irony, and Solidarity*, p. xiii.

[60] 1 Peter 3:15.

The Darkening of the Intellect: Four Ways of Sinning Against the Light

Donald DeMarco

At the beginning of his *magnus opus*, *The Degrees of Knowledge*, Jacques Maritain cites the rather pessimistic view of a Jesuit friend concerning man's reduced capacities for metaphysical thinking. According to this view, man, since the fall of Adam, has become so ill-suited for metaphysical thinking that the intellectual apprehension of being must be looked upon as a mystical gift, indeed, a supernatural gift awarded only to a few privileged persons. While Maritain himself regards this view as an evident example of "pious exaggeration," he nonetheless warns of certain methodological problems the metaphysician must solve and specific cultural temptations he must resist. But most of all, Maritain stresses the need for a virtuous disposition on the part of the metaphysician, as well as the need for a certain "spiritual light."[1]

As an astute philosopher, Maritain knows that if the fundamental act of grasping being is something reserved for the privileged, then education, in its strictest and most elementary sense, is equally esoteric. Consequently, education, for the most part, would inevitably be rooted in idealistic principles, that is to say, in principles that do not spring from any contact with reality. By contrast, Maritain's philosophical realism, as well as his Christian optimism, strongly incline him to take a more positive view about the prospects of both metaphysics and education. He understands that metaphysical thinking, like moral virtue, although difficult to acquire, becomes

---

[1] Jacques Maritain, *The Degrees of Knowledge*, trans. under the supervision of Gerald B. Phelan (New York: Charles Scribner's Sons, 1959), p. 2. Hereafter cited as *DK*.

easy to exercise once acquired. With this distinction in mind, there is no need to read any pessimism in the following assessment of his concerning the status of metaphysics in the modern world:

> Three centuries of empirio-mathematicism have so warped the intellect that it is no longer interested in anything but the invention of apparatus to capture phenomena—conceptual nets that give the mind a certain practical dominion over nature, coupled with a deceptive understanding of it; deceptive, indeed, because its thought is resolved, not in being, but in the sensible itself . . . thus has the modern intellect developed within this lower order of scientific demiurgy a kind of manifold and marvelously specialized touch as well as wonderful instincts for the chase. But, at the same time, it has wretchedly weakened and disarmed itself in the face of the proper objects of the intellect, which it has abjectly surrendered.[2]

Hope remains, nevertheless, for, as Maritain avers, the intellect has not been warped (nor can it be), in its nature. The root of the problem is not in the intellect itself, but in the cultivation of bad intellectual habits. Maritain makes the same point in his book on St. Thomas Aquinas: "The disease afflicting the modern world is above all a disease of the intellect."[3] Yet, it is not the kind of pathology that impairs the intellect's essential structure. However radical the disease may be, as Maritain goes on to say, it "remains of the accidental order, of the order of operation, and cannot affect it in its essential condition."[4]

Despite its magnitude, the problem—a "pathogenic upheaval" as Maritain calls it—remains essentially correctible.[5] "Only let the intellect become conscious of the disease and it will immediately rouse itself against it."[6]

For this disease to be overcome two things are needed: first, a proper disposition on the part of the subject, and second the presence of light. With regard to the former, courage and humility are needed: courage, "to face up to extramental realities, to lay hands on things, to judge about what is"; and humility, "to submit [the intellect] to be measured by things."[7] With regard to the latter, light is needed, that principle of manifestation, as St. Thomas calls it, which makes the intelligibility of things evident. The proper dispo-

---

[2] Ibid., p. 3.
[3] Jacques Maritain, *St. Thomas Aquinas*, trans. and revised Joseph W. Evans and Peter O'Reilly (New York: Meridian Books, 1960), p. 89. Hereafter cited as *STA*.
[4] Ibid., p. 93.
[5] *DK*, p. 72.
[6] *STA*, p. 93.
[7] *DK*, p. 108.

sition of the knower, and the capacity to be witness to the light and to realize what the light illuminates, as Maritain explains, are profoundly interwoven.

Humility is not a popular virtue in the modern world, whereas courage is
greatly admired. Many believe that these two qualities are actually incompatible with each other. Humility, they fear, interferes with courage. In
being willing to allow extramental reality to be the measure of truth, rather
than oneself, one places severe limitations on individual creativity, and
therefore negates the courage needed in order to be oneself. This presumed
antagonism between humility and courage is epitomized in Nietzsche's
heroic individualism: "Love yourself through grace," he writes, "then you
are no longer in need of your God, and you can act the whole drama of Fall
and Redemption to its end in yourself."[8]

Maritain sees no disjunction between humility and courage. On the contrary, he regards them as interdependent. When one exercises the humility
needed to allow something other than the self—extramental reality—to be
the measure of things, one does not, by the same stroke, divorce either humility from courage or self from self-realization. Although something other
than the self serves as the measure of truth, it is only through the self,
through the decisive employment of one's active intellect, that such a realization can take place. One brings to bear on extramental being a light that
emerges from one's own active intellect.[9] A confluence of two streams of
light occurs. As Maritain states, "even in our own case it is still the intellect—the intellect that illumines, a created participation in God's intellectual light—that makes things intelligible in act and which, by means of
things and the senses, determines the intellect that knows." The intellect
has the extraordinary capacity to see what it itself expresses, to be "transparent with its own transparency".[10] It may be this very transparency of the
intellect that occasions some people either to fail to realize its existence as
part of their own being, or its function as illuminative of that which arises
from outside their being.

For Maritain, the light by which the intellect first comes into contact
with being is also the light which, upon analysis, provides the most natural

[8] Friedrich Nietzsche, *Morgenrothe*, n. 79.

[9] St. Thomas writes in *In Aristotelis Libros De Sensu et Sensato* (ed. Marietti),
lect. 1 no. 1: "Quae vero a nobis a materialibus conditionibus sunt abstracta, fiunt
intelligibilia actu per lumen nostri intellectus agentis." ("Those things which are abstracted by us from material conditions, become intelligible in act through the light
of our agent intellect.")

[10] *DK*, p. 109.

and effective refutation of idealism. On the other hand, there is a second or subsequent light, not the light that manifests what is, but a reflexive light that shines on our awareness of that which is. To treat the second light as if it came first and deserved primacy, is preposterous in the truest sense of the word (*prae* + *posterius*: putting "before" what should come "after"). It results in excluding extramental reality and closing the mind in on itself. It results, therefore, in idealism. Consequently, according to Maritain, "Idealism sets an original sin against the light at the beginning of the whole philosophical edifice."[11]

The consequences of this original sin against the light, this darkening of the intellect, as it were, are dire, for, as Maritain contends, it is metaphysics that reveals authentic values and their hierarchy, provides a center for ethics, binds together in justice the whole universe of knowledge, and delineates the natural limits, harmony and subordination of the different sciences.[12]

Maritain uses his image of sinning against the light most advisedly. He also welcomes its employment by other writers. In *The Degrees of Knowledge*, for example, he approvingly quotes Garrigou-Lagrange, who accuses Descartes, the founder of modern idealism, of "committing a sin against the Holy Ghost or the redeeming light in the spiritual order".[13] In *St. Thomas Aquinas*, he includes the encyclical *Aeterni Patris* in which Pope Leo XIII denounces the intellectual sins committed against the light, while urging his readers to dispel the darkness of error.

Gerald B. Phelan states that the cause of the malady afflicting the modern mind that Maritain examines in *The Degrees of Knowledge*—a work whose French-to-English translation Phelan himself supervised—"is a suicidal decision of philosophers to disown completely the proper function of the intelligence and to place as the first condition of all knowledge an initial sin against the light."[14]

In its most fundamental implication, the act of sinning against the light represents a neglect, if not an outright rejection, of that illuminating factor which allows the intellect to establish its vital contact with a world outside of itself. The immediate philosophical consequence of this intellectual sin is idealism, along with its innumerable sub-species. A secondary consequence

[11] Ibid., p. 108.
[12] Ibid., p. 4.
[13] Ibid., 78. Cf. R. Garrigou-Lagrange, "Le réalisme thomiste et le mystère de la connaissance," *Revue de Philosophie* (1931): p. 14.
[14] Gerald B. Phelan, *Jacques Maritain* (London: Sheed & Ward, 1937), p. 14.

is a neglect or rejection of God who is the light par excellence in which man participates in order to gain knowledge of reality. In this regard, both Maritain and St. Thomas have emphasized the significance of the Psalmist's words: "The light of Thy countenance, O Lord, is signed upon us."[15]

These two implications associated with sinning against the light—the epistemological and the theological—are also found in the thought of John Henry Newman. In Newman's case, in contrast with that of Maritain and St. Thomas, their clearest articulation is more personal than intellectual, more dramatic than dispassionately philosophical.

While Newman was in Sicily in 1832, he had fallen victim to a severe fever which lasted for three weeks. Utterly convinced he was going to die, he made final arrangements with his Italian servant. In a memorandum he wrote many years later, Newman recalled the unlikely and unexpected words he kept saying to himself during the time of this critical illness: "I shall not die, I shall not die, for I have not sinned against the light . . . God has still a work for me to do."[16] In reiterating these words, he may have been unconsciously reproducing Psalm 118 verse 17: "I shall not die, but I shall live, and declare the works of the Lord." At any rate, subsequent events were to prove beyond any question that he did, indeed, have much work to do for the Lord.

When his condition had greatly improved, Newman left Sicily and began sailing for home. He crossed the Mediterranean bound for Marseilles. But his ship was becalmed for an entire week between Corsica and Sardinia in the Straits of Bonifacio. It was on this occasion that Newman penned his most endearing poem, which begins as follows:

> Lead Kindly light, amid the encircling gloom,
>   Lead Thou me on!
> The Night is dark, and I am far from home—
>   Lead Thou me on!

The poem brings many things to mind: Newman's own loneliness, depressed spirit, and homesickness, as well as the darkness of the world, the darkening of man's intellect, and the eclipse of God. The enveloping multilayered darkness moved Newman to recognize, with great emotional force, both the necessity and compelling significance of light.

---

[15] *DK*, 126, and Psalm 4, 7. Cf. *Summa Theologiae* Ia, q. 79, a. 4.

[16] John Moody, *John Henry Newman* (New York: Sheed & Ward, 1945), p. 32; John A. O'Brien, "John Henry Newman: Scholar of Oxford," in *Giants of Faith* (Garden City, New York: Doubleday, 1957), p. 146.

In *Education at the Crossroads*, Maritain makes the comment that it is not likely that "if God spoke, it was to say nothing to human intelligence."[17] Here, Maritain is presenting what he regards to be one of the main tasks of education in the modern world, namely, elaborating the organic relationship between theology, rooted in faith, and philosophy, rooted in reason. "Newman was right," Maritain remarks, "in stating that if a university professes it to be its scientific duty to exclude theology from its curriculum, 'such an Institution cannot be what it professes, if there be a God'"[18] "University Education without Theology," Newman writes in his book *On the Scope and Nature of University Education*, "is simply unphilosophical. Theology has at least as good a right to claim a place there as Astronomy."[19]

In the contemporary world of education, it is commonplace for philosophy and theology to be divorced from each other. Yet, the greater and more paralyzing divorce to which these disciplines are subject is the one which separates them from their own proper sources of light. Philosophy, especially in its epistemological roots, suffers in two ways: from *relativism*, wherein the intellectual light is deemed too weak to distinguish truth from error; and from *Skepticism*, wherein the intellectual light is deemed so weak that truth cannot be distinguished from nothing. On the other hand, theology also suffers in two ways: from *cynicism*, which rejects God's light and replaces it with something negative; and from a form of *nihilism*, which rejects God's light as well, but replaces it with nothing. Together, these four ways of sinning against the light occupy a dominant place in the world of contemporary education. It may be a decisive step toward exorcising these sins and allowing the intellect to reestablish its relationship with its proper object, as Maritain contends, by letting the intellect become more conscious of the nature of the problem. With this in mind, a brief examination of each of these four sins against the light may prove helpful.

Relativism

Allan Bloom, who holds that "education is the movement from darkness to light,"[20] makes the following unabashed statement at the beginning of his best-selling book, *The Closing of the American Mind*: "There is one

---

[17] Jacques Maritain, *Education at the Crossroads* (New Haven, Connecticut:Yale University Press, 1943), p. 82.

[18] Ibid.

[19] John Henry Cardinal Newman, *On the Scope and Nature of University Education* (London: J.M. Dent & Sons Ltd., 1943), p. 33.

[20] Allan Bloom, *The Closing of the American Mind* (New York: Simon & Schuster, 1987), p. 265.

thing a professor can be absolutely certain of: almost every student entering university believes, or says he believes that truth is relative."[21]

The students to whom Bloom refers do have values. But the light by which they grasp them appears so faint that it does not provide these young relativists with the conviction that such values are more real than their opposites. Consequently, they withdraw from judging certain things to be true or good and others to be false or evil. This twilight mentality, however, has not proven to be particularly disconcerting. In fact, it is usually taken to indicate the presence of a virtue, that of "open-mindedness." Professor Bloom would have relativists abandon their world of shadows and come out into the light where the distinction between truth and falsity, good and evil, becomes sharp. But relativists try to justify their opposition to making such sharp distinctions in the interest of preserving their attitude of equality toward everyone and everything. Rather than judge what is good, they prefer to judge that it is good not to judge. Nonetheless, the ideological world of equality, tolerance, and open-mindedness thereby constructed is precisely that, an ideological construction, having no foundation in reality and offering no practical guidelines by which people can conduct their lives.

When Plato, at the beginning of Book VII of his *Republic*, drew a sharp distinction between the darkness of the Cave and the brilliance of the noontime sun, he was anticipating, in his own way, St. Paul's remark that "Light and darkness have nothing in common." Light and darkness are not equal. Therefore, the relativist position that deems them to be so fails to demonstrate the virtue of open-mindedness and illustrates the vice of closedmindedness.

To be open-minded without any prospect of grasping truth, to be always in a state of intellectual suspense, defeats the purpose of being openminded and reveals a condition of empty-mindedness. In this sense, an "open mind" is not more fulfilling than a empty stomach. To be always open is to be always empty.

Skepticism

A relativist may have his values but he does not hold to them with enough strength that he would have any reason to object to a contradictory set of values. A skeptic would not be sure he had his own values, however subjective and tenuous their basis might be. The relativist can say "this is true for me, but perhaps not true for you," whereas the skeptic would say, "I'm not sure this is true for either of us".

[21] Ibid., p. 25.

In Christopher Derrick's witty and insightful book, *Escape from Scepticism: Liberal Education as if Truth Mattered*, the author claims that "most colleges and universities today" provide "an indoctrination in scepticism, a form of compulsory miseducation that paralyzes and imprisons the mind."[22] He relates a personal anecdote involving a conversation he had with two young philosophy majors from American "liberal arts colleges of repute." The students professed their skepticism to him, insisting that the mind cannot know any truths whatsoever of an objective order. When it was time for the students to take their leave, they expressed concern about getting to the train station on time. Professor Derrick calmly pointed out that if there is no real and knowable world within which their train could function in objective terms of time and space, their anxiety is entirely unfounded. This comment irritated them a little. They felt that philosophy and liberal education is one thing, perhaps nothing more than amusing intellectual games, but the practical business of catching trains is quite another.

Skeptics, very much like relativists, find virtue in their unenlightened state. As a result of being doubtful about everything, the skeptic is never able to secure enough reality ever to offend anyone. Therefore, in presuming himself free from any dogma, he prides himself in being broad-minded and above discrimination.

Maritain, following Aristotle and Aquinas, distinguishes between a doubt that is lived or exercised, and one that is signified as a hypothesis that should be examined. He rejects the possibility of doubting everything, for that would include one salient fact—the essential ordination of the intellect to being—which one already knows. "Realism," he writes, "is lived by the intellect before being recognized by it."[23] Universal doubt cannot lead to a grasp of being; it remains closed within itself as an endless circle of doubt. Critical doubt, on the other hand, is a bulwark against skepticism because, as Maritain argues, it shows that universal doubt is unrealizable, and that the mind grasps its proper object prior to any reflexive activity.

Cynicism

Plato explained that anyone who entered the Cave after being in the sun, his eyes still blinking from their exposure to the light, would appear foolish when he tried to educate those who knew nothing other than a world of

---

[22] Christopher Derrick, *Escape from Scepticism: Liberal Education as if Truth Mattered* (Chicago: Sherwood Sugden & Co., 1977), p. 47.
[23] *DK*, p. 79.

shadows. "Wouldn't they all laugh at him," asked Plato, "and say he had spoiled his eyesight by going up there, and it was not worthwhile so much as to try to go up?"[24]

The cynic takes a hostile view of light. He sees it as a liability, a source of presumption and error. He much prefers the comfort of the Cave.

Richard Neuhaus conjures up the image of Plato's Cave when he speaks of the mythical but ubiquitous "Totheline U." "Totheline" symbolizes the cave mentality of contemporary higher education where "conformity and cowardice" are more valued than the kind of creative and courageous scholarship educational institutions need in order to exercise their proper responsibilities. According to Neuhaus, "the academy today is, in very large part, the enemy of the intellectual life."[25] In fact, it may be difficult to imagine anything more anti-intellectual than the rigid party line that characterizes the groves of contemporary academe. At "Totheline" one cannot begin to speak in an enlightened way about issues such as abortion, contraception, euthanasia, feminism, homosexuality, chastity, justice, culture, aesthetics, and so on, without being accused, in effect, of imposing an alien light, thereby causing extreme discomfort. Just as a good pair of sunglasses filters out harmful ultra-violet light, a good pair of academic blinkers is supposed to screen out the harmful light of truth. The object of education for the cynic, then, is to keep people in the dark where they are comfortable, and away from that dreadful agent of illumination known as "light" which can cause only disruption, pain, embarrassment, and guilt.

The notion that light is an enemy of knowledge is not without its champions in science. In 1927, physicist Werner Heisenberg formulated his famous "Principle of Indeterminacy" which states that it is not possible, in principle, to determine both the position and the velocity of a particular electron. The reason for this is that photons of ordinary light exert a violent force of electrons thereby altering their position and velocity. The scientist who views the electrons with an extremely high-powered electron microscope is not seeing things as they are in themselves (or as they would be if he had not tried to see them). His act of seeing intrudes upon them. Light actually *interferes* with knowing the electrons in their objectivity. It is, therefore, an enemy of knowledge.

Intense or excessive light is known to cause a wide range of discomforts and diseases from sunburn to cancer. Light can be irritating, blinding, glar-

---

[24] Plato, *Republic* VII 517b.
[25] Richard Neuhaus, "Against Peer Fear," *First Things* (May 1993): p. 53.

ing, dazzling, and distracting. In Johann Peter Hebel's *Nibelungen*, Brunhilda epitomizes the cynic's aversion to light. Upon reaching the bright lands of Burgundy, having left her own country where an eternal night reigns, she exclaims:

> I cannot get accustomed to so much light,
> It hurts me, I feel as though I am going about naked,
> As though no gown here would be t hick enough![26]

The fact of the matter is that science does not support a cynical view of light. Light that interferes with the knowing process or causes harm in some way is not light as *a principle of manifestation*, but light as a physical entity. The cynic fails to understand how light is truly a source of illumination.

Nihilism

The strongest opposition to light comes from the nihilist who simply denies that it exists. In essence, as Marion Montgomery has expressed it, nihilism is the isolated mind encountering the void.[27]

The form of nihilism that is enjoying a great deal of popularity in North American colleges and universities at present is a form of literary criticism which assumes metaphysical significance known as *deconstructionism*. It is the creation of the post- Sartrean generation of Parisian Heideggerians, notably Jacques Derrida, Roland Barthes, and Michel Foucault. The word "deconstruction" is derived from Heidegger's call for the destruction (*Destruktion*) of ontology, or the metaphysics of being. Derrida originally used the word "destruction" before settling on "deconstruction."[28]

Deconstructionism reduces the world to the word, or reality to a text. The deconstructionist approaches a text, therefore, as if it had no referents, either to the world, to the author, or even to the meaning of the words themselves. As one disciple puts it: "meaning is fascist".[29] Derrida, himself, in *Of Grammatology*, states, "There is nothing outside the text" (*"Il n'y a rien hors du texte."*). To deconstruct is to unmask, demystify, dismantle, and above all, strip clean of any reference to the transcendent. It is not to elucidate. There is no such thing as the real world; the text is all. In his excellent

---

[26] Richard Peter Hebel, *The Nibelungs*, "The Death of Siegfried," Act II, scene 6.

[27] Marion Montgomery, "Deconstruction and Eric Voegelin," *Crisis* (June 1988).

[28] Jacques Derrida, *Of Grammatology* (Baltimore, Maryland: Johns Hopkins University Press, 1976), p. xlix.

[29] David Lehman, *Signs of the Times: Desconstruction and the Fall of Paul de Man* (New York: Simon & Schuster, 1991), p. 58.

study of deconstructionism, David Lehman speaks of its "relentless nihilistic drive" to assert its dogma that nothing can be known.[30] Deconstructionism rests on the fundamental principle of "wall-to-wall textuality."[31]

The great enemy of deconstruction is "logocentrism," particularly the Logos in The Gospel according to St. John.[32] The light of reason that shines from the *logos* is anathema for self-respecting deconstructionists, for it is alleged to be a principal source of meaning, direction, and purpose, both in the course of the universe and in the lives of men.

Deconstructionists, themselves, view the process of reducing being to a void not so much as nihilistic but as a way of escaping what they call the "closure of knowledge." Therefore, they see placing a text in the abyss (*mettre en abîme*) as achieving an abyss of freedom. They are intoxicated by the prospect of deconstructing all limitations and never hitting bottom.[33] By their eager acceptance of "undecidability" and their penchant for putting words "under erasure" (*sous rature*), they do not experience despair, but presume themselves emancipated from the tyranny of all authority, floating on a wing of limitless creativity. It is nihilism, so to speak, with a happy ending.

Many critics of deconstructionism see it as an intellectual fad, an academic cult, a philosophy of the absurd, or more imaginatively, "the squiggle of fancy French mustard on the hot dog of banal observation."[34] Walter Jackson Bate, Harvard University's most prestigious literary critic, speaks for many when he denounces deconstructionism as representing "a nihilistic view of literature, of human communication, and of life itself."

The phrase in Genesis, "Let there be light," has a twofold significance. It signifies the Light by which the world came into being, and "light" as a principle of manifestation, that by which it is possible for human beings to know things that have come into being, and to embark on that path which leads from the light of knowledge to the Light of the Creator.

Creative Light makes the world a reality: illuminating light makes it knowable. In the absence of illuminating light, nothing can be known and no advantage can be gained, not the "open-mindedness" that relativists assume, or the "broad-mindedness" that skeptics suppose, nor the "freedom from discomfort" that cynics presume, or the "abyss of freedom" that de-

---

[30] Ibid., p. 77
[31] Ibid., p. 106.
[32] Ibid., 42.
[33] Derrida, *Of Grammatology*, p. lxxvii.
[34] Lehman, *Signs of the Times*, p. 22.

constructionists allege. If nothing can be known on an intellectual level, then nothing can be gained on a practical one. "If your eye is worthless, your whole body will be in darkness."[35]

In dealing with the question concerning whether it was fitting that light was made on the first day, Aquinas, with his customary directness and simplicity, states: "That without which there could not be day, must have been made on the first day."[36] Just as there can be no day without light, so too, there can be no education without intellectual enlightenment. Consequently, the various sins against the light—relativism, skepticism, cynicism, and nihilism—are also sins against education.

[35] Matthew 6:13.
[36] *Summa Theologiae* Ia, q. 67, a. 4.

What Happened To The
Catholic University?

Curtis L. Hancock

In October of 1993 at the college where I teach, a Jesuit institution lo-
cated in the Midwest, a day was selected to celebrate the importance of
science in Catholic education. To honor such an occasion, the College invited a speaker, making sure that just the right person would be present to
symbolize the Catholic University's commitment to science. Among the
ranks of Catholic thinkers, of course, are several names from which one
could readily select a celebratory speaker. William A.Wallace and Stanley
L. Jaki come to mind. These names, however, were passed over. To honor
these proceedings my college chose Stephen Jay Gould. You may or may
not be surprised to learn that I was one of only two or three faculty members who seemed disturbed by this, and I was the only professor whose
disturbance inspired a written protest sent to the administration. Mind you,
I was not upset that Stephen Jay Gould came to our campus and spoke to
our faculty and students. He is an innovative and important member of the
scientific community and his voice should be heard. As an instructor, I
have even used his book, *The Mismeasure of Man*. What I found objectionable was that he was put forward as a symbol of science for Catholic
education: this notwithstanding the fact that during his talk he predictably
mocked Christianity, dismissing it as one of the principal interferences of
scientific inquiry. I found it also objectionable that he was given the
last word, that the situation was set up in such a way that he would not
have to reply to criticisms of his anti-Christian world view. I would certainly welcome him as a visiting scholar, for there he would have to
answer questions addressing his philosophical views about science, some
of which are antithetical to a Christian account of nature and of the human
person and are objectionable on purely philosophical grounds to boot. As

81

it was, the situation, it seemed to me, was arranged in a way that was intellectually dishonest and an offense to the mission and identity of Catholic education.

Why were faculty and administrators so indifferent to these proceedings? Once I answered this question, I began to realize what exactly had happened to the Catholic university. The sad truth is that faculty and others were indifferent simply because they agreed with Stephen Jay Gould. Many of those in attendance may not have known the details about his scientific claims, and they may not have known what the terms of their agreement entailed, but they were sympathetic nonetheless with Gould's world view, and by "world view" I mean simply a philosophical perspective on the universe, a claim about the first principles explaining the way things are. To explain the current state of the Catholic university, many changes have to be identified, only a few of which I can analyze here. But it seems to me that one of the principal changes is the acceptance, at least tacitly, of the substance of the naturalistic philosophy of Gould and his colleagues (e.g., Carl Sagan and Richard Dawkins) in regard to the actual substance of classroom instruction and in the determination of what counts as respectable intellectual discourse. Christian education has been undermined by naturalism, the view that nature, defined empiriologically as only matter in motion, is sufficient to explain both the non-living and living orders of things, including the nature of the human existent. That naturalism is inconsistent with Christianity is made evident by its central credo, which has been outlined nicely by the biologist J. Baird Callicott:

> What is now known about nature—from astronomy and astrophysics, geology, chemistry, and biochemistry—is not consistent with the hypothesis that the world was created out of nothing. . . . Indeed the evidence overwhelmingly supports the idea that the universe came gradually to be what we now find it to be—rather than coming into its present state all of a sudden—and that it is much larger, much older, and differently arranged than Genesis would lead one to suppose. Further, neither comparative anatomy and physiology nor the fossil evidence support the idea that human beings are a case apart from other creatures (which, of course, from a more informed point of view, are not "creatures" at all, in the literal sense of the term, but "evolvants"). . . . [T]he same natural processes which account for the physical structures and behaviors of other species account equally well for the physical structures and behaviors of human beings. . . . From the point of view of evolutionary theory as it has been extended in twentieth-century science, there is a historical continuity of human with animal life, *and* of animal with plant life, *and* of life *in toto* with nonliving chemi-

cal compounds, *and* so on right down to the most elementary physical constituents of nature.[1]

These are the words of Callicott, but they express exactly Gould's view, the position that he promotes in his books and that he advocated during his talk that October day at my college. As you can see from Callicott's words, this is a position holding that physics and chemistry are *sufficient*, not just *necessary*, conditions for the emergence of life and higher consciousness. Accordingly, neither life nor man requires God's special creative acts. The existence and the nature of the universe do not depend on God's creative activity. Nor does the universe rely on His providence. Of course, this inspires one to ask: What exactly is left of Christianity if one agrees with Callicott that it is not necessary to posit either creation or a Providential Creator? The obvious answer is "nothing," since these beliefs, along with a few others associated with them, are the non-negotiable core of Christian theism. Hence, those Christian educators who regard naturalism as an axiomatic component of sound education today have, in fact, nullified the role of Christian doctrine in actual instruction.

Still, Christians, even when thrown into the arena with the naturalist lions, are a resourceful lot, and have cleverly devised an escape route, an illusory one but desired by some nonetheless. This exit appears in the supposition that, while the substance of naturalism must be accepted, an area of religious discourse can nonetheless be staked where God and Christian doctrine still have at least emotional appeal. This has led to that particular sort of qualified naturalism which attempts to make God an object of speculation provided such speculation is regarded as extra-scientific. Phillip E. Johnson calls this type of naturalism "theistic naturalism," a perspective which gives to Callicott everything that belongs to the realm of knowledge and leaves to metaphysics and religion the realm of irreducible, groundless belief, where they can never be subjects of rational inquiry. This may seem to be an attractive compromise, but in fact it is a Faustian bargain, at least in terms of the educational mission and identity of a Catholic institution. And I never cease to be amazed at how zealously today Catholic intellectuals aim to strike this bargain, which concedes "to Darwinism the role of telling the true history of the development of life" and consigns God to a metaphysical realm which can only be spoken of poetically.[2] For those still

---

[1] J. Baird Callicott, "The Search for an Environmental Ethic," in Tom Regan, ed., *Matters of Life and Death*, 2nd ed. (New York: Random House, 1986), p. 387.

[2] See Phillip E. Johnson, "Creator or Blind Watchmaker?" *First Things* (January 1993): p. 9.

interested in such extra-scientific speculations, those incorrigibly religious souls who will not give up their childhood superstitions, such talk about God might be of interest. For example, one might still believe that God is *possibly* the originator of the universe, although it is assumed that this belief is *in principle* indemonstrable, since metaphysical and axiological claims are only so much poetry. Neither God nor the other *praeambula* of the faith—such as soul, immortality, freedom (issues which directly contradict naturalistic orthodoxy)—can be subjects of rational demonstration. Hence, when Catholic educators embrace theistic naturalism, they in effect reduce God to a philosophical irrelevancy. In terms of actual instruction, instead of being told that the universe is God's creation, and that man is God's special creation, and that science is possible because it recognizes the order of God's creation—just the kinds of truths you would expect to be advocated by Catholic intellectuals—students are led to believe that physics explains everything about which human beings can make genuine assertions, that is, statements that are not mere poetry but are really true or false.[3] Accordingly, God, creation, and His providential activity fade ever more into the shadows when the content of curricula are discussed. Since it is politically incorrect to challenge naturalism publicly, there is little opportunity to bring these issues to the attention of the academic community. Hence, Catholic educators go about their business blissfully thinking that they can have Gould's naturalism and God too. But in fact, the best naturalism will allow one is to grant God in an irrelevant and marginalized sense. Such is God's fate on today's naturalized Catholic campus. It is true that there is some residual lip service to Christian orthodoxy, usually spoken about obliquely in the school bulletin, at commencement, and at other formal occasions, when a little poetry is called for, when a little symbolism fills an emotional void. But even these moments are becoming less frequent. Ideally, these awkward occasions and embarrassments are to be offset by having the likes of Stephen Jay Gould speak on campus once in a while to debrief us. This will assure again that in terms of identifying substantive intellectual allegiances, naturalism prevails.

As I have suggested, the University has not been altogether critically

[3] Theistic naturalism grants only poetic, not logical, truth to religious utterances. Poetic truth cannot be contradicted, and thus is compatible with contrary accounts of the same subject in different narratives. Logical truth can be contradicted, and thus is incompatible with opposite accounts of the same subject. On the distinction between poetic and logical truth, and on its application to religion, see Mortimer J. Adler, *Truth in Religion* (New York: Macmillan Publishing Co., 1990).

aware of this change. Many faculty and other members of the Christian intellectual community have been duped, I fear, into thinking that they have no choice but to accept Stephen Jay Gould on his own terms. They surmise that at this stage in the twentieth century, an educated, rational mind simply cannot reject naturalism. Christianity, if it is to eke out any continued intellectual respectability, must simply embrace it. Herein lies the mistake. These educators mistake naturalism for science. The rhetoric of naturalism has been so successful that it has convinced academics that what is in fact a philosophy, or perhaps even more precisely, an ideology, is in fact a science. Specifically, they mistake the philosophical supposition that reality is merely physics for the demonstrated truths of science. It is understandable, of course, why many Christians might succumb to this rhetoric, given the esteem science has enjoyed over the past few centuries. And it is certainly the case that every rational mind must accept the truths of science. The problem, however, is that often doctrines pass for science that are really "scientific" in name only. While whatever is scientifically true is in harmony with Christian theological and philosophical understanding, it is also the case that a given age may accept a body of philosophical assumptions about science that are questionable and problematic, if not untenable. Naturalism seems to rest on a number of these assumptions. But many of our colleagues accept naturalism at face value, failing to realize that there is a non-negotiable core of Christian doctrine that could be compromised by the naturalist's world view.

This is very evident in the attitude many Catholic educators have toward Darwinian evolution, a point Alvin Plantinga has effectively made in some recent articles.[4] Had Gould quoted Richard Dawkins, who claims that "It is safe to say that if you meet someone who claims not to believe in evolution, that person is ignorant, stupid or insane (or wicked, but I'd rather not consider that)," he would have elicited mainly nods from the audience.[5] Propaganda about "the fact" of evolution, which Gould announces repeatedly in his writings, is powerful rhetoric aiming to sideline, if not negate, metaphysics and religion once and for all. As Callicott's quotation makes clear, there is no room in Darwinian evolution for God, creation, human souls, or the working out of salvation. Hence, if Darwinism is science, Christianity

[4] See Plantinga's "On Christian Scholarship," presented at the University of Notre Dame, Spring, 1990; "The Twin Pillars of Christian Scholarship," the Stob Lectures of Calvin College, 1989; and "Christian Scholarship and Secularization, summarized in *The Christian Educator* (January 1992): pp. 3–4.

[5] Plantinga, *The Christian Educator*, p. 4.

is either nullified or reduced to irrational fideism. Catholic educators have failed to understand that, however much one must credit Darwin for advancing our knowledge of natural history in important respects, one must also guard against giving away too much to his legacy. Of course, I am not saying that evolution should not be part of the description of natural history and even of the biological history of the human species. But it seems to me incoherent to maintain that Christian doctrine and a sound Christian philosophy can make evolution, as understood by the Darwinists (such as Callicott), the official doctrine. As I said above, orthodox Christianity is committed to the view that man is specially created. And a sound philosophy must acknowledge that neither the human intellect nor the will is reducible to matter in motion. In other words, if humans differ in kind and not in degree from the other animals, the human person requires special creation because the human species is discontinuous, in key respects, with the rest of nature. Accordingly, evolutionary theory might be part of the story of natural history, but it is not the whole story. I find it interesting that many philosophers who have virtually a congenital disposition to be critical and to analyze positions until all of their weaknesses are exposed, become curiously docile, even servile, when evolutionary claims and other "received" doctrines of naturalism are supposed. The most enthusiastic advocates of Darwinism whom I know personally have read nothing of the work of Phillip E. Johnson, for example, who shows that their doctrine fails to measure up to standards of empirical falsifiability and that their view, rather than being factual, is really only a theoretical interpretation of nature which happens to have a certain explanatory power. Those few I have met who have some acquaintance with Johnson, dismiss his work *a priori*, declaring that it is another effort at "creationist science," whatever that is. And whatever it is, I assure you, Johnson has nothing to do with it.

This disposition toward naturalism is tantamount to a prejudice. As Plantinga has put it: "In contemporary academia, evolution has become an idol of the tribe; it serves as a shibboleth, a litmus test distinguishing the benighted fundamentalist goats from the enlightened and properly acculturated sheep."[6] Being lumped with the former provokes a horror compared with nothing else for the contemporary intellectual. This is also true of many Catholic intellectuals, who have endorsed the policy followed by Catholic administrators that Catholic schools should mirror the curricula of secular schools so as not to risk this benighted condition.

[6] Ibid.

Whatever the faults (and I'm sure there were many) of the monopoly of Thomism on the philosophy curricula three or four decades ago, Thomistic philosophers were keenly aware of the hazards of getting in bed with the naturalists. However, after Vatican II, a spirit of openness may have inspired philosophers to think that Christianity could absorb any "-ism." To think otherwise was to be "divisive," a complaint I hear daily in some context on campus, a curious protest since history shows that almost all cultural achievements, especially those in philosophy and religion, have been divisive, pitting son against father, as the Gospel observes.

This condemnation of divisiveness brings to mind another "-ism" that many Christian academics imbibe today. I refer to relativism, which enjoys a symbiosis with naturalism, since the latter, so relativists maintain, spawns the fact/value distinction. According to this distinction, it is the proper purview of science to describe or report factually what is known about the world. That water is made of hydrogen and oxygen and that Red Square is in Moscow are examples of such facts. While statements of value, such as "democracy is the best form of government" and "it is wrong to lie," are subject to scientific inventory (that is to say, science can catalogue those who, as a matter of fact, report such prescriptive claims), there is nothing within the bounds of science to provide such remarks any kind of justification. Hence, they exist only as brute preferences. Accordingly, the term "value" has no cognitive content; if it had such content, it could be scientifically verified. This view, the offspring of positivism, has been debunked for some time by philosophers, but it is still surprisingly fashionable among the social scientists, even though they often contradict themselves in trying to abide by it, for every psychologist knows that mental health, freedom from cognitive distortions, and overcoming neuroses are better than suffering from them. But these incoherences have deterred few from accepting the relativizing effects of the fact/value distinction. It has become, I fear, a staple of the culture of college life. It even influences curricula. It begets the assumption that the content of the humanities is ultimately so much opinion, beyond even the possibility of justification, since it concerns values, and things not subject to scientific measurement and experimentation. The humanities, as a result, are merely the chaff winnowed away after the cognitive kernels of science have been harvested. Accordingly, the humanities devolve into free-for-alls in which people talk at each other about different points of view without really communicating, because, even if there is agreement, it cannot presumably be achieved based on any real demonstration. This leads to the dismal result that college disputes, even about curricula and academic matters that pertain directly to students, become matters of politics only. Disagreements become clashes of Nietzschean wills, wherein that view is "best" which survives the political struggle. Rationality and knowledge are despaired of. All that remains is politics, which lately has become that curious academic variety of fascism, political correctness.

In order to cope with competing political views, academic leadership has let back in the door one value standard, political expediency, which has the unfortunate effect of nullifying the Catholic university's power to be counter-cultural. If one carefully reads speeches composed by Catholic university administrators today, they often subscribe to the safe course of letting prevailing political sentiments dictate mission and policy. This is an abdication of leadership, of course, based on the mistaken judgment that the role of the educator is to adopt and foster trends in academic pop-culture. The classic Socratic mission of education—to foster self-knowledge and critical awareness so as not to be popular culture's willing thrall—seems overlooked by these academic leaders.

The same fate that befalls the other humanities awaits theology and philosophy. All disciplines break apart in the vortex of relativism unless they can claim some association with naturalism. Hence theologians, after exiling religious doctrines to the outer reaches of fideism, are anxious to demonstrate that what is left of their discipline must enjoy respectability on naturalist terms. Theology in practice, then, becomes sociology of religion, the kind of study reflected today in the writings of Joseph Campbell, Harvey Cox, Hans Kung, and Wendy Doniger O'Flaherty. Accordingly, religion can only meaningfully be talked about descriptively, complete with all the relativistic implications that follow from this sociological approach. One theologian told me that the philosophical demand to regard religious claims as assertions (as true or false) is an intellectual disease. This is an error, she asserted, because it assumes that religion is about beliefs. Philosophy of religion courses are especially pernicious because they subject religious doctrines to examination, fostering the mistaken supposition that religion consists of beliefs or assertions. Following Campbell, she stated that to assume religion is doctrinal ("credal") is to mistake religion for superstition. "Today," my colleague insisted, " we know that religion is really psychology, an orientation toward faith, not about propositions or credal statements." It apparently did not bother her that her own account of religion was expressed in propositional and credal terms or that her expression "orientation toward faith" could not mean much unless it involved specific commitments (beliefs). But her view generates more than just questions about coherency. How can one justify that theology be a part of an educational curriculum if her conception of religion is correct? By her own admission, theology seems to have become "religious studies," a part of sociology. If theological doctrines in and of themselves preclude rational examination, then theology disqualifies itself as an academic discipline. Education presupposes that students are being led (from the Latin *ducere*) to something true, not just to psychological dispositions or to sociological descriptions of religious cultures. I fear my colleague's view is a thinly veiled pretext for ideology, another version of deconstruction. If rational examination and argument are removed from theology, then students must become merely passive hearers of arbitrary interpretations of religion. Theology becomes a political instrument. At worst, this becomes manipulation to professors' agendas, which often reflect the latest political and theological fads.

The same tendency to reduce their discipline to relativistic, sociological descriptions appears not just among the theologians but among the philosophers as well. This has particularly dire consequences for the Catholic university. Once philosophy becomes reduced to merely a sociological, psychological, or historical phenomenon, it loses its ability to defend truth and to combat error, and thus it forfeits its rightful role as the integrating and regulating discipline in the curriculum. The philosopher becomes a prisoner of cultural and personal perspectives, and the best he or she can offer is interpretations. Reduced to mere words, philosophy becomes a battleground of baseless convictions. The nominalist legacy of modern philosophy begets only so much postmodernist gamesmanship.

To illustrate consider a recent article by Nicholas Lobkowicz entitled "What Happened to Thomism?"[7] The article argues that because Thomists naively clung to the view that philosophy involves the attainment of truth, the "advancements" of the discipline passed them by. Lobkowicz's preference for anti-realist philosophies that reject Thomistic realism speaks volumes about what happened to the Catholic university. Because his view of philosophy is so popular, it is no surprise that realism is ignored and that the Catholic university has paid a price for that ignorance. To elaborate, consider that in Lobkowicz's article philosophy is defined not as an awareness of things as they really are but as the interpretation of reality through conceptual categories. Thomism, he says, was eclipsed because it assumes that it can construct models that comprehensively explain experience. But

---

[7] Nicholas Lobkowicz, "What Happened to Thomism?" *American Catholic Philosophical Quarterly* LXIX (Summer 1995): pp. 397–423.

these models stand only so far as Thomistic language gives them authority. Other philosophical perspectives are equally satisfactory on their own terms, and Thomists cannot effectively criticize them without begging the question, without presupposing again their own language, models, and categories.

It requires only a moment's reflection to recognize the Enlightenment assumptions at work in this view of philosophy. Lobkowicz has assumed that philosophy is a construction by the human mind. On his view, Thomism happened to succeed ideologically for a while because it bullied many in the philosophical community into accepting its dictatorial constructions of "truth." Lobkowicz is now here to expose this tyranny for what it was. He is making explicit what many philosophers grasped implicitly, which caused them to ignore Thomism and hasten it into decline. These philosophers, like Lobkowicz, enjoy the *gnosis* that since all philosophical projects depend on distinct perspectives and chauvinistic lexical principles, there are as many philosophies as there are perspectives and lexicons. What right does Thomism have to argue that its perspective is special?

Because, Lobkowicz tells us, different philosophers work with different paradigms, they may disagree. But this disagreement is never absolute, nor resolvable in favor of any one position. A philosophical argument may be problematic for one philosopher's set of assumptions but quite acceptable from another point of view. It all depends on the context and categories which give rise to the argument. Consider, for example, the ontological argument. "It is not simply valid or invalid, but rather valid in some contexts and invalid in others. One may, of course, then discuss these contexts or assumptions, but after some time one reaches a point at which one is no longer discussing the truth or falsity of a conclusion, or for that matter the validity or invalidity of an argument, but rather the applicability of a conceptual framework, the ways of speaking about our common experience."[8]

Of course, if philosophy is not an inquiry into truth or falsity, why is Lobkowicz's appeal to common experience even relevant? Philosophy has become only so many anchorless, competing interpretations. This is the triumph of perspectivalism, with the presumption of course that Lobkowicz's perspective is somehow authoritative.

Lobkowicz's article is instructive in that it inadvertently identifies why the Catholic university has declined. The reason lies in the fact that it has

[8] Ibid., p. 413.

become overrun by Lobkowiczeans. To discuss Lobkowicz is relevant because the fate of Thomism is tied to the fortunes of the Catholic university. When Thomists are replaced by Lobkowiczeans education pays dearly. Philosophy suffers because, once bankrupted by Enlightenment pathologies, it is distorted into a postmodernist, nominalist game. Philosophers become helpless to challenge their peers or to exercise philosophy's power to justify the mind's contact with reality and value. Moreover, and it is especially in this regard that the eclipse of Thomism and the rise of Lobkowiczean philosophy has undermined the Catholic university, philosophy has lost its power to address and challenge (and also defend) other disciplines. In fact, the other disciplines (especially the humanities) have become mired in the relativistic mud because the philosophers, having talked for years like Lobkowicz, have given them their relativistic rationale. The unforeseen result for the philosophers is that, once these other disciplines accept the skeptical, relativistic doctrines of Lobkowicz's perspectivalism, they no longer have any use for philosophy. Philosophy, then, has succeeded ironically in deforming and marginalizing itself, and is much beleaguered by its enemies on today's Catholic campus.

I am reminded of a recent experience. A friend of mine who teaches at a Catholic university told me that his department of philosophy was much under fire in the curriculum reform taking place at his school. He asked me why I thought faculty outside the department of philosophy could hold the discipline in such disdain. My answer was simple and direct. His colleagues do not appreciate philosophy, I said, because they took his courses. There they drank only Lobkowicz's brew, which drugged them into believing that philosophy is only so much interpretation—about what we're not sure. Hence, they went home and interpreted philosophy out of existence. Who is the Lobkowiczean philosopher to protest?

Philosophy has been undermined by the Enlightenment skepticism which despairs of any knowledge of reality. If the Catholic vision of education is to be renewed, philosophers must take the lead and courageously reassert the mind's adequacy to know God's creation. If this is not done, Catholic universities will go the way of so many Protestant schools, institutions like Harvard and Columbia, which originally were conceived as seminaries to inform the mind about the things of God. We can do our part to prevent this from happening, if we remain faithful to the realist vision of philosophy. That is what inspired Jacques Maritain. It is still the best hope for the Catholic university.

The Elements of Discord:
The Sine Qua Non of Education

Gregory Kerr

Thus the chief task of education is above all to shape man, or to guide
the evolving dynamism through which man forms himself as a man.
. . . [E]ducation needs primarily to know what man is. . . . Man is a
person who holds himself in hand by his intelligence and his will. . . .
A person possesses absolute dignity because he is in direct relationship
with the realm of being, truth, goodness, and beauty. . . .

Jacques Maritain, Education at the Crossroads[1]

The moment one touches a transcendental, one touches being itself. . . .
It is remarkable that men really communicate with one another only by
passing through being or one of its properties.

Jacques Maritain, Art and Scholasticism[2]

In the face of multiculturalism and widespread relativism, this paper will
argue, along with Allan Bloom in *The Closing of the American Mind*, that
for educators to be effective, they cannot espouse a relativism. Rather they
must, among other things, examine, explore and provoke their students to
explore the principles underlying human discourse and discord and make
them explicit so that their students will know and communicate more effectively and thereby become more authentically human.

Inspired by ideas of Maritain on the transcendentals, Bernard Lonergan

---

[1] Jacques Maritain, *Education at the Crossroads* (New Haven, Connecticut: Yale
University Press, 1943), pp. 1, 5; 7–8.

[2] Jacques Maritain, *Art and Scholasticism and The Frontiers of Poetry*, trans.
Joseph W. Evans (Notre Dame, Indiana: University of Notre Dame Press, 1974),
p. 32.

on cognitional method,[3] C.S. Lewis on the moral law[4] and Allan Bloom on education,[5] we will attempt to explore some of those principles that underlie human discourse and even human disagreement, thereby disclosing the very conditions of possibility for any ideology or criticism of one. Even the most avid critic of traditional Western education can be shown to be using transcendental notions of unity, truth, goodness and beauty. If education is about criticism at all, then we need the transcendentals and all that they imply about human nature.

To put it concretely, if we are criticized by an extremely politically correct, multicultural feminist who claims that we are hypocritical, biased, androcentric, imposers of ideology and offensive, we might respond by saying that if we are really hypocritical, then it must mean that we are not consistent (i.e., have integrity or unity). If we are biased, then it must mean that we are *not* seeing the whole truth of reality and *ought* to be. If we impose our ideologies, then we are doing something we ought not to be doing and this implies that humans ought to seek, know, and freely will the good as well as allow others to do so. Finally, if we are criticized for being offensive, we presume that we appear ugly in some way and that we are faulted for that. Now we do not wish to start by criticizing the postmodern attitude *per se*. No; actually we wish for the present purpose to agree with them. We want to consider for a moment that perhaps we are biased and narrow-minded. The real question is, "What then is our obligation?" Critics think that the traditional educator has an obligation to take their advice. But if they are even partly right, whence comes this obligation?

I had a startling experience recently. I was teaching a argument that I had adapted from an introductory philosophy text.[6] The argument was in-

---

[3] Lonergan presents many criticisms of modernity by relying upon what he calls "cognitional method" in his book, *Insight*. The problem with most philosophical problems is that the philosophers do not take into account the very conditions of possibility for the origin of their theories, i.e., their own acts of insight, understanding and judgment. See *Insight: A Study of Human Understanding* (New York: Harper & Row, Publishers, 1958).

[4] See C. S. Lewis's powerful argument for a natural lawgiver in Mere Christianity (New York: MacMillan Publishing Co., 1952).

[5] Allan Bloom makes a powerful critique of relativism and how it closes the minds of students in *The Closing of the American Mind* (New York: Simon and Schuster, 1987), pp. 25–43.

[6] David Stewart and H. Gene Blocker, *Fundamentals of Philosophy* (New York: MacMillan Publishing Co., 1992), p. 107.

spired by Plato and it argued for the existence of immaterial things. I summarized the argument as follows:

> If the physical world were all that there is, then our moral judgments would not be based upon anything.
> If our moral judgments were not based upon anything, then they would be meaningless.
> But our moral judgments are meaningful.
> Therefore, they must be based upon something.
> Therefore, the physical world is not all there is.

The basic move is to accept moral judgments as the primary datum and then to argue about what reality must be like in order to make sense of them.

When I had finished, the students responded by saying, in effect, "Well, this argument is androcentric!" What they meant was that because Plato was coming from a certain point of view, namely that of a male, that somehow undermined the argument. Now rather than taking issue with "androcentric," I forwarded the argument to include their objection and I asked them, "But is it wrong to be androcentric?"

"Yes," was the reply.

"Then what accounts for the idea that we ought not to be androcentric, that we should not see things from merely our own point of view, either as male or female, but try to be open and embrace other viewpoints?"

I think some of the students in that class came to see that they could not both embrace the thoroughgoing relativism of postmodernism and still make the kind of moral judgments they were making and eagerly desired to make.

Postmodernists today want to say that some viewpoints are oppressive and therefore wrong; but what meaning can "wrong" have in their vocabulary? What could it mean other than they do not like the exercise of power of certain people and they would like to have more of it themselves or that they just feel bad about the arguments against them?

II

We propose here to give a sketch of a philosophy of education based upon the principles of Jacques Maritain. Of course, we will not be doing what Maritain has done so well in *Education at the Crossroads*, but we shall outline what we take to be some of the central tenets of education and argue that these are basic to any education and the failure to recognize them does not mean that they will not be taught, but will be taught badly and without proper *prise de conscience* due to them. For if one does not take the time to study and explore his philosophy, it does not mean that he does not have one, only that he has an unexamined and "biased" one. So too, if one does not examine the implicit underpinnings of one's education, it is not that he will not have any knowledge, but that it will be fragmentary and underdeveloped.

Recently, a colleague said to me that every time one's computer re-saves a file on the hard disk it saves it in a different position on that disk, so that the same basic file appears on different areas on that disk. He also told me that there are certain programs one can purchase that will join like files together on the disk. I think that many of our human philosophies have within them views and opinions that are perceptive but scattered, and we do not always check to see if they align or go together. For example, we all have students who will tell us, in one and the same breath, that they believe that God exists but also that, "who's to really say whether God exists or not?"[7] Of course, they continue, "it all depends upon your belief." Such people are, in my opinion, people who do not have their "files" or thoughts together. And, of course, the examination of these problems is precisely one of the major functions of philosophy. What we ask here is "What are the fundamental principles of a sound education?" We believe we can answer this question by examining the basic principles or attributes that a good "paper" or "position" ought to have.

Any paper is a bad paper if it presents views that undermine its own claim to reasonably present a position or theory.[8] Some papers contain certain positions which undermine any attempt to justify those positions. In short, these writers cut off the very branch they are sitting on.

Now, in the presentation of any theory or paper, certain things are implicitly assumed and affirmed even if explicitly they are denied. There are certain properties—if we can call them that—of a position or theory that *have* to be there. They are the necessary conditions of any "possible" theory.

---

[7] Norman Melchert has recently created a provocative dialogue on this question of relativism, exploring all the various issues, entitled *Who's to Say? A Dialogue on Relativism* (Indianapolis, Indiana: Hackett Publishing Co., 1994).

[8] This argument is similar to that of C. S. Lewis in his "The Cardinal Difficulty of Naturalism" in *Miracles* (New York: MacMillan Publishing Co., 1960). If we may improvise a bit, it runs thus: (1) No belief that is caused by non-rational mechanisms alone is a belief that is reasonable to accept; (2) All theories that hold that the universe began by a big bang accident are theories that are caused by non-rational mechanisms alone; Therefore, no theories that hold that the universe began by a big bang accident alone are reasonable to accept.

No one disputes that in the college or university setting that students should and do present papers and positions on topics. When a student gives an instructor a paper, he or she expects that the instructor will evaluate that paper. Now, assuming that the instructor is not a dictator or one who merely gives A's to those who fully agree with him, B's to those who partly agree with him and so forth, but actually grades the papers upon something other than his or her philosophical vision, we might just ask what does he grade them on? If he admires the Socratic method, he will not merely "teach" or impart theories to the student and expect him to regurgitate them, but rather will be concerned with the student's development of their own abilities to reason, to know and to appreciate. As any instructor knows, merely imparting theories short-circuits the learning process. But what properties should a paper have?

We argue that a good paper must: a) present a representation of reality, facts that correspond to the way things are; b) be clear about the values it is exploring and defending; c) have a unity and avoid internal contradictions; and d) have a beauty—not merely regurgitate the same old truths or values all over again but come with a new perspective and fresh insight.

These criteria, well-known as the transcendentals, are according to St. Thomas and Maritain, the property of every real being. We would claim that they are also the property of a good paper and thus a sound education. We argue for this by examining what papers would look like if they violated these transcendental properties at will. We propose some *reductio ad absurdum* arguments to show that no one can communicate without these for long. According to Maritain, it is precisely through the transcendentals that we can communicate at all.

Take the transcendental of the good. For instance, suppose a paper were to claim that nothing is really good or that good and evil are only by-products of our minds, culture, time, or "will to power." If that were the case, it would be hard to figure out why the paper should be written at all. Why do people write essays explaining their point if to hear their point is not any better—in a real sense—than not to hear it? It is like saying that even though my theory has no real value to it, you should listen to it anyway.

The paper may make a stronger relativistic claim. It may claim that those who believe in objective values will necessarily force or impose their view upon others or, at the very least, be arrogant or foolish. For, as the argument runs, if you really think that you know absolute values—or, as some would claim, make any value distinctions at all—you would be inclined to insist that everyone agree with you.

In response, we might say that if we should not impose my view upon another and that this is really wrong, then there is real wrong. You have claimed that we have broken some rule. If we have broken some rule, then some rule exists that neither you nor I have made. You may be right that I should not be intolerant but you have cut off any reasonable way to argue for that.[9]

A second response would be to assert that if I believe in objective values or a moral law, then I believe that humans are moral beings and that they can only be moral by freely knowing and choosing what is good. Now, if I know that this is the case, how can I but realize that to impose my view precisely undermines the very same view.[10]

But once *any* value is asserted as a real and objective good, it behooves educators to help students to ascertain the parameters of that good so that we and the students may be able to draw the line between genuine tolerance and apathy. We need to learn the meaning and the limits of tolerance and how this good relates to other goods. We should learn how tolerance is a real moral principle and how it is not simply a matter of personal ideology or preference of Western, well-educated males.

The second property is truth. It may be claimed by a paper that the knowledge of all of reality is a matter of interpretation, that all truths are simply expressions of particular culture or are bound by language, and that no one can really say what is ultimately real. But here again it is a position that undermines the possibility of writing a paper of any value. Every paper assumes a set metaphysic. It presumes that the items it talks about are, at least for the moment "real." It must assume something is real! As Chesterton has put it in a similar point about evolution:

> If evolution simply means that a positive thing called an ape turned very slowly into a positive thing called a man, then it is stingless for the most orthodox; a personal God might just as well do things slowly as quickly, especially if, like the Christian God, he were outside time. But if it means anything more, it means that there is no such thing as an ape to change, and no such thing as a man for him to change into. It means that there is no such thing as a thing. At best there is only one thing, and that is a flux of everything and anything. This is an attack not upon faith, but upon the mind; you cannot think if there are no things to think about.[11]

---

[9] Bloom argues a similar point about prejudice in *The Closing of the American Mind*, p. 35.

[10] This is very similar to a major point of John Locke's *A Letter Concerning Toleration* (Indianapolis, Indiana: Bobbs-Merrill, 1955) New York: Image, 1959), pp. 34–35.

Even practically speaking, no paper can be skeptical here. For one must know certain things to be true in order to doubt other things. Everything cannot be up for grabs! For if this were the case, then one's world view would be like the confused grey image on a television set on the wrong channel. Further, if this were true, then I could write that Derrida really is a neo-platonist and Marx a covert capitalist and might be legitimate in saying so. It might be alright to say that there were no such things as slaves, mass murders, racism, dominance of one group of people over another. Furthermore, what would be the meaning of a "group of people"? If truth is relative to culture, who determines what constitutes a culture? May I not make my own? You may suppose that all views of truth are but the expression of the will to power, but then must not the "will to power" be a real reality? Nietzsche certainly talks about power, life, decadence as if they are "real" things and not his own interpretations. No, even for Nietzsche there is objective truth, the drive of life, and not even he would want us to dispute that. Sometimes I wonder, if the views of postmodern relativists were totally true, how we could possibly misrepresent them? After all, their views are external to us and beyond our subjective consciousness.

The third property of a good paper is unity. While unity concerns many things, what is perhaps the most important is what falls within the domain of logic. One can criticize any paper that is incoherent, a paper where a student flatly contradicts himself or has theories whose implications do so. We would rate poorly a paper that claimed that postmodernism was the best philosophy to live by because it helped us live up to our nature as human beings. Yet there are those who criticize logic. In a very provocative article by Barry Barnes and David Bloor entitled "Relativism, Rationalism, and the Sociology of Knowledge,"[12] the authors make a powerful argument concluding that:

> Logic, as it is systematized in textbooks, monography or research papers, is a learned body of scholarly lore, growing and varying over time. It is a mass of conventional routines, decisions, expedient restrictions, dicta, maxims, and ad hoc rules. The sheer lack of necessity in granting its assumptions or adopting its strange and elaborate definitions is the point that should strike any candid observer.[13]

[12] Barry Barnes and David Bloor, "Relativism, Rationalism and the Sociology of Knowledge," in Martin Hollis and Steven Lukes, eds., *Rationality and Relativism*, (Cambridge, Massachusetts: The MIT Press, 1982), pp. 21–47.
[13] Ibid., p. 45.

My reaction to the article puzzled me. I was very impressed by the authors' arguments against the universal cogency of logic. If ever there was a well-supported and well-reasoned argument, it was here. And I was all prepared to believe them except for one thing. They informed me that there really was no such thing as an objectively good argument. They were only using their social conventions to persuade me to their side. They had created a brilliant argument only to show me that there were no such things as brilliant arguments. They had proved to me that there was no such thing as proofs. Later on, I wondered why they should not want to invent a logic all their own! After all, some techniques of persuasion are more effective than others. Are the authors bound by any rules? Is there any obligation or reason for the readers to listen to someone if they think reason is simply a matter of cultural or personal preference? Well, I do like listening to the preferences and tastes of others. Indeed, much of what I do know and appreciate in the fine arts has come from such suggestions. I can imagine a man saying that everything is a matter a taste, but a man certainly cannot argue that. If he does he is lying. His actions say that I am obliged to assent to his reasoning and at the same time that no form of reasoning should oblige me.

The last area is, perhaps the most difficult to explore and that is the domain of beauty. Just as all things are one, true, good, they are also beautiful. A good paper should not simply reiterate the truths and values that have been said before in the same way. We expect or hope the student to present his or her own opinion or angle on the truth and values above. If Maritain and St. Thomas were right in stating that clarity, proportion and integrity are criteria of beauty, might we not expect these attributes in papers as well? Might we not expect the papers to have clarity or to shed light on some issue? Might we not expect the ideas treated in the paper to be proportionate or well-balanced, to have treated other sides of the issue, especially opposing ones? Might we not expect the paper to have integrity and to have every issue covered that needs to be covered within the scope determined by the thesis and not to leave any relevant questions unanswered? Beauty has been defined by Maritain as the "radiance of all the transcendentals united"[14] Thus, if a student has found new ways to creatively han-

---

[14] Maritain, *Art and Scholasticism*, 173 n. 66; "A vrai dire il est la splendeur de tous les transcendantaux réunis" (*Art et Scholastique*, p. 225, n. 66). The phrase first appears in the footnotes of *Art et Scholastique* in the second edition of 1927, Paris: L. Rouart. May we suggest at this point the significance of "réunir"? According to Cassell's *French and English Dictionary*, the primary meaning is "to reunite." The beautiful brings the transcendentals back together. It is interesting that Cornelia N.

dle ideas that are true and valuable, then we might say that his paper is "beautiful."

In addition, we think it is not enough that students state a position that is true, good and beautiful, they should also give arguments why it is. Unless their paper states what everyone already knows to be true and valuable, they need to state the reasons why they are so. It may even be claimed that they should be able to trace their truths or values back to their first reasons or principles.

If we have been at all accurate thus far, what we have just shown is that for any theory to do well, it must rely upon assumptions of unity, truth, goodness and beauty. If these notions, as well as the realities seen through them are important, then instructors are obliged to provoke student insight in how to evaluate and explore these regions of human inquiry for themselves. In short, the instructor should try to help the student to see the things that are true, grasp the things that are good and beautiful, and understand the reasons behind these.

III

Now if the transcendentals are, in some manner, the property of good papers, they are what we as educators wish to inspire and elicit from our students. We want them to produce theories that are one, true, good and beautiful.

Are we imposing on them when we do so? No. Just as we have shown that the transcendentals are *naturally* the properties of a good paper, and insofar as all humans desire to communicate themselves—whether in papers or, for that matter in any other form—to others and insofar as they desire to do it well, it is natural and indeed liberating to educate in this way.

So if a human is a being who, to communicate himself, must rely upon the transcendentals, we can be sure that they are of his own human nature. If an instructor elicits a movement on the part of the student, it is precisely upon the tracks or roads of his own human nature. Human nature, as Norris Clarke, Gilson, Lonergan and Maritain have shown time and time again, aspires along the lines of the transcendentals—and we claim by three dif-

---

Borgerhoff, who worked with Maritain on Creative *Intuition in Art and Poetry* and *The Responsibility of the Artist*, translates the same phrase as the "splendor of all transcendentals gathered together," in *An Introduction to the Basic Problems of Moral Philosophy* (Albany, New York: Magi Books, 1990), p. 69. Cf. *Neuf leçons sur les notions premières de la philosophie morale* (Paris: Pierre Téqui, 1960), p. 63.

ferent means: towards the true and the understanding of the real which includes himself as knower, towards the good and the fulfillment of his own nature and this includes notions of his liberty and responsibility, and towards the beautiful and that valuable intelligibility of things not yet comprehensible but which is a reflection of the gift of existence that runs through all things.

Maritain lays special emphasis upon the last drive.[15] He does so because it underlies all of the other drives. Beauty is that which is the first to invade the preconscious root of the human spirit to ignite and inspire it to form all of its products, whether theoretical concepts or moral actions. A teacher must protect and encourage that.

Educators want to provoke growth in human beings, to make them better. They wish to provoke insights in students to help them first to understand and to judge what is truly real and to evaluate their own "maps" of reality; second, to understand what is truly good and that which will make them more responsible and free; and third, to appreciate the beautiful and to help them penetrate the surfaces of things and discover that "there is more in heaven and on earth than are dreamt of in their philosophies."

In short, when an educator does this, he does not impose his biases upon students, but rather provides an opportunity for the students to become more themselves, and, as a result, become better judges of reality, and better judges of values, including the value of tolerance. Finally, a motto may come to mind, "Give a man a fish and you have fed him for a day, teach him how to fish and you feed him for a lifetime." We want to teach him how to "know" truth, goodness and beauty simply and feed him for an eternity.

---

[15] Maritain, *Education at the Crossroads*, pp. 42–44; 52; 61.

The Catholic College:
At the Crossroad or
at the End of the Road?

R. J. McLaughlin

The Problem

The Catholic college is gravely ill, perhaps terminally so. The very titles of James T. Burtchaell's probing study, "The Decline and Fall of the Christian College," and Kenneth Woodward's more anecdotal commentary, "The Catholic College: What happened? A Parent's Lament," suggest that something has gone awry.[1] Jesuit Michael Buckley certainly thinks so and has written perceptively on the subject.[2] Philip Gleason has long been an intelligent voice in the chorus.[3] George Marsden's scholarly examination of the gradual erosion of religious traditions at mainline Protestant universities has to be dispiriting to Catholics also, especially when they read it in conjunction with Burtchaell's essay.[4] Though Church historian David O'Brien takes a rather benign view of developments (possibly because of a more lat-

---

[1] Burtchaell's two-part essay appears in *First Things* (April 1991): pp. 16–29 and (May 1991): pp. 30–38, Woodward's in *Commonweal* (4 April 1993): pp. 15–18. Burtchaell first studies the process by which Vanderbilt University gradually lost its Baptist character and then, using the stages of change at Vanderbilt as a model, seeks to alert Catholics how dangerously far along the same path they have come.

[2] Michael Buckley, S. J., "The Catholic University and its Inherent Promise," *America* (29 May 1993): pp. 14–16.

[3] Philip Gleason, "The Crisis of Americanization," in Philip Gleason, ed., *Catholicism in America* (New York: Harper and Row, Publishers, 1970), pp. 133–53; "What Made Catholic Identity a Problem," Marianist Award Lecture, University of Dayton, 1994.

[4] George Marsden, *The Soul of the American University* (Oxford University Press, 1994).

itudinarian conception of Catholicism as well as a more optimistic view of American culture), he leaves us with no doubt that the changes in Catholic higher education of the last thirty years have been profound and sweeping.[5]

The essays gathered by Theodore Hesburgh under the title of *The Challenge and Promise of a Catholic University* are for the most part hopeful but all acutely aware of difficulties.[6]

[5] David J. O'Brien, *From the Heart of the American Church* (Maryknoll, New York: Orbis, 1994). O'Brien gives other relevant sources, especially in the notes to Chapter 6. The book has much valuable information and interesting argument, though one sometimes wishes for a sharper distinction of argument and history.

To identify O'Brien's benchmark of the authentically Catholic, one should study the first chapter closely. There O'Brien expresses nervousness over proposals that there is "some foundation—reason or faith—on which ideas [can] be erected and sustained" (p. 5). Distrustful of philosophy, especially epistemology (ibid.), and not too comfortable with theology either, he prefers to arrive at his understanding of the Church by concrete appeal to history. Prominent in this approach is his own autobiography—in which family, the Catholic Worker movement, the Catholic Committee on Urban Ministry, and the 1976 Call to Action Conference play important roles (pp. 7–11); these help explain O'Brien's paradoxically strict requirement that Catholic education, or at least Jesuit education, be rather directly aimed at promoting peace and justice (Ch. 10). Though O'Brien allows parenthetically that texts and institutions may be "precious" (p. 14), his approach seems frankly historicist; and he admits that he is not particularly bothered by the accusation that his is a "cultural Catholicism" (ibid.). He stresses that the Catholicism that he knows is American. If what has happened to Catholic colleges in the last thirty-plus years is that they have become more American, that is nothing to worry about—unless Americanization is inherently secularization (e.g., p. 22). But O'Brien finds too much good in the larger American culture to see as threatening many of the changes that bother Burtchaell, Woodward, Gleason and others.

See also David O'Brien and Michael Buckley, "A Collegiate Conversation," *America* (11 September 1993).

[6] Theodore M. Hesburgh, C.S.C., ed., *The Challenge and Promise of a Catholic University* (Notre Dame, Indiana: University of Notre Dame Press, 1994). Father Hesburgh's opening essay, with its stress on the key roles that Catholic theology and philosophy play in Catholicizing education, its insistence on the compatibility of intellectual openness and academic freedom with institutional religious commitment deserves attention. Other highlights of this valuable book merit special comment.

David B. Burrell, C.S.C., developing what Hesburgh has to say on commitment, argues that if all inquiry is tradition-directed, one of the merits of universities with a Catholic tradition is that they can serve "to open conversation more widely."

Richard McBrien calls attention to some of the key difficulties that Hesburgh and some other Catholic college presidents had with the 1985 Proposed Schema for a Pontifical Document on Catholic Universities.

Frederick J. Crosson discusses the issue of academic freedom in the context of the religiously inspired university.

Ralph McInerny sees the Ellis essay (see n. 10) as skewing the conversation in the direction of ever greater educational homogeneity and secularism.

I begin these remarks a bit nostalgically, not so much out of a romantic desire to caress the past as to mark the distance that we have come and to suggest features of an older model that may be adaptable to present constraints. In the fall of 1948, just out of the Army a few months, I arrived at St. Michael's College in the University of Toronto. The society in which I found myself was solidly intellectual and at the same time deeply religious. The program of studies was challenging, the system of annual examinations spread over a month daunting. The priest-professors of the Congregation of St. Basil, on top of their theological studies, had graduate degrees from the most eminent North American and European universities.[7]

Joined with them in the academic enterprise were such distinguished scholars as Etienne Gilson, Anton C. Pegis, and Ignatius Eschmann in philosophy, and Herbert Marshall McLuhan in English. Jacques Maritain was an occasional visitor, and his writings gave form to the undergraduate curriculum in philosophy. Gerald B. Phelan would soon return from a stay at Notre Dame, and Joseph Owens was about to begin his distinguished teaching career at the Pontifical Institute of Mediaeval Studies. All these men set the highest standards of scholarship. The classroom treatment of religion was scrupulously academic, and no trace of apologetics crept into theology. Outside the classroom, of course, religious practices were encouraged. In those days, happily prior to the establishment on our campuses of a distinct chaplaincy personnel, every priest-teacher could be seen at the altar and was available for confession and spiritual direction.

George Marsden, lamenting that Catholic universities have let so much of their heritage slip away, contends that the fundamental task is to build a respected tradition of Christian education and in all disciplines to recruit faculty disposed to wonder about the implications of Christian faith to their explorations of reality. He has hope that such a project will attract the necessary donors.

Wilson Miscamble, C.S.C., sees faculty hiring as the critical issue for colleges that would retain a Catholic identity and calls for postdoctoral programs on the model of the Lilly fellowships conducted at Valparaiso University, to prepare young scholars to make distinctively Catholic contributions.

Indispensable reading on what is required for a Catholic college is, of course, Pope John Paul II's encyclical *Ex Corde Ecclesiae*, in *Origins* 20 (4 October 1990).

See also Margaret and Peter Steinfels' interesting contributions in *Origins* 25 (24 August 1995). And particularly valuable, both for its description of Notre Dame strategies for safeguarding the religious tradition and for its analysis of thinking that puts the tradition at risk, is David Solomon, "What Baylor and Notre Dame Can Learn from Each Other," *New Oxford Review* (December 1995): pp. 8–19.

[7] The Basilians included John Madden and Laurence K. Shook in English, Armand Maurer, Ralph MacDonald (whom Maritain praises in the foreword to *The Degrees of Knowledge*), John Kelly, Victor Brezik, and Robert Miller in philosophy, Eliot Allen and Wilfrid Dore in theology.

Like Sertillanges, we saw our secular studies and our religious life each feeding the other.[8] The entire resident student body was expected to turn out for Mass six mornings a week, and Sunday nights would see us by the hundreds in St. Basil's church for university sermons often of a quality to warm Cardinal Newman's heart. Sometime before the Dublin lectures on university education, St. Michael's already had established the house system that Newman was to recommend. Many of the houses were literally that, wonderful old Victorian mansions of a sort to encourage camaraderie and the informal exchange of ideas. Of course there were also fun and games in abundance. But study—that is what the place was principally about. One event of my freshman year captured the spirit nicely: the Arts Banquet, a dinner for students and faculty celebrating the accomplishments of the year, featured an address by none other than Jacques Maritain, who chose the occasion to share his latest ideas on the role in art and morality of knowledge through connaturality. I had the good sense to know that the ideas were above me; but I was grateful to be in an institution that so respected the intelligence of its students as to challenge them in this way.[9]

This picture that I paint does not square well with that suggested by John Tracy Ellis in his influential 1955 essay, "American Catholics and the Intellectual Life." Admittedly, south of the Canadian border, where Catholic colleges exist apart from large state universities, education could not be quite the same. Still, in the fifties and early sixties across the United States hundreds of institutions were doing something like what St. Michael's was doing: providing an education that was Christian in more than motivation and attendant spirit, marshalling all forces, curricular and extra-curricular, to serve this purpose. No doubt Ellis was correct in maintaining that these colleges had failed in preceding generations to produce their share of people who would be in the vanguard of creative intellectual activity. No doubt he was correct too in identifying ghettoism as an ingredient of the Catholic mentality that interfered with the intellectual greatness—especially if greatness was to be on the model of the leading secular research universities. But the education supplied by Catholic colleges was one that served well

---

[8] A.G. Sertillanges, O.P., *The Intellectual Life: Its Spirit, Conditions, Method*, trans. Mary Ryan (Washington, D.C.: The Catholic University of America Press, 1987). First published in 1946, this book has a tone that seems a bit dated now, but its content remains valuable. Would that it could be required reading for teachers and campus ministers.

[9] No doubt, like many another recalling his undergraduate days, I look through rose-colored glasses. But articles in such magazines as *Jubilee* (January 1958), *Sign* (April 1961), and *Time*, 25 January 1963, support my general appraisal.

the needs of the typical undergraduate who sought, among other things, a Christian perspective on the world.[10]

Today perhaps no change in Catholic colleges is more obvious to the casual observer than the dramatic reduction in the number of priests, brothers and nuns serving as teachers and administrators. In the fifties these religious were major forces, especially at small undergraduate colleges. No longer. At St. Michael's today not a single member of the Congregation of St. Basil remains on the undergraduate faculty. St. John Fisher, where I now teach, has but three Basilians teaching full time, none likely to be called young. Even a much larger community like the Jesuits suffers comparably. Only twenty-nine Jesuits are expected to finish doctoral studies in this academic year—for staffing all departments of all twenty-eight Jesuit colleges and universities across the country. The expected number for the following year is about the same; then the drop is precipitous to thirteen and nine for the following two years.[11]

Now, absent this living endowment of low-cost teachers, the colleges have to experience financial strain. This is part of the reason why in New York State there is, to my knowledge, but one college founded as Catholic that has not chosen over the last twenty-three years to distance itself from its original Catholic moorings in order to qualify for State financial assistance in the form of Bundy money. David O'Brien reports that across the country for diverse reasons religious communities have simply given their schools away.[12] Replacing the once impressive array of Catholic colleges we now have throughout the United States religiously independent schools claiming vaguely to be in the Basilian, Jesuit, Vincentian, Josephite or some other religious tradition. Ironically for us in New York, just in the last three years State budgetary curtailments have reduced the flow of public money to a near meaningless trickle—though the religious disavowals remain to affect membership on governing boards, advertising, recruitment of students and faculty, range of course offerings, content of curricula, classroom emphases, fund-raising, and more.

[10] John Tracy Ellis, *Thought* 30 (1955): pp. 351–388. Apropos of this essay Ralph McInerny fairly observes: "Ellis did not ask how Catholic universities could be better Catholic universities, however; he asked how they could be more like their secular counterparts, many of which had been founded under religious auspices and then drifted away." See McInerny's essay in Hesburgh, ed., *The Challenge and the Promise*, p. 176.

[11] Report of the Jesuit Conference, 21 August 1995, Washington, D.C. The picture is bleaker still if not all of these new Ph.D.'s are university-bound.

[12] Cf. O'Brien, *From the Heart*, p. 76.

Of course, even did not our law constrain a secularizing of institutions coming to the public trough, the shortage of priests, nuns and brothers interested in teaching (even teaching theology) would leave us confronting much the same problem. And even if there had been no shortage of religious, the Second Vatican Council with its accent both on new roles for the laity and the value of working with non-Catholics on common concerns was enough to ensure growing diversity of academic personnel and therefore of ideas about how a college should operate. Besides, Ellis's tracing of Catholic intellectual inadequacies to a ghetto mentality had already got college leaders thinking that maybe they should turn more to the leading secular universities for models and for personnel. Newly recovered appreciation, thanks again partly to Vatican II, of the freedom and dignity of all people and widespread acceptance of the standards of the AAUP meant that the many new voices on campus were sure to be heard. These would often represent a greater commitment to the now quite secularized disciplines than to the cause of religiously-inspired education of the whole person.[13]

Within the college, then, we can see with O'Brien three main obstacles to a concertedly Catholic educational program: "separate incorporation [giving the college a legal status independent of the Church and her agencies], professionalization [making faculty appointments according to criteria internal to each discipline, following the practice of the best secular schools without much attention to specifically religious concerns], and internal diversity."[14]

However, what makes the future of Catholic colleges particularly ominous are forces extending beyond the schools themselves. The last thirty, forty, fifty years have brought such profound cultural and religious changes that it is harder now for the average citizen, Catholic included, to see the point of Catholic education. The laudable post-Vatican-II emphasis on what we have in common with out "separated brethren" has understandably distracted us from what is distinctively Catholic. And as concern for the distinctively Catholic erodes, we cannot be surprised that concern for the dis-

---

[13] George Marsden considers the "methodological secularization" of the disciplines at graduate schools a major factor in the erosion of religious traditions at undergraduate schools. See especially Chapter 9 of *The Soul*. Note that faculty indifference to religious issues was occasioned, paradoxically, by John Tracy Ellis's clarion call for a new commitment to intellectual excellence on the part of Catholic scholars (see n. 10).

[14] O'Brien, *From the Heart*, p. 118.

tinctively religious wears away.[15] Moreover, across society the popular confusion of truth with one's awareness of the truth and the confusion of our right to hold an idea with the soundness of the idea have contributed to relativism that shies away from unflinching intellectual commitment, religious or secular. Of course, one does not have to be religiously indifferent or an intellectual relativist to wonder whether the vast educational project of an earlier American church is still worth the effort. Are not most people basically pretty decent? Do not most Americans, whatever their religious adherence, accept the life-liberty-and-pursuit-of-happiness motif, give elbow room for private pursuits (like religion?), act justly and display civic friendship? Why should Catholics hesitate to participate in the common educational enterprise at public universities?

Granted that the young may encounter more challenges to their faith at the public university, modern technologies, especially in communication, ensure that at an early age these people will already have been exposed to many of the ideas and values against which parents of an earlier age wanted Catholic colleges to protect them. The protectionist argument for Catholic higher education may never have been the best, but it is one that used to resonate in the psyche of many a Catholic parent. Its undermining means that we can expect fewer parents nudging their sons and daughters in the direction of Catholic colleges and fewer contributors thereto.

With the fortress mentality out of vogue, we are disposed to think of Catholicism less as a way of being set apart from the world than as a special way of being in the world, caring for it, working hand in hand with non-Catholics in all that promotes the common good.[16] Amen. And echoes of St. Augustine's *City of God* suggest that at least the best minds always knew this.[17]

Such considerations give David O'Brien a certain equanimity in the face

---

[15] I am talking here about what in fact occurs and am in no way suggesting that Catholics should see Protestants or other non-Catholics as the enemy or that they should not seek projects on which they can collaborate with people of other faiths or of no faith.

Apropos of my remark that seeing the point of Catholic education is becoming harder I should add that Woodward (see n. 1) is far from being the only parent to lament what has become of most Catholic colleges. Schools claiming to be Catholic ignore the concerns of this constituency at their peril.

[16] See the *Pastoral Constitution on the Church in the Modern World* in Walter M. Abbott, ed., *Documents of Vatican II* (New York: Herder & Herder, 1966), p. 200.

[17] St. Augustine, *City of God* XIX.17.

of the progressive secularization—he calls it "Americanization"—of our religious colleges.[18] Of course, one may accept the ideals of openness and ecumenism and service to one's fellows and still suspect that some kind of religious and intellectual ivory tower is a wise stopping-off place for those who seriously want to make the best contributions. But the ivory-tower image is out of favor, and O'Brien is certainly not alone in thinking that the kind of education that Church institutions used to provide is no longer what is needed. The life-expectancy of most Catholic colleges looks short. And the reasons go well beyond the often self-destructive policies[19] of the schools themselves to the religio-cultural sea- changes that have occurred, especially in the last thirty years.

The Principles

The death of the coherently and concertedly Catholic *college*[20] cannot, however, be allowed to mean an end to Catholic higher *education*, which *in*

---

[18] See note 5.

[19] Some of the self-destructive policies that I have in mind are: (a) failing to include in its charter a statement to the effect that a college belonging to the Basilian, Franciscan, or other such tradition has a continuing *special* and *pervading* interest in informing students about and cultivating appreciation of the Catholic intellectual heritage; (b) failing to make Catholicism, or at least intelligent goodwill for the project of Catholic education, a factor in hiring (though, if special interest in the Catholic heritage ideally should be felt throughout the curriculum, no candidate's attitudes toward that aspect of the college mission should be a matter of total indifference); (c) largely abandoning courses in Catholic theology in favor of courses in methodologically neutral religious studies; (d) reducing or abandoning requirements in Christian philosophy and religious studies in order to become more marketable to transfer students from community colleges, and thus losing the most obvious curricular indicator that the school belongs in the Catholic tradition of higher education; (e) failing to advertise the institution's abiding special interest in Catholicism (where it is still honest to do so); (f) doing little in its community outreach programs to cultivate in adult Catholics an ever deeper appreciation of their heritage and its implications for contemporary culture (and thus ensuring that the number of people disposed to support the Catholic college will gradually diminish).

[20] The Franciscan University of Steubenville (OH), St. Thomas Aquinas College (Santa Paula, CA), and St. Thomas More College (NH) are among a handful of colleges in clear reaction to the general trend that I have described. Cf. Samuel Casey Carter, "Ten Colleges to Consider," *Crisis* (January 1995): pp. 33–36. Time will tell whether these new or newly reshaped institutions are as concerned with being colleges as they are with being Catholic. Carter's list of identifiably Catholic colleges includes some well-established schools: St. Anselm College (Manchester, NH), Assumption College (Worcester, MA), Loyola College (Baltimore, MD). In connection with the newer and smaller ventures in particular, one longs for a way of adapting the Toronto scheme of religious colleges within the non-denominational (or multi-denominational) university so as to mitigate the very real dangers of undue insularity.

one form or another simply must survive and flourish. The requirement of
religious education follows from the obligatoriness of religion itself. St.
Augustine credits Cicero with recognizing what Plato's *Euthyphro* earlier
suggested and what St. Thomas clearly teaches: justice demands religion.[21]
Anyone who admits the existence of a Creator and yet fails regularly to go
down on his knees in humble thanks and adoration fails to pay what is due,
is unjust. And since we don't come into this world already knowing that it
is a created world or that all that we are and have we owe to God, we need
to be taught! So given that the existence of God is indeed demonstrable,
philosophy by itself comes to see religion and religious education as oblig-
atory. It is not surprising that even a pagan like Plato made provision for
regular religious worship in the program of his Academy.[22] And what reason concludes faith gives us additional basis for affirming: "Go and *teach*
all nations," said Jesus.

Many will object that the conviction that there is a loving God to whom
we should be ready to confess our dependence can be adequately inculcated
at mother's knee, that feelings of indebtedness and love count for more than
sophisticated theorizing about God. But surely Newman was right in refusing to reduce religious convictions to sentiment,[23] right too in warning that
the person who receives a college-level education in everything but theology will be hard pressed not to think of God-talk as somehow intellectually
suspect, hardly meeting the requirements of an adult mind. He will come to
disparage religious knowledge.[24]

That instruction in religion itself should matter to any Church is obvious. But if all that mattered were our knowing Church doctrine, the history
of Christian involvement in education from the very first centuries after
Christ would be unintelligible. I am thinking of such early Christian apolo-
gists as Justin Martyr and Clement of Alexandria, of a Father of the Church
like St. Basil—all of whom recognized that Christian wisdom must enter
into dialogue with pagan wisdom. I am thinking of those Irish monasteries
where in the darkest of the dark ages humble monks laboriously copied secular as well as sacred manuscripts in order that a precious heritage not be

[21] Cf. Augustine, *City of God* II.21 and XIX.21–23; and Thomas Aquinas,
Summa Theologiae IIaIIae, q.81.
[22] Cf. Josef Pieper, *Leisure: the Basis of Culture* (London: Faber and Faber,
1952), p. 77.
[23] John Henry Newman, *The Idea of a University*, Daniel M. O'Connell, S.J., ed.
(New York: The America Press, 1941), Discourse 2.
[24] Ibid., Discourse 3.

lost. I am thinking of the role of Irish and English monks in the Carolingian renaissance. I am thinking of the first universities of the West, the work of bishops and their clergy. I am thinking of the role of St. Francis de Sales in establishing the first high schools. I am thinking of all those Benedictines, Dominicans, Franciscans, Jesuits, Basilians, Sisters of St. Joseph and Mercy, and others male and female, who out of religious inspiration have undertaken to teach not just theology and Christian philosophy but literature and history, mathematics, physical and social sciences, art. Theology may be the first interest of the Christian intellectual; it cannot be his only interest. While recognizing with Aristotle that the little that we can know of God is much more worthwhile than the abundance that we can know of terrestrial things,[25] we see all knowledge, even of the least created thing, as in principle revelatory of the Creator. We have a religious stake in secular learning.

It is difficult to emerge from a study of the middle ages in particular without seeing in the Catholic Church one of the greatest friends higher education has ever known. Of course, then and now the Church occasionally sins against education.[26] Still, that friendship with learning, based not on changing circumstance but on principle, the principle that *truth is in its Primary Instance divine and has revealed Himself not just in His handiwork to the person of reason but also in the history of the Jewish people and in Jesus Christ and the tradition of His Church to the person of faith*—such friendship, such devotion to learning cannot be allowed to wither just because Catholic colleges as we have known them are in trouble.

In all of this I am presuming, as Maritain and others have maintained,

[25] Aristotle, *Metaphysics* VI.1 1026a 21–23; *Nicomachean Ethics* X.7 1177a 12–19.

[26] The treatment of Galileo and the Inquisition stand out as sorry episodes in the life of the Church. In recent times the denial to Father Charles Curran of the right to teach as a Catholic theologian in a Pontifical university was unfortunate public relations even if it was defensible control of the content of instruction at a school professing to teach Catholic doctrine. Of course, conflict between the official magisterium of the Church and individual theologians conscientiously seeking deeper understanding of God's revelation can be expected to recur in every age. Ideally such conflicts are resolved in some other way than by appeal to force. One thinks here of the turmoil in the thirteenth-century University of Paris when Latin Averroists were talking of one Agent Intellect for all men and Gerard d'Abbeville and Geraldini were denying the very right of mendicants to teach in the university. The Dominican response (to the latter issue, at any rate) was to pull their best man out of his work in the Roman province and rush him back to Paris in the middle of an academic year—that an intellectual quarrel might be resolved at the properly intellectual level. See James A. Weisheipl, O.P., *Friar Thomas d'Aquino* (Garden City, New York: Doubleday, 1974), pp. 237–239.

that education at any level is concerned more with the making of a human being than with the making of a worker or a citizen *or a Christian*; that any educational institution should make its appeal principally to the intellect[27]; that the perfection of the human person entails the acquisition of a whole panoply of virtues, moral as well as intellectual; that the college or university cannot be indifferent to the moral bent of its students even as it concentrates its efforts on chemistry, biology, mathematics, history, philosophy, theology and other such intellectual virtues.[28] I stand with Maritain also in affirming that merely human virtue is not enough: having a destiny beyond the natural we need the theological and moral virtues that "God works in us without us."[29] I stand with St. Thomas in affirming that even naturally knowable truths about God such as are the business of metaphysics, most people are not going to succeed in grasping, certainly not in a timely fashion or without many mistakes unless they are guided by God's *super*natural revelation.[30] I thus stand with Gilson in my misgivings about young people's studying philosophy in an unChristian or a-religious setting.[31] I stand with Newman, and with Gerald B. Phelan in the essay which Maritain cites in *Education at the Crossroads*, in holding that theology should be central to the educational enterprise and that to ignore its insights is to embrace a distorted view of reality as a whole.[32] Finally, I stand with churchmen from St. Thomas to Theodore Hesburgh in respect for the freedom of intellectual inquiry and thus insist that the Catholic college must have a certain autonomy vis-a-vis the bishops as well as the state and recognize that, once faculty members are given tenure, the mere fact that they come to harbor unpopular views is no reason for dismissing or otherwise punishing them—at least provided that these views are compatible with the

---

[27] Jacques Maritain, *Education at the Crossroads* (New Haven, Connecticut: Yale University Press, 1943), pp. 1–7; 9–10.

[28] Ibid., pp. 24–28; 93–97.

[29] Jacques Maritain, *Science and Wisdom* (New York: Scribner's, 1940); *Moral Philosophy* (London: Bles, 1964), pp. 71–91.

[30] St. Thomas Aquinas, *Summa Theologiae* Ia, q. 1, a. 1.

[31] Etienne Gilson, "St. Thomas and Our Colleagues," in *The Gilson Reader* (NewYork: Doubleday-Image, 1957), pp. 278–297.

[32] Gerald B. Phelan, "Theology in the Curriculum of Catholic Colleges and Universities," *Man and Modern Secularism* (New York: National Catholic Alumni Federation, 1940), pp. 138–142. In a recent article James Heft, S.M., Provost of the University of Dayton, sharply distinguishes theology from religious studies and argues that it is the former that is crucial to the Catholic identity of a college or university. See Heft, "Theology in a Catholic University," *Origins* 25 (28 September 1995).

stated purposes of the college as made plain to the faculty member at the time of his initial appointment.[33]

Applications

The issue, then, concerns not whether education needs to make provision for faith but how it may best do so in the concrete circumstances in which we now find ourselves. A first point to note is that if the learning and teaching activities are not in some way Catholic, then the college simply is not Catholic. And because the classroom is the principal place for these activities, it is the classroom that pre-eminently needs religious influence. Wherever there is plausible hope of maintaining a college as distinctively Catholic, this means, at a minimum, that sympathy for religiously-inspired education generally and a Catholic approach in particular is normally a necessary condition for appointment to the faculty. Hence, even though departments can be expected to chafe sometimes at what they will perceive as administrative interference, presidents and academic deans must involve themselves in every faculty appointment, lest the overall purposes of the college be lost sight of in departmental enthusiasm for a candidate's special disciplinary expertise.

Whether the administrators of a college be Catholic, or at least deeply

[33] The Christian, especially the Christian intellectual, should have a passionate devotion to the truth. But one of the truths that he recognizes is that, because free choice is a mark of human dignity, he must respect the free ways in which others seek the truth. Efforts to force people to think one way rather than another are not only counterproductive, they are unjust. Cf. the proemium to the moral part of the *Summa Theologiae*, where St. Thomas makes freedom the keynote of all morality: it is precisely as intellectual beings who determine our own lives that we are in the image of God.

What Theodore Hesburgh says in the opening essay of *The Challenge and Promise of a Catholic University* about university autonomy and faculty freedom seems by and large correct, but the degree of autonomy from episcopal authority appropriate to a college or university that takes seriously its profession of being Catholic is difficult to formulate and more difficult to work out in practice. Catholics, after all, hold that it is through the Church that God's revelation is conveyed to them. The prospects of a college's remaining in any significant sense Catholic without a corporate link to the Church are slim indeed, as James T. Burtchaell argues in the essay cited in n.1. See especially Part II of Burtchaell's essay, *First Things* (May 1991), p. 35.

Also, something more needs to be said about the parameters within which the faculty exercise their freedom to teach as they see fit. Trustees, presidents, academic deans, academic departments have a role here. That the setting of parameters is legitimate Ralph McInerny makes abundantly clear in the Hesburgh volume (pp. 183–84).

familiar with and supportive of the Catholic educational project, matters enormously—for how can they husband faithfully a tradition that they little know or care for? Besides, presidents, academic deans, deans of students, and others can set a tone—to say nothing of a budget—that either supports or impedes the project of Christian education. And now that the governing boards ultimately responsible for appointing top administrators can no longer count on the availability of qualified members of the founding religious community, it becomes increasingly important that they too have a deep understanding of the Catholic educational project. Still, in another sense, whatever their legal status, administrators and trustees are essentially of secondary importance. Their purpose is to facilitate the effective coming together of faculty and students.

Similarly, insofar as the students' spiritual lives need feeding in the liturgy and insofar as the institution as such needs on certain occasions to mark liturgically its religious commitment, the role of a campus minister is unquestionably important (though the sacraments could be made available in a neighboring parish). Ideally, as in the past, chaplains at schools claiming to be in some way Catholic would be many, every priest-teacher regularly being seen at the altar, visibly symbolizing the harmony of reason and revelation. Today, however, not only are the priest-teachers fewer and fewer in number but the conduct of liturgies often falls to one or two non-teaching priests. The result is that students find it harder to see connections between their religious lives and their academic lives. Now and then from the pulpit they need to hear a word said for studiousness, ardor for knowledge, intellectual honesty; they deserve to be treated to deeply theological meditations on the Trinity, on Truth Himself, on creation—topics less likely to occur to the minister who is not actively engaged in the life of scholarship and teaching. In a word, because the campus minister's ministry is to the campus, it is campus life—a life centered on learning and teaching—that he should care to make or keep Christian.[34]

Of course, much learning and teaching go on outside the classroom—in dormitory common rooms, on playing fields, in the cafeteria, through a

[34] The campus minister should probably take a leading role in organizing food drives for the hungry, money-raising projects to help people in physical or spiritual need, service programs for staffing houses of hospitality, abortion hotlines, etc. For students must not come to think that Catholicism is a matter of merely intellectual adherence without practical consequences. Nonetheless, it remains true, as *Ex Corde Ecclesiae* points out, that the college's basic way of serving society is at the intellectual level, seeking an ever deeper grasp of the truth and communicating it to others as effectively as possible.

wide variety of co-curricular activities. Setting an appropriate moral tone (according to which civility, friendship, respect for the free workings of human intelligence, truthfulness, and other virtues serve good learning) must be an institutional aim[35], though recent propagandistic excesses of the politically correct on our campuses stand as warning against heavy-handedness and the de-Christianizing of virtue.

Probably most of the colleges claiming to be in a Catholic tradition are already too diversified to be recalled to a coherently and concertedly Catholic education.[36] So we seek alternatives that may not be ideal but will keep the concerns of Christian faith in more prominent and clear focus than is the case on avowedly secular campuses. Imagination is called for. And we need to act now before we lose any more support for key votes in our faculty assemblies and boards of trustees.

Given that over the years the personnel of any college or university change completely, for any school to maintain its character it must tell its story again and again. The story is about those who founded the institution and why, about great professors, about outstanding students, about alumni. It is told to incoming freshmen; it is repeated on state occasions. The college seal, explained to each new group, will become a visible reminder of what the institution stands for. If the school is named for a person, all should know who that person was and why his name attaches to the school. For the still-more-or-less-Catholic colleges telling the story must involve reference also to the centuries-long intellectual tradition in which even the newest of them participates.

In the interest of telling the story to faculty, representatives of forty-five

---

[35] Probably every college recruits the academically strongest students that it can hope to attract, and probably no college wittingly accepts those whose level of civilization assures that they will be disruptive influences on campus. In a similar way every college serious about Catholic education must make special efforts to recruit Catholic students. For it is Catholics whom such institutions exist directly to serve. Cf. Burtchaell, "The Decline and Fall . . . II," *First Things* (May 1991): p. 38.

[36] Given the religious diversity of faculties and student bodies in today's Catholic college, any efforts that the school makes to return to its religious roots must take care to avoid injustice to its non-Catholic members, who in joining its ranks had perhaps little reason to think that the school's religious tradition would have at this late date any significant impact on the teaching or learning that went on there. Still, if over the years an institution continued saying, however vaguely, that it was in some way Catholic, efforts now to put substance into the words cannot come as a total surprise. And, after all, sensitivity to the feelings and the conscience of others should extend not just to non-Catholics but also to all those Catholics on campus who are understandably saddened, even angered, over policies that have eroded religious features of the college.

colleges—Jewish, Protestant, and Catholic—have for several years been meeting at Valparaiso University for a conference on religion and higher education sponsored by the Lilly Foundation. An offshoot of this group is the Collegium, based at Fairfield University, which holds summer seminars on Catholic education. The Jesuits of the Maryland province have been meeting annually for the same purpose. Faculty at Basilian schools have had one such meeting; others are contemplated. Many schools have held at least sporadic colloquia in which faculty members discuss among themselves the significance of the Catholic rhetoric of their mission statements.

As a tactic for salvaging something of the tradition some colleges have established programs or institutes that would gather together faculty and students who desire to focus their attention on the Christian patrimony and its lessons for today. Christ College at Valparaiso may be worth studying in this regard. So too the Christian Culture Program at St. Michael's College in the University of Toronto. The St. Ignatius Institute at The University of San Francisco probably has some lessons for us. And there must be other models. My chief misgiving about such programs or colleges-within-the college is that they may aggravate the problem by further marginalizing religion. Those involved in them are too apt to be thought of by the majority of students, and perhaps faculty, as eccentric, not engaged in the same sort of serious scholarship as is the rest of the school. So a college-wide academic program is preferable. Maybe with the right personnel, planning, and college-wide support solid interdisiplinary concentrations in Christian culture could substitute for the traditional minor and for part of the core requirements in a student's academic program.

Scholarships in Catholic studies of one sort or another, though awarded to but a few outstanding students, might stimulate broader interest in things Catholic among many students. Thus my own college is seeking funding for what we propose to call the Jacques Maritain scholarships in Christian philosophy.

We also look to endow a chair to support a visiting professor of Catholic studies. Because it is the educational process as a whole that should be Catholic, this proposal is for a multidisciplinary chair. One semester the visitor might be a professor of literature looking for intimations of the divine in Dostoevski, Gerard Manley Hopkins, Georges Bernanos, Flannery O'Connor, and others. Another semester might bring an historian to examine interactions of Christians and Muslims in the Middle Ages or a sociologist to probe the joint impact of the civil rights movement, Vatican II, and the Vietnam war on the American Catholic psyche. Another semester might feature an Avery Dulles helping students to understand more deeply what faith and church are or a Charles Curran examining moral issues that arise in today's hospitals. Another semester a philosopher from Blackfriars, Oxford, might examine the possibility of knowledge that transcends sense experience; or somebody like Stanley Jaki might weigh the relevance of Stephen Hawking's physics to the Christian conviction that this world is created by God. The enthusiasm of first-rate scholars should be contagious. Our hope at St. John Fisher is that on a regular basis various departments would be thus stimulated to reflect on the significance of Christian faith for their disciplines.

There is no question here of the non-theologian's being expected to do amateur theology in the science or history or literature class. But perhaps we can still hope for English teachers who (even if not themselves particularly sympathetic to things Catholic) will in their passing comments invite students to wonder if the relativist critical theories deriving from Jacques Derrida are compatible with the Christian commitment to the sacredness of a particular Text; or for economists whose *obiter dicta* will alert students that rejection of the concept of illusory marketplace services[37] may entail rejection of the sort of objective morality basic to Christianity and recently reaffirmed in *Veritatis Splendor*, or for physicists whose asides will make clear that talk of a Big Bang has nothing to do with the issue of creation as Christian philosophers and theologians understand it. Only to the extent that teachers are aware of the tradition can they be expected not unwittingly to undermine it. Like the faculty conferences and seminars, the visiting professor idea is aimed at increasing awareness of and support for the tradition.

Conclusion

Almost no college today is Catholic in the pervasive way that many once were. It is easy to suppose that the slide to complete secularism is inexorable and that the Catholic public should now redirect its energies and resources to more promising projects. Still, almost none of colleges founded as Catholic is yet completely secularized either. Generally speaking, can something both academically and religiously worthwhile be salvaged? I am uncertain. But I hesitate to abandon the effort, lest I help to ensure the very outcome I seek to avoid.

---

[37] Yves R. Simon, *Work, Society, and Culture* (New York: Fordham University Press, 1971), pp. 122ff.

Maritain: Philosophy, The Catholic University and Truth

Robert E. Lauder

It is no accident that in recent years several important books have appeared exploring and examining the university. I think immediately of George M. Marsden's *The Soul of the American University*,[1] David J. O'Brien's *From the Heart of the American Church*,[2] Jaroslav Pelikan's *The Idea of the University*,[3] Douglas Sloan's *Faith and Knowledge*,[4] and Allan Bloom's *The Closing of the American Mind*.[5] Because of his distinguished career in Catholic higher education sections of the autobiography of Father Theodore M. Hesburgh, *God, Country, Notre Dame*[6] can also be added to the list. There is a crisis in education. The contemporary world has problems to spare and it is difficult to make some kind of hierarchy or list in order of their importance. But if we look to the needs of the present and toward what must happen if the future is to be better then university education has to be near the top of the list. The amount of discussion that

---

[1] George M. Marsden, *The Soul of the American University: From Protestant Establishment to Established Belief* (New York: Oxford University Press, 1994), p. 462.

[2] David J. O'Brien, *From the Heart of the American Church: Catholic Higher Education and American Culture* (Maryknoll, New York: Orbis Books, 1994), p. 212.

[3] Jaroslav Pelikan, *The Idea of the University: A Re-examination* (New Haven, Connecticut: Yale University Press, 1992), p. 238.

[4] Douglas Sloan, *Faith and Knowledge: Mainline Protestantism and American Higher Education* (Westminster: John Knox, 1994), p. 336.

[5] Allan J. Bloom, *The Closing of the American Mind* (New York: Simon and Schuster, 1987), p. 392.

[6] Theodore M. Hesburgh with Jerry Ready, *God, Country, Notre Dame: The Autobiography of Theodore M. Hesburgh* (New York: Doubleday, 1990), p. 331.

Bloom's book caused less than ten years ago suggests something of the urgency that many educators sense in relation to contemporary education's failures. With great accuracy Bloom articulated the relativism that pervades the horizon of the contemporary student.

> There is one thing a professor can be absolutely certain of: almost every student entering the university believes, or says he believes, that truth is relative.If this belief is put to the test, one can count on the students' reaction: they will be uncomprehending. That anyone should regard the proposition as not self-evident astonishes them, as though he were calling into question 2+2=4. Those are things you don't think about . . . The danger they have been taught to fear from absolutism is not error but intolerance . . . The study of history and of culture teaches that all the world was mad in the past, men always thought they were right, and that led to wars, persecutions, slavery, xenophobia, racism and chauvinism. The point is not to correct the mistake and really be right, rather it is not to think you are right at all.[7]

In my own reading of Bloom I was impressed by his perception that something was wrong but disappointed with his suggestions of how to combat it. Though I share Bloom's enthusiasm for Plato, I think that more is needed than a re-reading and reflection on some of antiquity's insights. What is needed is a philosophy of person that states forcefully essential truths about personal existence and can make clear the crucial role that university education can play in the life of a person and indeed in the life of a society in which it exists. The philosophy of Jacques Maritain is such a philosophy.

In his marvelous book, *Crossing the Threshold of Hope*, Pope John Paul II succinctly characterizes the positivist mentality:

> Positivism has not only been a philosophy or a methodology, it has been one of those *schools of suspicion* that the modern era has seen grow and prosper. Is man truly capable of knowing something beyond what he sees with his eyes or hears with his ears? Does some kind of knowledge other than the strictly empirical exist? Is the human capacity for reason completely subject to the senses and internally directed by the laws of mathematics, which have been shown to be particularly useful in the rational ordering of phenomena and for guiding technical progress?
>
> If we put ourselves in the positivist perspective, concepts such as *God or the soul* simply lose meaning. In terms of sensory experience, in fact, nothing corresponds to God or the soul.[8]

---

[7] Bloom, *The Closing of the American Mind*, pp. 25–26.
[8] Pope John Paul II, *Crossing the Threshold of Hope* (New York: Alfred A. Knopf, 1994), p. 244.

Unfortunately the positivist mentality still pervades our students' visions. Perhaps threatening circumstances shed new light on old realities or at least help us to appreciate more deeply what we have that is of value. At this moment the role of the Catholic university never seemed more important. Yet it is in crisis. In terms of crisis it is, to borrow Maritain's phrase, "at the crossroads."[9] In this essay, using Maritain's philosophy of person, truth, and education, I want to highlight three aspects of Catholic university life that are especially important today: 1) the Catholic university's commitment to the liberal arts; 2) its commitment to philosophy; and 3), its commitment to specifically Catholic studies.

In reflecting on the unique contribution that a Catholic university can make to a student I re-read a description of a contemporary person that highlights what a Catholic university does *not* want to produce. The description underlines what can happen in our secular humanistic, consumer culture which discourages serious reflection, especially serious reflection on self and what it means to be a person. The description, taken from Walker Percy's novel *The Moviegoer*, is the self-description of the main character, Binx Bolling. Catholic Thomistic-existentialist Percy touches all the bases and gives us a humorous but frightening image of a person who has not transcended the errors that bombard him every day:

> I am a model tenant and a model citizen and take pleasure in doing all that is expected of me. My wallet is full of identity cards, library cards, credit cards. Last year I purchased a flat olive-drab strongbox, very smooth and heavily built with double walls for fire protection, in which I placed my birth certificate, college diploma, honorable discharge, G.I. insurance, a few stock certificates, and my inheritance. . . . It is a pleasure to carry out the duties of a citizen and to receive in return a receipt or a neat styrene card with one's name on it certifying, so to speak, one's right to exist. What satisfaction I take in appearing the first day to get my auto tag and brake sticker! I subscribe to *Consumer Reports* and as a consequence I own a first-class television set, an all but silent air conditioner and a very long lasting deodorant. My armpits never stink. I pay attention to all spot announcements on the radio about mental health, the seven signs of cancer, and safe driving. . . .
>
> In the evenings I usually watch television or go to the movies. Our neighborhood theater in Gentilly has permanent lettering on the front of the marquee reading: Where Happiness Costs So Little. The fact is I am quite happy in a movie, even a bad movie. Other people, so I have

[9] Jacques Maritain, *Education at the Crossroads* (New Haven, Connecticut: Yale University Press, 1943), p. 120.

read, treasure memorable moments in their lives: . . . What I remember is the time John Wayne killed three men with a carbine as he was falling to the dusty street in *Stagecoach*, and the time the kitten found Orson Welles in the doorway in *The Third Man*.[10]

How not to produce Binx Bolling? The study of liberal arts has a special role. In discussing with contemporary students and educators the unique role of the liberal arts in education I stress that such study enables people to think, to reflect on what it means to be human. I believe that deeply and I might add statements such as "The study of the liberal arts humanizes us" or "The study of the liberal arts personalizes us." I believe that too but Robert Hutchins when he was the President of the University of Chicago put forth the case for the liberal arts more profoundly. His articulation of the value of the liberal arts includes implicitly the philosophical vision of person that Maritain had. Hutchins wrote:

> The object of education is the production of virtue; for virtue is that which makes a man good and his work good, too. As virtue makes a man and his work good, so also it makes him happy, for happiness is activity in accordance with virtue. As virtue makes a man good and makes him happy, so also it makes him a good citizen, and this is the aim of general or liberal education. The four cardinal virtues are justice, prudence, temperance and fortitude, and one description of them is that they are social virtues, the virtues that good living in society requires.[11]

Reading this today, and perhaps being startled by it, may reveal just how much the theory of value-free education has subtly influenced us. Hutchins goes on to stress that because a virtue is a habit it is acquired and strengthened by particular acts. A person becomes just by performing just acts, becomes temperate by being temperate. A person cannot acquire a virtue merely by listening to lectures in ethics. An individual can have a doctorate in ethics but not be a virtuous person. A person has all sorts of habits, good and bad, before he or she attends a university. However, Hutchins reminds us that virtues may be lost or weakened and, of course, may also be strengthened. A Catholic university will want to help students strengthen their virtues and diminish their vices. If good habits learned at a young age are to be strengthened, they need to be supported by reason. Stressing that this is where the connection between the moral and intellectual virtues is Hutchins wrote:

---

[10] Walker Percy, *The Moviegoer*, (New York: Avon, 1960), p. 191.
[11] Robert M. Hutchins "The University and Character," *Commonweal* 27 (22 April 1938): p. 710.

The great and specific contribution that a college or university can make to the development of virtue is in supplying the rational basis for it, that is, in developing the intellectual virtues. Wisdom, science and understanding, the three speculative virtues, and prudence, the good habit of the practical intellect, must be the focus of a university's educational endeavor. They are the criterion of teaching and research. The test of a good course is not whether it is amusing or informational or seems to contribute to financial success, any more than the test of a good research project is whether it is expensive and elaborate and produces large literary poundage. The real test of instruction or research is whether it has high intellectual content and demands intellectual effort. Otherwise it has no place in a university, for it cannot assist in forming those habits which a university is designed to foster.[12]

Hutchins went on to say that the special way that a university serves a democracy is in helping its students to think. He pointed out that economic and social injustice of his time were not due to the lack of resources or the failure of technology but to the weakness and absence of moral and intellectual virtues. The main issue of the day was a moral and intellectual one. I am tempted to note that the more things change the more they remain the same. In discussing education Maritain wrote: ˙

Education must remove the rift between the social claim and the individual claim within man himself. It must therefore develop both the sense of freedom and the sense of responsibility, human rights and human obligations, the courage to take risks and exert authority for the general welfare and the respect for the humanity of each individual person.[13]

Concerning the Catholic university's commitment to philosophy I would like to mix Maritain's philosophy of person with insights from the Roman Catholic existentialist, Gabriel Marcel. In reflecting on the role of a Catholic university I find Marcel's distinction between a problem and a mystery quite helpful. Many people on many days are preoccupied with problems; philosophy and the Catholic university call people to reflect on mystery.

Marcel claimed that there were four differences between a problem and a mystery.[14] A problem is always external to the self. It is out there. A question in physics or chemistry or mathematics does not involve direct reflection on the self. A problem deals with what is other than the self. A mystery

---

[12] Ibid., 14–15.

[13] Maritain, *Education at the Crossroads*, p. 89.

[14] Kenneth Gallagher, *The Philosophy of Gabriel Marcel* (New York: Fordham University Press, 1962), p. 30–40.

is internal and always involves the self. I can not reflect on the mystery of freedom without reflecting on my freedom; I cannot reflect on the mystery of death without reflecting on my death; I cannot reflect on the mystery of God without reflecting on my relationship with God. The second difference is that the mood in dealing with a problem is curiosity while the mood in dealing with a mystery is awe or wonder. Third, there is an answer to a problem; there is no answer or final solution to a mystery. With a problem I may not know the answer, you may not know the answer, but in principle there is an answer. With a mystery a person can go deeper and deeper and gain richer and richer insight but there is no final answer. Finally, a problem can be worked on by anyone. For example, I may work on a science problem for two hours and then hand over my research to someone else to work on for a few hours and that person in turn may hand his or her research over to someone else. Only I can think about mystery in my life. Only *I* can think about *my* death, only *I* can think about *my* freedom, only *I* can think about *my* relationship with God. Mystery is eminently personal.

Problems plague many people. A Catholic university with a strong philosophy requirement can call its students to deep reflection on mystery. In assessing his education from grammar school through university philosopher Sam Kean wrote:

> Although it was nowhere explicitly stated, I found the motto of education to be: *Dubito Ergo Sum* (I doubt therefore I am). And for years I sat with cramped muscles in hardwood chairs (with initials carved in them) and listened to lectures on the necessity for dialogue (no one laughed) and on the incarnate and engaged character of human existence.
>
> Scarcely ever in my quarter of a century of schooling was I invited to consider the intimate, personal questions which were compelling my attention outside the classroom.[15]

Philosophy can call people to reflect on the meaning of personal existence from a most profound and radical perspective that is uniquely philosophy's. In discussing philosophy's role in education Maritain wrote that:

> the highest aim of liberal education which is to make youth possess the foundations of wisdom. At this point I need not dwell on the vindication of philosophy. It is enough to repeat a remark often made indeed, namely that nobody can do without philosophy, and that, after all, the only way of avoiding the damage wrought by an unconscious belief in

---

[15] Sam Kean, *To A Dancing God* (New York: Harper & Row, Publishers, 1970), p. 39.

a formless and prejudicial philosophy is to develop a philosophy consciously. Furthermore metaphysics is the only human knowledge
which actually claims to be wisdom, and to have such penetration and
universality that it can actually bring the reader of the sciences into
unity, cooperation and accord, and if anybody honestly wishes to dispute the validity of this claim, he must perforce begin by knowing the
metaphysics that he challenges. In fine, education deals ultimately
with the great achievements of the human mind; and without knowing
philosophy and the achievements of the great thinkers it is utterly impossible for us to understand anything of the development of mankind,
civilization, culture and science.[16]

The mystery of self, the mystery of neighbor, and the mystery of God
are philosophy's preoccupations. Actually, philosophy can glory in the truth
that it does not reach final and finished truths about person, neighbor and
God. There is too much in an unlimited God for a finite mind ever to master a final truth about God and the Divine has shared too much of itself with
human reality for a limited mind ever to penetrate totally its own mystery.
In a fast-paced world, our technological society—one which may at times
slip into a technocracy—the wonder and awe that should accompany all
philosophical reflection are a special counter-cultural benefit that philosophy can provide. That no one can reflect on a mystery for someone else reminds us of a profound truth about a university: there is a sense in which no
one educates anyone else. The great teacher invites us, calls us, shares his
or her excitement with us. But all truth involves a commitment and no one
can make the commitment for anyone else. Philosophy calls students to
mystery, perhaps even tries to seduce to mystery, but education will not
happen without the student's self gift.

Those aspects of mystery which may at first seem repugnant to the student—that there are no final solutions, that the mood is awe and that reflection about self must be done by the self—are actually what makes philosophy such an indispensable blessing for the student in a Catholic university.
Philosophy calls the student to a new level of existence, a more reflective,
integrated and self-possessed way of existing.

Of course, liberal arts and philosophy can happen in universities other
than Catholic universities. Any program that incorporates them should be
applauded. But in the Catholic university, with its commitment to God's
Self-Revelation and the teaching of the Catholic Church, the liberal arts and

---

[16] Maritain, *Education at the Crossroads*, pp. 71–72.

philosophy should have a home that nourishes and nurtures them, indeed that sheds special light in their insights.

John Henry Newman was correct in placing theology as the queen of the sciences at the center of a University. Newman summarized his argument as follows:

> I have argued . . . first, from the consideration that, whereas it is the very profession of a University to teach all sciences, on this account it cannot exclude Theology without being untrue to its profession. Next, I have said that all sciences being connected together, and having bearings on one another, it is impossible to teach them all thoroughly unless they are all taken into account, and Theology among them. Moreover, I have insisted on the important influence which Theology as a matter of fact does and must exercise over a great variety of sciences, completing and perfecting them; so that, granting it be a real science occupied upon truth, it cannot be omitted without great prejudice to the teaching of the rest. And lastly, I have urged that, supposing Theology is not taught, its province will not simply be neglected, but will be actually usurped by other sciences, which will teach, without warrant, conclusions of their own in a subject-matter which needs its own proper principles for its due formation and disposition.[17]

Without theology we cannot have a Catholic university—yet the Catholic dimension should color everything. While leaving each discipline its own necessary independence the Catholic vision should permeate all studies. Years ago, not really facetiously, German theologian Romano Guardini said that a Christian climbs a tree differently than anyone else. I suggest that a Catholic university presents all academic disciplines differently because of the Catholic commitment which colors the Catholic university's identity.

However, I would like to echo the sentiments of other Catholic educators and suggest that at a Catholic university there should be much reflection on the Catholic imaginative tradition. Here I rely on David Tracy's insights into the analogical imagination.[18] Simplifying and summarizing Tracy's insights, Andrew Greeley has argued provocatively and persuasively that the Catholic imagination should be studied at a Catholic university.[19] There is a

---

[17] John Henry Newman, *The Idea of a University* (Notre Dame, Indiana: University of Notre Dame Press, 1982), p. 74.

[18] David Tracy, *The Analogical Imagination: Christian Theology and the Culture of Pluralism* (New York: Crossroad, 1989), pp. 405; 456.

[19] Andrew Greeley, "The Catholic Imagination and the Catholic University," *America* (16 March 1991): pp. 285–288.

significant difference between the Catholic imagination and the Protestant imagination. The former tends to emphasize the immanence of God; the latter tends to emphasize the transcendence of God. The Catholic imagination is analogical; the Protestant dialectical. Greeley wrote:

> The analogical or Catholic imagination, to summarize and simplify David Tracy, emphasizes the presence of God in the world. It perceives the world and its creatures and relationships and social structures as metaphors, sacraments of God, hints of what God is like. I often illustrate the theory by noting that Catholics have angels and saints and souls in purgatory and statues and stained glass windows and holy water, and an institutional church that itself is thought to be a sacrament. Protestant denominations, on the other hand, either do not have this imagery or do not put much emphasis on it. The Catholic imagination is defined by the practice of devotion to Mary the Mother of Jesus. To fall back on the mother tongue, *ubi est Maria, ibi est ecclesia catholica* ("where Mary is, there is the Catholic Church").[20]

It should be remembered that in naming the imaginations it is not being claimed that they are mutually exclusive or that either one exists completely, in a pure state, in any individual. The two imaginations represent emphases and tendencies but the differences in those tendencies and emphases are real and important. It would be a tragedy if faculty and students at a Catholic university were not widely exposed to the analogical Catholic imagination. There should be no fear that exposure to the Catholic imagination smacks of parochialism or narrowness. Nothing need be lost, weakened or trivialized in an academically strong curriculum by studying in depth what the Catholic imagination has produced. Andrew Greeley suggests five areas of study: 1) research and courses about the high culture of the Catholic imaginative tradition such as courses on Catholic poets, novelists, artists and film makers; 2) reflection on Mary and the saints; 3) reflection on traditional Catholic social teaching; 4) study of the unique American Catholic experience of immigration in the neighborhood parish and of the parochial school; 5) the establishment of artists, poets and writers from the tradition in residence on campus. Though a modest proposal, I think it is one good response to the secular atmosphere in which the Catholic university lives and breathes. I can attest to great enjoyment and apparent success in teaching a course entitled "Meaning, Mystery and Metaphysics in the Catholic Novel" which I created for St. John's philosophy department. I created the course after meeting an English major from a Catholic college

[20] Ibid., p. 286.

who not only had never read Graham Greene or Evelyn Waugh, but never even heard of them!

It is impossible to stress too strongly the contribution that a Catholic university can make in the contemporary world. Years ago, addressing youth concerning education, Maritain wrote what I will make my final word:

> the world, which hungers not only for bread but for the freeing word of truth, the world needs you, it asks you to be as courageous in the field of intellect and reason as in the battles of land and sea and air. What your intellect and reason have to win is something which is not to be measured or manipulated by scientific tools but grasped by the strength of rational insight arising from what your eyes see and your hands touch; a universe of realities which make your thought true by virtue of their very being, and not merely as a result of successful action. This is the universe of intelligible being and of the sacred character of truth as such. You will then be able to show the world how human action may be reconciled with and permeated by an ideal which is more real than reality. . . .[21]

---

[21] Maritain, *Education at the Crossroads*, p. 117.

On The Education of
Young Men and Women

James V. Schall, S.J.

> There are people who think that it is wonderful to have a mind that is
> quick, clever, ready to see pros and cons, eager to discuss, and to dis-
> cuss anything, and who believe that such a mind is that to which uni-
> versity education must give scope—regardless of *what* is thought
> about, *what* is discussed, and *how important* the matter is.
>
> Jacques Maritain, *Education at the Crossroads* [1]

> As an atheist, I preferred metaphysics because it is the supreme sci-
> ence, the ultimate crowning of reason. As a Catholic, I love it still
> more because it allows us to have access to theology, to realise the har-
> monious and fertile union of reason and faith. It was not enough for me
> to live, I wanted a reason for living and moral principles which were
> based on an absolutely certain knowledge. . . . Among all the sciences,
> it is metaphysics which, after all, seems to me best suited for a femi-
> nine mind with a gift for abstraction.
>
> Raïssa Maritain, *Raïssa's Journals* [2]

I.

Jacques Maritain wrote one book (*Education at the Crossroads*) and several essays (collected in *The Education of Man*[3]) on education. He consid-

---

[1] Jacques Maritain, *Education at the Crossroads* (New Haven, Connecticut: Yale
University Press, 1943), p. 53.
[2] *Raïssa's Journals*, presented by Jacques Maritain (Albany, New York: Magi
Books, 1974), pp. 110–111.

ered education to be an art, perhaps in its own way the finest of arts because its object, when perfected, was the most beautiful of all the earthly realities. The closest analogy to teaching, according to Maritain, is medicine.[4] Neither medicine nor education creates its respective subject matter or what it is to be healthy or complete once it exists. Each seeks to lead or guide a body or soul to what it ought to be when it functions normally. Once in its normal status, the healthy body or the healthy soul should be let alone to do those myriads of things that healthy minds and bodies do. Given that the body is healthy, it, that is the human incarnate person informing it, simply lives, does the things that healthy human beings do. When man, body and soul, is educated, he again simply lives, does the wondrous things free and healthy human beings can do or, more darkly, freely does the things they ought not to do. Knowledge as such, as Aristotle tells us, does not automatically mean that we will be virtuous.[5]

Education prepares our given faculties and capacities to do what they are made or created to do. Man does not cause or have control over what he is. What he is, is given to him by nature. Man does not make man to be man, Aristotle says, but taking him from nature makes him to be good man. We are astonished that such a being as ourselves exists in the first place. The drama of human existence, however, has to do with what this same human being, among his fellows, does with this given existence, because he can both know and rule himself in a curious freedom that enables him also to reject, revolt against what he is. The human good includes the choice of the human good. The human being can choose not to be what it is designed, purposed to be. The risk of human existence is its capacity to reject human existence.

Maritain holds that the teacher is indeed a cause in the education of youth, but an instrumental cause, necessary for the most part, to be sure, but not the principal cause of education. The student is the principal cause of his own education. Interestingly, Maritain shows a certain persistent, optimistic sympathy for students, not untypical, I suppose, of those who have no children of their own. He thinks everyone can be educated in the important things—not only can be but should be. He is, no doubt, willing to

---

[3] Jacques Maritain, *The Education of Man*, eds. Donald and Idella Gallagher (Garden City, New York: Doubleday, 1962). Most of Maritain's lectures and essays on education are also published in a French edition, *Pour une philosophie de l'éducation* (Paris: Fayard, 1959).

[4] Maritain, *Education at the Crossroads*, pp. 30–31.

[5] *Nicomachean Ethics* II.5 1105b2.

admit a small place for strict scholastic discipline. We have all heard the expression "spare the rod and spoil the child." Maritain evidently referred to this saying in his own attitude to physical discipline. "Education by the rod," he affirms, "is positively bad education." He then adds, amusingly,

> if from a love of paradox I were to say something on its behalf, I should only observe that it (the rod) has been able, actually, to produce some strong personalities, because it is difficult to kill the principle of spontaneity in living beings, and because this principle occasionally develops more powerfully when it reacts and sometimes revolts against constraint, fear and punishment than when everything is made easy, lenient and psychotechnically compliant to it.[6]

Maritain even wonders whether, from the opposite side, making things too easy for the student does not produce indifference and passivity in them. But he is much more concerned about inspiration, play, and the delight of seeing things for one's self. Neither "birch and taws (floggings)" nor the teacher himself ought to the the principal agents in education.

In *Education at the Crossroads*, moreover, Maritain cites some remarks of Professor F. Clarke of the University of London to the effect that a certain "stringency and tension" are needed in education. Clarke adds that "original sin may be more than an outworn theological dogma after all," that "of all the needs of democracy, some abiding sense of the reality of original sin may yet prove to be the greatest."[7] To this sober remark of Clarke about the existential condition of the subject of education, Maritain immediately adds that, as a Catholic, he agrees with him. Maritain has, nonetheless, one caution, namely, "that an abiding sense of the reality of the internal power of regenerating grace and faith, hope, and charity, may prove to be even more necessary."[8]

---

[6] Maritain, *Education at the Crossroads*, p. 32.

[7] Ibid., pp. 93–94. Clarke's book is *A Review of Educational Thought* (London, 1942).

[8] Ibid., p. 94. "Christian faith knows that human nature is good in itself but has been put out of order by original sin; hence it sees that Christian education will recognize the necessity of a stern discipline, and even of a certain fear, on the condition that this discipline, instead of being merely external—and futile—should appeal to the understanding and the will of the child and become self-discipline, and that the fear should be respect and reverence, not blind animal dread. And Christian faith knows that supernatural grace matters more than original sin, and the weakness of human nature, for grace heals and superelevates nature and makes man participator in divine life itself; hence it is that Christian education will never lose sight of the God-given equipment of virtues and gifts through which eternal life begins here below," Ibid., p. 131.

Maritain, in other words, is willing to talk about Christianity as if it were a legitimate topic of conversation and as if it has something both positive and necessary to contribute to education and to the understanding of what its subject matter is like. He does not, to be sure, want anyone to be forced to study theology in non-denominational schools, but he thinks anyone without a knowledge of theology simply would not understand the actual human record and probably not himself. "Modern philosophy itself . . . has burdened itself all through modern times with problems and anxieties taken over from theology, so that the cultural event of philosophy purely philosophical is still to be waited for."[9] That is, all actual philosophy not only bears the mark of some theological consideration, but, to use Maritain's perceptive phrase, "philosophy purely philosophical" always reveals itself to be somehow incomplete even for its own purposes.

II.

I have entitled this essay, "On the Education of Young Men and Women." Maritain of course speaks rather of the "education of man," using that word to mean, in context, any person, male or female, of a rational human nature. He does not make too much of the differing ways of approach to the highest things that we might find in say a Gertrude von le Fort's *Eternal Woman* or even in some of his own wife, Raïssa's writings. However, we find one striking exception to this general approach. In 1941, George Schuster was inaugurated President of the then all-women Hunter College in New York. On this occasion, Maritain was invited to give an address which he entitled, "The Education of Women."[10] This essay develops a thought that, as we cited in the beginning, he had already learned from his wife about the place of metaphysics in the education of young women. I think it worthwhile to recall the principal points that Maritain makes about the education of young women because it shows both its importance and, in an indirect way, what he thinks about the education of young men.

To introduce this topic, however, let me begin with a classic text about the education of young men and young women. Charlie Brown is worried about his slow reading and is seeking an excuse that would not redound to his own unwillingness to work at it. Linus, it seems, has been to the opthamalogist who has explained to him the dubious relation between glasses and slow learning. Charlie was hopeful his problem was caused by

---

[9] Ibid., p. 74.
[10] Maritain, *Education of Man*, pp. 154–158.

lack of glasses, in which case, of course, he was not responsible. However, there may be more serious reasons at work here. Charlie, with some concern, asks Linus, "You say my being a slow reader is not caused by needing glasses?" Linus replies, "Probably not." Linus continues authoritatively to a puzzled Charlie, "Slow reading in children is often the result of 'mixed brain dominance'. . . . A person is right-handed because the left side of his brain is dominant. . . . " In the third scene, Lucy appears from nowhere intently listening as Linus proceeds, while Charlie hesitantly puts his hand on his chin, "Now if you are ambidextrous or if you have been forced to write with the wrong hand, this may produce 'mixed brain dominance'. . . . " Linus concludes triumphantly to a bewildered Charlie, "If this is true, we can rule out poor vision as the cause of your slow reading." The last word, however, as we might expect, goes to the ever logical Lucy who asks Linus the really worrisome unspoken question bothering Charlie Brown about the slow learner, "Have you ruled out stupidity?"[11] If I might put it this way, Maritain in his various discussions about the education of young men and women does largely downplay both original sin and stupidity as the major problems, or at least as insurmountable ones. He affirms, for instance, that "in a social order fitted to the common dignity of man, college education should be given to all, so as to complete the preparation of the youth before he enters the state of manhood."[12] I am not sure whether Maritain ever goes into the problem of the private or public financing of such a system, assuming that he is in fact right that everyone should go to college. He does, however, have some reservation about his own thesis: "Exacting from all pupils the same degree of rigorous study and progress in all items of the curriculum is most unwise."[13] A natural "apathy" toward many studies will probably be normal.

What about the lazy student, someone we have all met at one time or another, perhaps in ourselves?

> Laziness must be fought, of course, but encouraging and urging a youth on the way which he likes and in which he succeeds is much more important, providing, however, that he be also trained in the things for which he feels less inclination, and that he traverse the entire field of those human possibilities and achievements which compose liberal education.[14]

[11] Charles Schulz, *Nobody's Perfect, Charlie Brown* (New York: Fawcett, 1963).
[12] Maritain, *Education at the Crossroads*, p. 64.
[13] Ibid., pp. 64–65.
[14] Ibid.

Maritain's educational project, then, though formidable, is weighted on the side of learning because it is itself a delightful and worthy thing to do.

III.

Maritain begins his lecture at Hunter College, delivered in the midst of World War II, by remarking that "culture today stands in need of defense."[15] As the subject of culture has both progressed and degenerated since Maritain's time, we need to see that for Maritain the word culture includes wealth, technology, industry and scientific equipment. But primarily it means knowing "*how* and *why* to use these things for the good of the human being and the securing of his liberty."[16] Culture is primarily inner formation. To develop inner strength is another way of talking about what the classics called the virtues, both of mind and heart. The soul cannot be destroyed by force. "The soul yields only when it so wills. Culture implies the pursuit of human happiness, but requires also that we know in what this happiness consists."[17] These are words directly from Aristotle and Aquinas. Culture includes the habits of our tradition. "Culture consists in knowing, but it does not consist only in knowing; it consisted even more in *having known*, and in the forgetting of a great many things because we know them too well and because they have passed down from memory into the very marrow of our bones."[18] Included in culture is the liberty that the founders of the American Republic knew. If we do not know the reasons for living and for dying we will not keep our culture.

Maritain next acknowledges that not everything can be learned in books, but he insists that books and lectures "are an indispensable and basic vehicle of what man should know, and that without schools worthy of the name, there is no culture."[19] Maritain recalls Goethe to emphasize the priority of being over having, something John Paul II often emphasizes. Action follows being. Maritain suggests, carrying out the implications of this position, that the mission of the school respecting culture is greater in women's colleges than in men's, a statement of much interest when men are not allowed to have colleges.[20] What is the reason for this? It is because, Mari-

---

[15] Maritain, *Education of Man*, p. 154.
[16] Ibid.
[17] Ibid.
[18] Ibid., pp. 154–155.
[19] Ibid., p. 155.
[20] Ibid.

tain thinks, women have more leisure for "being" than men do. He calls it
their great "privilege and duty."[21] Somewhat in the tradition of Tocqueville,
he remarks as a foreigner that America is known for being a land favorable
to youth and a land favorable to women. Since women are so important for
culture, Maritain thinks, the teaching of young women is "doubly important
and significant."[22]

Maritain, moreover, sees no truth in the idea that at the level of intelligence women cannot attain the highest levels of excellence. He avers, however, that there is a welcome and necessary differentiation or complimentarity that is itself good for culture. "My already long experience as a
professor has shown me," he continues,

> that often young women enter into the realm of knowledge with an in-
> tellectual passion more ardent and a love of truth more disinterested
> than young men do. If they are usually less gifted than men for the
> constructive synthesis and the inventive work of reason, they possess
> over them the advantage of a more vital and organic feeling for knowl-
> edge. When they love truth, it is in order to bring it down into life it-
> self. When they love philosophy, it is because it helps them to discover
> themselves and the meaning of existence; and they well understand the
> saying of Plato, that we must philosophize with our whole soul.[23]

Young women have more need of unity, Maritain thinks, the result of which
means that an overly departmentalized education is more damaging to
women than to men. He cites his old teacher Henri Bergson who did not
think that women were in fact "more gentle and compassionate than men"
and supposes Bergson was right in this, but Maritain does think women are
"less naive and more courageous in the face of public opinion" than young
men.[24]

The complimentarity of male and female is not seen as an opposition but
as a necessity. Men have perhaps better judgment, women more intuition.
The prodding and perception of women often disconcert but without it
human culture would lack its richness. To teach the same discipline to
young men and to young women reveals often that "the same discipline is
received in different ways," a result that is a source of richness for the culture.[25] Raïssa Maritain's notion that metaphysics is to be a preferred study

---

[21] Ibid., p. 156.
[22] Ibid.
[23] Ibid., pp. 156–57.
[24] Ibid., p. 157.
[25] Ibid.

for women suggests the truth of Jacques Maritain's remarks about how differently and more ardently young women receive the same subject matter. "It was not enough for me to live," Raïssa Maritain wrote in 1919; "I wanted a reason for living and moral principles which were based on an absolutely certain knowledge."[26] On reading this, one cannot help recalling John Paul II's wonderful reflection in *Veritatis Splendor* on the rich young man who asks what he must do to be saved.

Very often, Maritain observes, young women may not realize the long historical and intellectual effort it takes to bring "the human person, in woman as in man, to a consciousness of its dignity."[27] Christianity played an original role in woman's emancipation when the Gospel was preached to Greek and barbarian, to male and female alike. Maritain can be blunt at times: "The sense of human dignity is the mark of every civilization of Christian origin and foundation, even when our fickleness of mind causes us to forget it."[28] Maritain sees that the political notion of human dignity follows from the Christian notion of each person's supernatural destiny, not vice versa. Even in the natural order, following Aristotle, there is something in each person that transcends the state.

> The human person, even though it be part of the political community, has within itself values and a calling which transcend the political community, for they are things that rise above time. Truth, beauty, wisdom are sovereignly useful for the State, they are not at the command of the State. The State must serve them, just as the State must respect in each one the fundamental rights of the person.[29]

Since there are things in the natural order that already transcend the state, the state is limited. All of these natural things in turn are put into proper place, however, only when the supernatural destiny of actual men is understood in the light of man's "philosophy purely philosophical."

Maritain ends his little essay on "The Education of Women," then, not with an exhortation to women in particular but again to all those who would be educated, men and women. He calls what he stands for "a democratic education." This is "an education which helps human persons to shape themselves, judge by themselves, discipline themselves, to love and prize the high truths which are the very root and safeguard of their dignity, to respect in themselves and in others human nature and conscience, and to con-

---

[26] *Raïssa's Journals*, presented by Jacques Maritain (Albany, New York: Magi Books, 1974), pp. 110–111.

[27] Maritain, *The Education of Man*, p. 157.

[28] Ibid., p. 158.

[29] Ibid.

quer themselves in order to win their liberty."[30] If we reflect on this vision of education, does it not seem, in retrospect, that Maritain's project has largely failed, at least as an institutional project?

The famous first two sentences of Allan Bloom's *The Closing of the American Mind*, written some forty-five years after Maritain's lecture at Hunter College, are worth recalling here: "There is one thing a professor can be absolutely certain of: almost every student entering the university believes, or says he believes, that truth is relative. If this belief is put to the test, one can count on the students' reaction: they will be uncomprehending."[31] Maritain's proposals remain pertinent precisely because they put the relativist belief "to the test."

IV.

Maritain's elaborate program for all levels of education endeavors to spell out the various stages of teaching according to the age and maturity of the student. He is also interested in graduate and post-graduate education. If we return to the question of the education of young men, as I mentioned, we will find very little specifically written on this subject. What we do find is rather a detailed description of the person who is to be educated, almost as if to say that we cannot educate man unless we know what he is. I want to say something about Maritain's understanding of education from the side of his presentation of what the man, male and female, is who is capable of being his own primary cause of his education. In conclusion, I want to turn to Maritain's description of the famous "Thomist Circles" which were held between 1919–1939 at Versailles and Meudon while Maritain was teaching at the *Institut Catholique* in Paris. I want to mention these Circles in particular because, I think, they represent something that is becoming more and more of a necessity in the context of the political correctness of modern university life, namely some sort of alternative to the university, alternative not as a counter-institution, but as a human initiative that transcends the intellectual disorders that everyone confronts.

In his essay, "The Christian Idea of Man and Its Influence on Education," as well as in some remarks he made on Plato and Descartes, Maritain takes pains to set down the sort of being who is to be educated. He earlier affirmed that "education is by nature a function of philosophy, of meta-

[30] Ibid.
[31] Allan Bloom, *The Closing of the American Mind* (New York: Simon and Schuster, 1987), p. 25.

physics."[32] This is no doubt one of the reasons that the penchant for metaphysics in the education of young women is so pronounced in the Maritains. If we do not know what or who it is to be educated, the whole effort will easily go awry. This understanding also hints at the importance of there being no philosophy that it itself "purely philosophically philosophical," that is to say, that the philosophic life, the highest life of the philosophers, however valuable, cannot itself be identified with the happiness to which each human person is intrinsically ordained.

What I appreciate in Maritain here is his willingness to state the uniqueness of the Christian understanding of man. Not unlike John Paul II in *Crossing the Threshold of Hope*, or Augustine in *The Confessions*, Maritain states clearly his understanding of competing views of man. Christianity, thus, does not hold the "transmigration of souls." This view would eventually mean that each of us is eventually everyone else, even every other thing. The Christian alternative is a version of the Greek philosophic idea of the immortality of the soul. "After the death of the body the human soul lives forever, keeping his own individuality."[33] But this understanding of immortality is not all. Faith holds that "the body will rise up and be united with the soul again." Even in the state after death, the immortal soul is not in a state of completion, a completion that would necessitate both body and soul. Both against Hinduism and Platonism which find the soul to be the essence of man, the Christian idea includes at all times the body, or the whole person, as the completion that is really implied by man's initial dignity as a being made for nothing less than God. Descartes's notion that the individual is only mind is likewise to be rejected as incomplete. This excursus into philosophy is important. A lofty understanding of man's soul at the expense of his body is not a Christian alternative. Christian philosophy grounds the whole educational enterprise by placing both body and soul in right perspective with regard to the final end of the whole person.

"Christian education does not worship the human body, as the ancient Greeks did," Maritain writes,

> but it is fully aware of the importance of physical training as aiming at a sound balance of the whole human being; Christian education is intent on making sense-perception, which is the very basis of man's intellectual life, more and more alert, accurate, and integrated; it appeals confidently to the deep, living power of imagination and feeling as well as to the spiritual power of reason; it realizes that in the develop-

[32] Maritain, *The Education of Man*, p. 41.
[33] Ibid., p. 129.

ment of the child hand and mind must be at work together; it stresses
the properly human dignity of manual activity.[34]

Maritain is careful to pay tribute to Plato and still make clear why a proper
understanding of education does not follow from the notion of innate ideas
or man's being as only a soul. Human souls do not preexist, nor are they replete with ideas the understanding of which is obscured by the body, so that
the highest understanding can only be had if the body is removed. In the
Platonic understanding the pupil "does not acquire knowledge from the
teacher, who has no real causal influence and who is at best only an occasional agent; the teacher only awakens the student to those things which he
already knows, so that to know is nothing else than to remember."[35]

Maritain thinks that this Platonic system treats the human being as if he
were an "angel." He also notes that Plato in the *Laws*, far from stressing
this angelic knowledge, seems to propose an extraordinarily detailed list of
things to which the citizen has to conform, something that implies a lack of
an active practical intellect responsible for the judging of particular cases in
which normal human life usually happens. Maritain's alternative is that of
Aristotle which proposes a more realistic understanding of the relationship
of teacher and pupil. "The teacher does possess a knowledge which the student does not have. He actually communicates knowledge to the student
whose soul has *not* previously contemplated the divine Ideas before being
united to his body; and whose intellect before being fecundated by sense-
perception and sense experience, is but a *tabula rasa*, as Aristotle said."[36] It
is of some importance to spell out this background understanding of what
man is because it alone can justify the combining of man's physical and
spiritual sides in one whole, all of which are essentially related to one another because of an end that itself transcends not only the state but philosophy, without being hostile to either.

V.

Maritain thinks that there is an intimate relation between the pursuit of
truth, of education, and the spiritual life. The higher the level of education
the more deeply the things of the spirit—now taken in the Christian sense
of the incarnational unity and destiny of each person—need attending to.
Maritain, for all his praise of philosophy, does not think that by itself it can

[34] Ibid., p. 130.
[35] Maritain, *Education at the Crossroads*, p. 29.
[36] Ibid., p. 30.

succeed in keeping human dignity among men. "Thus we may understand the paradox that natural law exists, as the very basis of morality, and that nevertheless no effort of reason to establish among men a firm system of morality based only on natural law has ever been able to succeed. . . . "[37] Some evidently paradoxical relationship exists between the supernatural and man's natural inability in this life, at least, to be natural. This paradox, this dilemma, is certainly pertinent to Maritain's organization of the "Thomistic Circles." He notes that throughout history, in India, China, Europe, among Quakers and Catholics, that "wise men living in solitude and contemplation gather together disciples who come to listen to them either for a certain number of years or at certain times of the year."[38] Within the Catholic tradition, Maritain thought that the times especially required the formation of spiritual centers wherein spiritual life and instruction could be developed. This sort of experience would also be advisable for university students and boys and girls during vacation time.[39]

In his *Notebooks*, Maritain describes his own experiment with this sort of program that combines study, prayer, conversation and a sort of family environment. These study groups met once a month at the home of the Maritains. They were designed for "those men and women for whom the spiritual life and studies in wisdom (philosophical and theological) had a major importance and who wished to devote themselves as much as they could to pursuing them."[40] The formal structure for these groups, its written constitution, is printed in the Appendix of the *Notebooks*.[41] It included even a private vow of prayer and devotion, though there was no idea of a religious congregation. The people who attended are listed by Maritain as they appear in one or other meeting. They were a "varied ensemble." They included

> young persons and old persons, male students and female students, and professors—laymen (in the majority), priests and religious—professional philosophers, doctors, poets, musicians, men engaged in practical life, those who were learned and those who were uneducated— Catholics (in the majority), but also unbelievers, Jews, Orthodox, Protestants. Some were already experts in St. Thomas, others were

---

[37] Maritain, *The Education of Man*, p. 116.
[38] Maritain, *Education at the Crossroads*, p. 84.
[39] Ibid., pp. 85–86.
[40] Jacques Maritain, *Notebooks,* trans. Joseph W. Evans (Albany, New York: Magi Books, 1984), p. 133.
[41] Ibid., pp. 290–297.

serving their apprenticeship with him, others knew nothing about him
or almost nothing.[42]

There was a climate of friendship and liberty.

The atmosphere was not that of class or convent or seminar, nor were
they "guests of a more or less stiff intellectual trying to offer them seats and
passing out drinks and cigarettes before the exchange of ideas." Rather, the
success of these afternoons and evenings was largely due to the presence of
Maritain's wife. "They were received in the hearth of a family, they were
the guests of Raïssa Maritain. Such meetings and such a work in common
are inconceivable without a feminine atmosphere," Maritain wrote. Not
only Raïssa was present but her sister Vera and her mother. Raïssa is described as present, taking an active part in the discussion, "always dis-
creetly, but with the mad, boundless love of truth which burned in her."
This peculiar phrase "mad, boundless love" appears often in Maritain's
notes almost by way of challenge to those pedestrian souls who are not
ready or willing to engage in the real drama of human existence in the
knowledge and love of God.

What was the subject matter of these circles? They always concerned
some great theological or philosophical issue, usually based in a text of St.
Thomas or John of St. Thomas. "The fundamental idea was to being into
play at one and the same time, in the concrete problems and needs of our
minds, things we knew to be diverse in essence but which we wanted to
unify within us; reason and faith, philosophy and theology, metaphysics,
poetry, politics and the great rush of new knowledge and of new questions
brought by modern culture."[43] Maritain himself prepared the night before
or on Sunday morning a brief exposition of the matter to be discussed. His
notes contain outlines and sketches of what he had to say. He gives a list of
the subject matters for the first ten years of the circles ranging from angelic
knowledge to human knowledge of singulars, the desire for the vision of
God, speculative and practical knowledge, justice and friendship, the Trinity, person, the Incarnation, free will, and the analysis of the voluntary
act.[44] There was a constant effort to clarify language, to appeal to direct experience, but a "fierce search for intellectual rigor."

What did Maritain conclude was the most important thing that he himself learned from this experience of the Thomist Circles?

[42] Ibid., p. 134.
[43] Ibid., p. 135.
[44] Ibid., p. 136.

The experience of our study meetings taught me a very precious thing: namely, that discursive and demonstrative argumentation, doctrinal erudition and historical erudition are assuredly necessary, but of little efficacy on human intellects such as God made them, and which first ask to *see*. In actual fact, a few fundamental intuitions, if they have one day sprung up in a mind, mark it forever (they are intemporal in themselves), and they suffice . . . to make a man unshakably strengthened in the love of St. Thomas and in the understanding of his wisdom. I observed this in a good number of our friends, whose example I take to be decisive.[45]

Maritain seems to imply that his academic experience, at its highest level, requires spiritual experience. We must first ask to "see" before we shall see.

VI.

Maritain's experience in the Thomist Circles seems to confirm his experience in teaching young women as well, in anticipation of confirming Bloom's remark that the unhappiest members of our society are the students in the twenty or thirty best universities. They are unhappy because with the presuppositions of their philosophy, there is nothing left to see. Raïssa Maritain as a young woman loved metaphysics because it was "the ultimate crowning of reason." She loved it more because it gave her access to something more, something higher, not higher than reason, but to a reason that is higher than human reason. Jacques Maritain thought it made a difference what kind of education we had. Education is not merely something of the soul, yet it is of the soul. What is really important is not a quickness of wit or a specialization of knowledge. What really matters is what is thought about, what is discussed, and how important the matter is.

That St. Thomas could guide us in sorting out things of importance to discuss, Maritain had no doubt. We can say without too much exaggeration that today graduates of most universities—public, Catholic, private—simply have never had the things that really matter clearly and adequately exposed to them. Yet, each student has to desire to know and has to suspect, at least, that he is not really encountering the great questions and, what is more important, the great answers. Education is not just a series of questions. Rather it is mostly a series of answers. When the Platonist tells us that our knowledge is innate, or when the Hindu tells us that we are already incarnate, or the Cartesian that we are only mind, we must be ready to see something else. No doubt there is an intimate relation between moral life

---

[45] Ibid., pp. 136–137.

and intellectual life. When the habits of our human wholeness are not in order, we will not be likely to think straight. But our bodies can be perfectly healthy and we can will not to see.

An access to "a reason for living" is, among us, the most important of the things we can receive from education. We should not doubt that the original sin that Professor Clarke speaks of, or the stupidity that Lucy Van Pelt suspects, or the relativism that Allan Bloom observes the best students embrace uncomprehendingly, can deflect us. Still, even the most perceptive theoretical knowledge and education will little avail us as we actually are, as Maritain said in his *Notebooks*, unless, like Augustine, "we first ask to *see*." What we have yet to see when we already see is what education is really about and this seeing itself requires our first knowing what we are and, yes, praying for what we want to be. If we do not know some purpose for ourselves, we will not be able to fulfill that great Socratic admonition to "know ourselves," for we cannot know even ourselves by knowing only ourselves.

"The task of the teacher," as Maritain says, in a final sentence that we can properly apply to Maritain himself, is not one of "birches and tawes," but "above all one of liberation."[46] What really matters are the right answers to the right questions. The endeavor of the twenty-first century may well be that of finding new Thomist Circles, new families, new universities, new monasteries, yes, new on-line systems wherein the right questions and the right answers can be asked. But what is important is not the technology of it all, but the seeing, the desire that we see, the discipline and grace of life that enables us even to want to see.

[46] Maritain, *Education at the Crossroads*, p. 39.

Studiositas,
The Virtue of Attention

Gregory M. Reichberg

At the entrance to the first ring of Hell, Dante reads the famous lines in-scribed above the outer portal to that accursed city, an inscription which concludes with these famed and ominous words: "abandon every hope, ye who enter here." Perplexed and troubled, Dante seeks clarification from his guide Virgil, who utters this simple phrase in response: "we have come to the place where . . . you will see the wretched people who have lost the good of the intellect." As if to offset the force of this harsh and enigmatic explanation, Dante confides how Virgil "placed his hands in mine, and with a cheerful look from which I took comfort, he led me among the hidden things."[1]

The good of the intellect: this is what the wretched people have lost. And if the loss of this good is the worst of all possible losses, imagine how im-mensely wondrous will be its gain! Yet for all its importance, Dante does not immediately tell us in what precisely this good of the mind consists, nor exactly how and where we may find it. But if we turn to his chief guide in matters philosophical and theological, St. Thomas Aquinas, we learn that *truth* is the very good of which Dante speaks: falsehood, Thomas teaches, is the ruin of the intellect, just as truth is its good.

Verum est bonum intellectus. Truth is the good of the intellect! This phrase appears time and again in Thomas's works. It bears ample repetition, because for him there is no human achievement more crucial then discerning the truth about our world, ourselves and God; St. Thomas is convinced that

---

[1] Dante, *Inferno*, trans. John Ciardi (New York: W.W. Norton & Company, Inc., 1977), Canto 3.

our very happiness hinges on this discovery: "No desire," he writes, "carries us on to such sublime heights as the desire to understand the truth," to which he adds this sharp admonition: "Let those men be ashamed, then, who seek human happiness in inferior things, when it is so highly situated."[2]

So happiness, our fulfillment as human beings, is in a very special way bound up with our personal commitment to truth. Every authentic good has its price, however. The joy of knowing truth is no exception. To find truth we must seek it ardently, and to be worthy of its company we must gain the strength of character requisite for its pursuit. Few philosophers have underscored this better than Plato, who, in the *Republic* especially, urges us to acquire the virtues of philosophic character—intellectual self-control, spiritedness, courage and gentleness—as part and parcel of the moral fiber that we must possess if we are to seek truth well. For instance, at the conclusion of *Republic* Book I we find Socrates chastising himself for his intellectual gluttony:

> I have not dined well. . . . As gluttons snatch at every dish that is handed along and taste it before they have properly enjoyed the preceding, so I . . . before finding the first topic of our inquiry—what justice is—let go of that and set out to consider [something else]. . . . So that for me the present outcome of the discussion is that I know nothing at all.[3]

This Socratic admisson is meant to teach us that the "appetite for inquiry must find gratification in a disciplined way if truth, . . . the mind's natural "nutrition," is to be obtained."[4] Essential to this intellectual discipline is the recognition that, despite the vast array of things which we may study in the course of our lives, we must not pursue these studies disconnectedly, but rather, whenever possible, we should strive to attain a synoptic vision, in which we see all these things in, to use Plato's words, "a comprehensive survey of their affinities with one another and with the nature of things."[5] Speaking in this same vein, Cardinal Newman tells his readers that "you must be above your knowledge, not under it, or it will oppress you, and the more you have of it, the greater will be your load."[6] And to bring home this

---

[2] *Summa Contra Gentiles* III, chap. 50.

[3] *Republic* I 354a–b. Translations from the *Republic* are those of Paul Shorey, reprinted in The Collected Dialogues of Plato, Edith Hamilton and Hamilton Cairns, eds. (New York: Bollingen Foundation, 1963).

[4] Richard Patterson, "Plato on Philosophic Character," *Journal of the History of Philosophy* 25 (1987): p. 328.

[5] *Republic* VII 537c.

[6] John Henry Cardinal Newman, *The Idea of a University* (Notre Dame, Indiana: University of Notre Dame Press, 1982), p. 106.

same point, he adds, with a characteristic touch of wry humor: "How many commentators are there on the Classics, how many on Holy Scripture, from whom we rise up, wondering at the learning that has passed before us, and wondering why it passed!"[7] If we are to be intellectually temperate, we must seek to feed our minds on not just anything and in any way whatsoever, but only on what is truly important, and according to the unity that befits our vocation to wisdom.

In addition to intellectual moderation, Plato urges us to cultivate intellectual spiritedness which consists, he says, in a keen desire for victory. The virtuous lover of truth "must be ready, willing, and able to 'do lengthy battle' on behalf of the truth."[8] Desire for victory in matters of the mind "is not to be confused [however] with victory of one's own views."[9] On the contrary, the virtuous inquirer is one who will "actually hope that insofar as his views are false they will meet defeat."[10] Thus "in the pursuit of truth one must not become angry or resentful at the proper refutation of one's own views."[11] Instead, "one ought to welcome as just . . . the revelation of one's own ignorance."[12] "Strength of spirit there must be for the intellectual enterprise, but a strength open to persuasion and even, as need be, to rebuke."[13]

Moreover, despite their willingness to engage in intellectual battle, virtuous inquirers will not "prosecute such victory savagely, harshly, or in anger at an opponent, but with gentleness and gracious good will."[14] Or, as Plato puts it, "he who would attain the highest understanding of truth and goodness must himself be orderly and gracious, 'friendly and akin to truth, justice, courage, and self-mastery,' presumably because only such a person will prove genuinely receptive to noble discourse, whose purpose is a thoroughgoing education of the soul to virtue" and truth.[15]

Finally, Plato tells us that the virtuous inquirer's love of victory must be accompanied by "courage to enter the fray."[16] "Courage finds a place within intellectual activity in two important ways: first, as the courage to

---

[7] Ibid.
[8] Patterson, p. 341.
[9] Ibid.
[10] Ibid.
[11] Ibid., p. 343.
[12] Ibid.
[13] Ibid.
[14] Ibid., p. 341.
[15] Ibid.
[16] Ibid., p. 345.

make one's convictions known, even under adverse circumstances; second, as perseverance in the face of long and difficult inquiry."[17]

Noteworthy in Plato's account of intellectual character is his focus on the appetitive side of truth-seeking. Each of the virtues mentioned above— intellectual moderation, courage, and gentleness—assures rectitude in the *desire* to know. As such, these virtues of philosophic character do not coincide with those virtues that Aristotle was later to term "intellectual virtues" or "virtues of thought," i.e., wisdom, understanding, science, art and prudence, which, with the exception of the last, are exclusively perfections of intellectual judgment. Thus the Stagirite draws a rather sharp distinction between the moral virtues on the one hand and the intellectual virtues on the other.

Hence, whereas Plato took care to posit moderation and courage within intellectual activity itself, to assure that the passions which arise within the mind's proper pursuits do not lead the mind astray, Aristotle, for his part, appears reluctant to follow his mentor's lead. In his treatment of moderation in the *Nicomachean Ethics*, for instance, Aristotle explicitly excludes from the scope of this moral virtue those pleasures which arise from knowledge and learning.[18] Even so, it is well worth observing that Thomas Aquinas does not exhibit this same reticence. Under the influence of St. Augustine, Thomas sought to integrate the Platonic teaching on intellectual character into his account of the moral virtues. Nowhere is this more noticeable than in his treatment of temperance in the *Secunda Secundae* of the *Summa Theologiae*. Surprisingly—given the Aristotelian cast of his ethics—Thomas widens the scope of this virtue to include not only the appetite for tactile pleasures, but what's more, the very appetite for truth as well:

> I answer that, as stated above [IIa-IIae, q.41, aa.3–5] it belongs to temperance to moderate the movement of the appetite, lest it tend excessively to that which is desired naturally. Now just as in respect of his corporeal nature man naturally desires the pleasures of food and sex, so, in respect of his soul, he naturally desires to know; thus the Philosopher observes at the beginning of his *Metaphysics* i 1: "All men have a natural desire for knowledge." The moderation of this desire pertains to the virtue of *studiositas*; wherefore it follows that *studiositas* is a potential part of temperance, as a subordinate virtue annexed to a principal virtue.[19]

---

[17] Ibid., p. 346.
[18] See *Nicomachean Ethics* III.10 1117b27–35.
[19] *Summa Theologiae* IIaIIae, q. 166, a. 2, c.

Thomas proceeds to explain that the name *studiositas* is taken from the noun *studium*. *Studiositas* designates a virtue which assures the moral rectitude of the *studium*, just as temperance is a virtue which assures the moral rectitude of the concupiscible appetite. Next, Thomas defines the *studium* as a "*vehemens applicatio mentis ad aliquid*," literally "a vigorous application of the mind to something."[20] Let's pause for a moment to consider the parts of this definition:

(i) *Vehemens*: ardent, intense, vigorous.

(ii) *Applicatio*: a joining, attaching, or applying; connotes a persistent or sustained contact of one thing to another. In Thomas's technical lexicon it designates *usus*, the voluntary employment of the soul's powers.

(iii) *Mentis*: of the *mens*, the mind, a shorthand reference to the human soul's cognitive faculties. *Applicatio mentis* thus signifies the voluntary employment of the cognitive faculties (sensory or intellective).

(iv) *Ad aliquid*: any item to which cognitive agents may be vitally joined by their engagement in willed acts of thinking or sensing. Thomas tells us that the items in question encompass things which are simply objects of cognition (through either theoretical speculation or sensory delight) or things which may be transformed by human labor.

Thus defined, the scope of *studium* is surprisingly vast: it signifies any voluntary engagement of the mind in cognitive endeavors, speculative or practical, sensory or intellectual. As such, the English term "study" does not faithfully translate the Latin *studium*; the former is more restrictive in scope, signifying as it does the cultivation of a particular branch of learning, science or art. Such scholarly activities are comprised under the heading of *studium* but not exclusively so, since in Thomas's usage *studium* denotes any purposeful application of the mind. Hence, on his account the *studium* also encompasses what we today call "work" or "exercising an occupation," either manual or mental, for here too the agent is intent upon something involving concentration and effort. In fact, the expressions "heightened attention," "concentration," or "vigorous mental occupation" are more suitable transcriptions for *studium* than its English cognate "study," for they convey without undue restriction the full breadth of this Latin word. Accordingly, to concentrate rightly, to occupy one's mind well, to attend to whatever truly warrants one's attention, is to exercise the virtue of *studiositas*.

The Angelic Doctor assigns a dual role to *studiositas*.[21] Its primary func-

---

[20] Ibid., q. 166, a. 1, c.

[21] On the dual role assigned by Thomas to *studiositas*, see *Summa Theologiae* IIaIIae, q. 166, a. 1, ad 3.

tion consists in curbing the appetite for knowledge, which easily tends to excess due to the pleasure experienced in acts of knowing. Here the virtue functions as a form of temperance or moderation. The opposing vice, *curiositas*, embraces two forms of cognitive immoderation: first, an inordinate appetite for pleasures arising within intellectual knowing, intellective *curiositas* (*circa cognitionem intellectivam*[22]), and second, an inordinate appetite for pleasures arising within the operation of the external senses and the imagination, sensory *curiositas* (*circa sensitivam cognitionem*, Thomas's version of the *concupiscentia oculorum* so vigorously condemned by St. Augustine).[23]

Thomas is not very specific about what kinds of knowledge ought to be sought, when and where and by whom. This is in keeping with his keen sense of the limitations of moral science, which cannot direct action in particular instances. The virtue of prudence alone can fully disclose how a specific person ought to pursue speculative inquiry within the context of his or her life. Nonetheless, Thomas does venture to propose four criteria to guide our moral judgments concerning the concrete exercise of the speculative intellect.[24] These criteria are stated negatively, as various forms of intellective *curiositas*:

(1) A speculative inquiry becomes excessive when it entails neglect of other studies, studies which are necessary for the acquittal of one's personal and social duties. Thomas cites the case of a judge who is so enamored of geometry that he arrives in court ill prepared to hand down informed decisions in prosecution of justice.[25] Examples of this sort could easily be multiplied. The point is that virtue requires a studious attention to the matter at hand, a sense of priority in knowing what one's mind should be on in the present circumstances, and the willingness to develop and to apply competent knowing in the accomplishment of the responsibilities incumbent on one's vocation.

Likewise, the other extreme ought also to be avoided, namely an obsessive engagement in professional activities, to the neglect of more lofty callings. Aquinas holds that a life well-lived requires an attention to "higher

---

[22] Ibid., q.167, a. 1.

[23] Ibid., q.167, a. 2.

[24] Ibid., q.167, a. 1.

[25] "[Q]uando propter occupationem in studio alicujus scientiae impeditur ab executione officii ad quod tenetur; sicut judex si propter studium geometriae desisteret a causis expediendis. . . . " *Scriptum super Sententiis* III (ed. Mandonnet/Moos), dist.35, q. 2, a. 3, ad 3, no. 1205.

things," an aspiration to weave wisdom into the tapestry of daily life. The love of wisdom can presumably manifest itself in different ways, according to the diversity of individuals and cultures. For some this will involve the study of philosophy and theology, for others an engagement in spirituality and prayer within a religious tradition, or for still others an openness to the sapiential dimension of existence through a participation in the fine arts.

(2) Since human beings acquire understanding by learning from others, virtuous knowing requires a vigilance in regard to the *sources* of instruction; for knowing can become inordinate, Thomas writes "when a man studies to learn from one by whom it is unlawful to be taught, as in the case of those who seek to know the future through the demons." [?] To advance a more contemporary example one could cite the controversy surrounding the morality of using scientific data which Nazi scientists procured by means of cruel experiments on human subjects. Should access to these materials be barred because their source was morally blameworthy?

In any event, the question about the sources of knowledge is actually broader than is at first blush indicated by Thomas's example. Indeed it concerns the overall question of how tradition, authority, and the social context of learning are integrated into a virtuous pursuit of truth. For instance, Thomas remarks that one manifestation of pride is the unwillingness to receive instruction from others—whether from fellow men or from God. On a positive note, Aquinas considers the social dimension of learning to be of such vital importance that he assigns a special virtue to regulate this domain. This is *docilitas*, which consists in moderating the appetite for knowledge so that the learner is receptive to instruction within the context of an ongoing intellectual tradition. This virtue is attached to the cardinal virtue of prudence, although Thomas suggests that it should accompany the cultivation of the intellectual virtues in their entirety.[26]

(3) The pursuit of knowledge becomes immoderate when a man desires to know the truth about creatures, without referring this knowledge to its due end, namely the knowledge of God. This should not be read as a condemnation of the desire to uncover the secrets of nature through an investigation of secondary causes. In the *Summa Contra Gentiles*, Thomas devotes several chapters to explaining why the assiduous study of creatures is a praiseworthy pursuit.[27] Moreover, the stress here is not on some intellectual error regarding the relation between creatures and God, or even igno-

---

[26] On this, see *Summa Theologiae* IIaIIae, q. 49, a. 3, esp. ad 1 and 2.
[27] See in particular, Book II, chap.1–4.

rance concerning God as creator. Instead, the focus is on a disordered *will*, which moves the process of knowing toward an ultimate end other than the infinite truth which is God. Just as the avaricious person seeks an unbounded satisfaction in unlimited finite goods through the acquisition of wealth, likewise the intemperate inquirer seeks full intellectual satisfaction in dwelling upon the inexhaustible variety of natural phenomena. Both place their last end in something other than God, the first in the accumulation of material possessions, to the exclusion of spiritual possessions; the second in the enjoyment of science to the exclusion of wisdom.

(4) Finally, Thomas names a fourth variety of intellective *curiositas*, which occurs when a man studies to know the truth above the capacity of his own intelligence, since by doing so men fall easily into error. Thomas does not give any examples to illustrate the nature of this vice. It clearly has an affinity with pride (*superbia*), because the prideful person hopes to achieve some good beyond the measure of his or her inner strength.

Previously I noted that *studiositas* has two roles, of which the primary is to curb the appetite for knowledge, for reasons that we have just now considered. By contrast, in its secondary role, *studiositas* reinforces intellectual desire. Here it functions as intellectual courage. In fact the very name *studiositas* is taken from this secondary role, inasmuch as the *studium* signifies a tenacious application of the mind (*vehemens applicatio mentis*).

Thomas does not expressly name the vice opposed to keen interest in truth and the strength needed for applying one's intellect in a consistently focused manner. He does however, give some indications on the unnamed vice of intellectual indolence and its remedy.

The essential problem here is to overcome the body's resistance to the effort involved in the acquisition of knowledge. By extension, however, any kind of difficulty encountered in the pursuit of knowledge is strengthened by studious fortitude, the difficulty that we face, for instance, in resisting the pressure to conform to prevailing opinions. Aquinas makes due note of this when he relates how the supreme act of fortitude, martyrdom, can encompass not only a witness to the divine truth of faith, but a firm adherence to truths of the natural order as well, when they are violently denied by others.[28] Finally, in addition to assuring endurance against fatigue and other pains incurred in the pursuit of truth, studious fortitude also fortifies the soul against the seductive attraction of sensible pleasures which can distract and dissipate its arduous quest for knowledge.

---

[28] On martyrdom for truth's sake, see *Summa Theologiae* IIaIIae, q. 124, a. 5, ad 2.

The implications of Thomas's teaching on *studiositas* for a sane theory of education are numerous. Fundamental, in my estimation, is his emphasis on the moral or ethical dimensions of knowing. In this respect, St. Thomas is very much the disciple of St. Augustine, whose *Confessions*, in particular, are replete with comments about the intentions which ought (and ought not) to guide the student in his or her pursuit of knowledge. Augustine faults himself, for instance, for having sought intellectual cultivation, not for the sake of insight about himself and God, but rather in order to impress his classmates and professors. Likewise, he faults his parents and educators for their misguided motives: they wanted to see him educated in order that he might achieve worldly stature, thus to secure for himself an ample income and the pleasant amusements money can buy. On the positive side, Augustine informs us that his reading of Cicero's *Hortensius* awakened in him a love of truth, an attachment to knowledge for its own sake, and that this love was the beginning of his journey back to God.

Aquinas's teaching on *studiositas* could also profitably be read in conjunction with an incisive essay by Simone Weil, "Reflections on the Right Use of School Studies with a View to the Love of God."[29] There she argues provocatively that "the development of the faculty of attention forms the real object and the sole interest of studies."[30] What matters most in education is not the acquisition of particular truths about particular subjects—although this clearly has its importance—but rather increasing the power of attention with a view to the highest and best use of the intelligence; this, for Weil, is a contemplative communion with God in prayer. Significantly, she does not equate the "power or faculty of attention" (clearly akin to Aquinas's *studium*) with simple will-power, i.e., the ability to concentrate despite one's inclination to the contrary.

> Contrary to the usual belief, it [will-power] has practically no place in study. The intelligence can be led only by desire. For there to be desire there must be pleasure and joy in the work. . . . It is the part played by joy in our studies that makes of them a preparation for the spiritual life, for desire directed toward God is the only power capable of raising the soul.[31]

Here Weil utters a profound truth. Since knowledge is actively sought only when it is desired, and the since desire springs from love—which is nothing other than to rejoice and delight in the good thing loved—it follows that

---

[29] In *Waiting for God*, trans. Emma Craufurd (New York: C.P. Putnam's Sons, 1951), pp. 104–116.
[30] Ibid., p. 105.
[31] Ibid., p. 110.

educators should strive above all to convey to their students the joy of knowing truth. It is precisely the experience of enjoyment in acts of knowing which enables epistemic agents to recognize the disinterested knowledge of truth as intrinsically good for the self. That recognition has an ethical dimension, because the moral life requires a firm attachment to the good of the intellect, wherein lies our ultimate beatitude. Intellectual enjoyment thus quickens the appetitive powers, rendering them auxiliaries of the mind's approach to the Living Truth.

Education: Restoring the Goal of Development to the Ideal of Learning

Joseph Koterski, S.J.

There are many reasons for pride over the present state of our universities, but equally many reasons for dissatisfaction. Sometimes the terrific successes of this glorious academic system can strike us as the systematically terrifying glorification of success that is merely academic. The luxuriant profusion of inquiry and the truly awesome discoveries of some research are as exhilarating on the campus as a simple walk down Broadway of Fifth Avenue for any visitor to New York City—the throb and hum cannot fail to affect heart and mind very deeply. But reflection on what goes on behind the glitz gives us pause.

Debates about a college's core-curriculum, for example, easily degenerate into turf-battles. These battles are fought by professors who regularly employ articulate arguments about their visions of what constitutes a desirable pattern of education for undergraduate students, but whose loyalties are actually stronger and clearer to their disciplines than to their institutions or to the ideal of a truly well-rounded education of young persons. But besides reminding us of the deep-seated stubbornness of human nature in all of us, reflection on this phenomenon points to a certain disintegration in the understanding of what "education" means. The diversification of disciplines over the centuries-long history of the university has certainly been fruitful for the resolution of countless theoretical and practical problems, but the task of giving and getting an integrated education has often been sacrificed in the fragmentation that professional competence inevitably requires.

My thesis is that the problem is not just a matter of weakening a given curriculum in the compromises made to find common ground, for instance, by reducing the portions devoted to philosophy and theology so as to increase the portions devoted to the social sciences, or by focusing less on broadly humane concerns so as to leave more time for studies in one's major. Even if this is often the ground of which we have to fight these important battles, it is not the ground I would choose if I could. These are important concerns, but in all honesty most current approaches to teaching even the liberal arts, philosophy, and theology do not sufficiently address the question of the formative and developmental aspects of learning. They too have taken on the marks of the modern, academic culture with all of its professionalism and have focused on the fact that there is so much to learn. Teachers of these subjects often adopt methodologies more appropriate to the specialized sciences in their teaching. Programs of values clarification, or ethics courses that ask students to educe some least common denominator principles of ethics from the analyses of the toughest and most controversial of current moral problems, are only the most egregious examples of the trendy inclination to think that morality is a subject that can be well-handled by sincere attempts at the objective (or even "sincere and sympathetic") presentation of vast amounts of "relevant data" and the careful contrast of "competing positions and arguments" for the sake of personal evaluation and selective appropriation by the relatively inexperienced minds of students who have vicariously been made aware of these "life options" by techniques of outcome-based education.

Even the teachers most successful at stimulating in students a personal engagement with the material taught are part of a university-system that has replaced the psychic and spiritual development of persons as the goal of education with the mastery of some set of "learnables" (not just facts, but various kinds of theories, sometimes highly complex—in short, whatever can be learned by observation or instruction). Nor are subsequent professional programs with extremely arduous training programs like law or medicine exempt from this criticism, for in fact they are not organized for the formation of the person but are specifically designed for the formation of professionals—and we certainly do want professional competence in these areas. Perhaps along the way the importance of a good bed-side manner in a physician or the indispensability of cultivating in every lawyer and potential judge a heart for justice can be poignantly suggested by personal contact in the course of an internship; but it is rightly regarded as not something one can be "taught" in a curriculum, and it is the rare exception among the courses designated as medical ethics and jurisprudence in medical schools and law schools that goes beyond discussion of the relevant code of professional conduct and the more successful ways of handling malfeasance and malpractice.

The privatization of moral ideals is so pervasive that even well-intending and deeply humane academics who personally hold profound notions about the meaning of human life and its relation to the Transcendent would question the notion that there is any normative vision of the person that could be desired as the goal of education, for education has come for them to be identified as the transmission of various learnables and the acquisition of the habits of thinking pertinent to a discipline, not the formation of the person. This is ultimately the reason, in my judgment, why ethics courses make so little impact on students—in theory it ought to be possible to convince people of what is right by giving them good reasons, and even to teach natural law ethics with an emphasis on the needs of civil life and without elaborate argumentation about the metaphysical grounds of natural law in the Author of nature; but in practice, all this will be in vain unless we accompany such teaching with initiation into *an entire pattern of life* that reinforces good reasons with virtuous practices and provides the sort of activity (such as religious ritual) that symbolizes these beliefs in a concrete way of living.

At the heart of the rejection of any demonstration of moral truths is a faulty conception of freedom, a libertarian conception, which, in my judgment, has to be dealt with by maturation of the person to the point of accepting duties, law and necessities in the fashion of a realistic adult. Until that degree of psychic maturity dawns, I doubt that other patterns of moral reasoning that deal with the objectively good and bad uses of one's free will are going to make much of a dent in a mind that has gotten stuck in an adolescent stage of confidence in one's own powers and abilities. In fact, I suspect that it is this which Aristotle meant by his remark that the young are not ready for ethics because of a lack of experience.[1]

My purpose here is to examine just one aspect of this phenomenon in light of the wisdom of thinkers like Jacques Maritain and Christopher Dawson on the proper conception of the purpose of higher education, for all too often the ideal of learning, noble as it is, seems to have crowded out the ideal of human development in our universities. They ought to be companions. Thus, I want neither to impugn the realm of unrestricted research, nor to praise it, though there are reasons for doing both. I want neither to attack nor to defend the prized claims of academic freedom, or the merits of one course of study rather than another. Rather, I want to raise a question about university education that is like the question we sometimes raise about tele-

---

[1] *Nicomachean Ethics* I.3 1095a2ff.

vision: granted there may be problems about the nature of many shows on TV, even if the content of a given show is unobjectionable, isn't there also a profound problem with the very form of this medium? Like the even more enticing new forms of electronic media, TV combines the excitement of oral and visual means of communication with the mass-market outreach, the dynamic flow of subjectivity, and the exact iterability that once made the print media so revolutionary, and this change in our communications has had profound effect on the way people get their information, how they relate to other people, and how they understand their society. This is not to claim, of course, that most of us who teach at the university level are any-where near as exciting as the videos which entertain our students and per-suade them about questions of value when they are not even noticing that such questions are in play. Sometimes the best we can hope for in practice is the growth of a taste for a live performance, the way going to a concert or a play is better than seeing even the best recording.

The similarity I have in mind here is the question of form. I am not rais-ing a Luddite objection to the classroom use of videos or the presentation of interesting lecturers by means of telecommunication—in fact, I rather welcome all sorts of things like that. My question is about form: has the form of higher education not been bent seriously out of shape by taking the purpose of such education to be learning, to the comparative exclusion of personal development? The prima facie case for this position is clear from some sociological considerations: the teachers at nearly all universities are unconnected with what goes on most hours of the day for their university students, and what care there is for these other hours is in the hands of stu-dent-development "professionals." The mere division of labor here implied is not in itself odious. In fact, it is interesting to see how advanced the tech-niques of personnel management now applied to student populations have progressed among student development staffs, but it is usually regrettable to see the ends for which they use their skills. The problem is thus a lack of insight and often a lack of agreement about what constitutes real virtue in persons, so that the "message" given to most university students either tends to be uniformly perilous when the usual unspoken "agreement" is in place that morals are an entirely private business of our students, or, at best, schizophrenic, as in those cases where academic instruction still talks a good line about objective morality but there is little in the organization of their residential life that reinforces or encourages the practice of such virtues as prudence, generosity to neighbors, real chastity, or moderation in pleasure-seeking.

As professionals in a given discipline, most academics now identify

themselves with their discipline and devote what time they can spare from
the busy-ness of their schedules to continued learning within their disciplines. Invariably they never have enough time for that as it is, what with
the bureaucracy of committee work and the countless administrative tasks
that spring up, let alone the vast time demands of modern technological living and the unavoidable consumption of time spent commuting—and all of
that secondary (I do hope) to questions of family and personal needs. Those
outside of academe never understand how teachers at a university consider
themselves working full-time when their formal classroom obligations
amount to six hours a week, or maybe nine, or (perish the thought) twelve!
And yet for such little contact time, increased by however many office
hours a professor keeps (and my observation is that such hours are precious
few for many), academic life is legitimately very busy already. The demands of keeping up in one's discipline, not to mention advancing the state
of that discipline by one's own research and publication, invariably make
us seek out the soft spots in the schedule that confronts us for extra time,
and I submit that the chief soft spot is found in the almost unquantifiable
labors of forming students, for we can much more easily justify the time
spent on the personal appropriation and transmission of learning. In fact,
we can even quantify much of academic work for purposes of tenure, promotion and salary-adjustment evaluations: teaching can be measured by the
number of students and credit-hours (and in some cases by peer or student
evaluations), service can be measured by the number of committees and the
amount of grants received, and scholarship can be measured by square-inch
published, multiplied by the degree of prestige of the press or journal. But
as I suggested earlier, my objection is not to any of these things in principle, any more than it would be to TV's content in principle, for there clearly
is programming of high quality available. These are generally good things
in themselves and essential to the modern university as presently constituted. We could not work without them.

My question then has to do with how we conceive the university and
whether our present conception has not contributed to the current cultural
morass by forgetting the developmental aspect of education in the present
concentration on learning. I do not mean to suggest that there is any absolute distinction between the learnables and the developmentals, for all
processes of learning (whether the techniques of pottery-making or blanket-
weaving in a "primitive" culture, or the technical know-how involved in
good writing, higher mathematics, and basic chemistry in our own "more
advanced" culture) do entail some genuine types of inner development, but
often so very little inner development of habits and virtues that this distinc-

tion is easy to use in practice to identify what would make for psychic or spiritual growth as opposed to advancement in technical understanding or in theoretical knowledge. The relative passivity of most college students in class, for example, suggests that there has been a certain psychic development promoted by our culture (the ability to sit still and cooperate in the course of primary and secondary education), but relatively little other psychic maturation can be presumed (witness the virtually unassailable moral relativism that meets even the best presented academic arguments to the contrary as a justification for lax moral conduct and religious indifference).

The great paradox of this situation is that the very affluence which has made university life and the other attainments of high culture (art, music, literature, and so on) possible (just imagine how utterly impossible these would be in a culture organized around the struggle for survival) has distracted educators away from the more difficult tasks of fostering personal growth and real psychic and spiritual development, in favor of transmitting what can be learned, not just in high schools, but in the smorgasbord of the university (just listen to our own complaining about what students didn't get on their last exam, despite our pellucid lectures!).

Perhaps a brief historical note will be helpful. The origins of the institution of the university in medieval cathedral schools shows the original intention of integrating all the learning with an entire way of living, and a religious one at that, whose structured habits of prayer and communal life were designed to live out the lessons of the classroom. The rise of universities as such already encouraged not just the ramification of the disciplines and the professionalization of the teachers but the compartmentalization of the lives of students. University life in the present day is simply reaping the fruits of these early seeds, now that the protective husks of the religious purposes present at the foundation of many institutions of higher learning have long fallen away.[2] It is no surprise that even prior to the Reformation the scholastic method that developed for theology and law in the medieval university was already being attacked for substituting logic-chopping and the mere training of the mind for spiritual maturity in habits of prayer and the formation of the whole person required for experiential knowledge of God. Not only did the whole raft of specialized studies that now rightfully claim to be departments in their own right emerge from philosophy, but

---

[2] See George Marsden, *The Soul of the American University* (Oxford: University Press, 1994).

"the university gradually transformed theology from a developmental to a learnable."[3] The very greatness of great scholastic theologians like Albert the Great, Bonaventure and Aquinas is much dependent on their early initiation as members of the new, reformed mendicant orders with well-discerned programs of forming their spiritual lives in the faith long before their years of university teaching and research. To chart the course of the evolution of the modern university is to trace the growth of what Dawson calls "the crisis of Western education"[4]—for the flourishing of the academy and its social dominance in all areas of professional and systematic knowledge was progressively emancipated from the authority of divine revelation and the mediation of institutions like church and family for the education of conscience (all this is now considered private and subjective). This has resulted in a population more highly cultivated in mental skills and technical knowledge than in faith, practical charity, or even a common morality. As Dawson put it in his 1947 Gifford Lectures, "We are faced with a spiritual conflict of the most acute kind, a sort of social schizophrenia which divides the soul of society between a non-moral will to power served by inhuman techniques and a religious faith and a moral idealism which have no power to influence human life."[5] Jacques Maritain makes a similar observation about the real goals of education: "What is most important in education is not the job of education, and still less that of learning. . . . The teaching of morality, with regard to its intellectual bases, should occupy a great place in school and college education. Yet that right appreciation of practical cases which the ancients called *prudentia*, and which is an inner vital power of judgment developed in the mind and backed up by well-directed will, cannot be replaced by any learning whatsoever."[6]

Perhaps the task of the philosopher is to seek wisdom about the formation that should be part of holistic education. But in the time that remains, let me turn from these more theoretical considerations to two practical suggestions. Without presuming to suggest any easy ways to rectify the whole situation, I would like to call attention first to the need to re-integrate the

[3] Paul Quay, *The Mystery Hidden for Ages in God* (New York: Peter Lang, 1995), p. 400.

[4] Christopher Dawson, *The Crisis of Western Education* (Steubenville, Ohio: Franciscan University Press, 1989).

[5] Christopher Dawson, *Religion and Culture* (New York: Sheed and Ward, 1961), p. 217.

[6] Maritain, *Education at the Crossroads* (New Haven, Connecticut: Yale University Press, 1943), p. 23.

average undergraduate's day at college. Our own modest efforts at Fordham University (not my idea, by the way, but a program in which I have happily been a participant the past two years, the brainchild of Fr. John Piderit, S.J., now the President of Loyola University of Chicago) are what occasioned this paper. I serve as "chaplain and tutor" at "Queen's Court Residential College"—the "Master" is my colleague and friend, Fr. John Conley, S.J., also in the Fordham Philosophy Department. Queen's Court is a lovely old stone building that houses 86 freshman (next year 145, when repairs are finished on a wing of the building now closed). Students have to choose to live there (there is no special screening process), pay a little extra for the special programs, and accept the policy that there will be no loud noise (guess who gets to help decide what loud is too loud?) twenty-four hours a day; we had about 200 applicants for the 86 positions this past year. Some, no doubt, come exclusively for the guarantee of quiet, but most by far quickly get into the swing of the place. Two of their classes (theology and literature in the fall, history and philosophy in the spring) are taught in a classroom on the ground floor—just having the teachers come to their residence makes a certain contribution to the integration of their studies and the rest of their living. We do not make any effort to regulate the whole of their days, but there certainly are plenty of "programs." At the top of the list is "Knight Court" (named in honor of the Queen, whose statue is in the courtyard), held every evening at 11:00 P.M. in "Bishops Lounge," a large hall on the first floor, so named from the stained-glass windows of the coats-of-arms of the bishops who have been graduated from Fordham over the years. It is a gracious commons, about a hundred feet long, with large tables, oriental rugs, a fire place, rimmed with book cases crammed with books of all sorts. By day the place is to be perfectly silent—a quiet, beautiful place to study. But by 11 P.M. (Monday through Thursday) about half our number chooses to assemble to hear one of their number who has been assigned speak from a lectern in the center of the room on a subject of his or her choice for ten to fifteen minutes, followed by cookies and milk—a bit of socializing before they return to studying or turn in for the day. We have had many stories about their families and about family vacations, but we have also heard about the rules for rugby, the way one figures out wind chill factor, and what it's like to work for the summer in the mail room of a maximum security prison in upstate New York. Knight Court is intended as an exercise in public speaking joined to a study break for socializing. But along with other such programs (for example, a formal debate called a "Disputatio," a talent show we call "Art Court," and the every other Monday "Common Dinner" which begins with pretzels and juice in the Master's

Suite for the host-floor and some invited faculty members and that continues with a short program and then dinner together in the Faculty Dining Room), our hope is to see the development of friendships and loyalty beyond what the average dormitory accomplishes in the direction of preparing modern cave-dwellers for apartment living. Thus far we have soft-pedalled religious programs, but there is a steady group who attends the Mass celebrated at Queen's Court on Thursday evenings (at 10:00 P.M.!). Fr. Piderit once led a twenty-mile walking pilgrimage from our Bronx campus to the Church that was frequented by St. Elizabeth Anne Seton at the very foot of Manhattan, and I hope to repeat that as soon as my walking legs are in shape! As you can see, we have a long way to go, and for all the enthusiasm this program arouses, I am quite sure that most of our 700 freshmen would not be interested, even if we had the buildings and the staff.

Secondly, I want to call your attention to a proposal by Father Paul Quay as an example of how the university could better serve the personal and cultural development of its students by reconfiguring one important element of the curriculum; he calls for a change in a discipline that ought to be most amenable to such change but will probably not be, university-level theology as taught in religious institutions. Instead of modeling itself on the methods of other disciplines, and thus often leaving students with the impression that there is an impressive body of speculation and perhaps even that there is some real knowledge there, but a body of theory that they generally do not find personally compelling, theology could organize its instruction as education in religion in a way more suitable to promote personal maturation (of mind, heart and whole person, individually and socially). Quay's idea is to focus this part of education on using the spiritual senses of the Scriptures that have been downplayed by Catholics and Protestants alike in favor of their literal (or historical) meaning over the centuries since the Reformation. The purpose of this concentration would be to bring about an understanding of: 1) the way the Scriptures present the life of Christ as recapitulating the whole life of Israel, but completely and perfectly where Israel's life was incomplete and imperfect; and then 2) the way they present a pattern of life in Christ as the way for the individual Christian and for any given culture to sanctify the stages of one's own life and the patterns of life and growth available to that culture. Without going into all the details to be found in this remarkable proposal, let me simply summarize Quay's insights as an expansion on the idea of "recapitulation by Christ and in Christ" introduced by St. Paul and championed by St. Irenaeus of Lyons. What Quay has discovered in this line of reading the Scriptures according to their diverse spiritual senses (including the literal meaning, which has been the main concern of modern exegetes) is a path to an authentic route of spiritual development, including the natural course of human physical and psychic development as well as moral growth in the virtues. What he proposes is a way of envisioning academic theological study that may well also assist growth in the life of faith.

A direct carry-over to some other disciplines (without any loss to their independence as appropriate) readily suggests itself, for what is intended here is formation in how to read the different levels of meaning in a text (rather like the work of literature), just as pondering life-stages now comes, if at all, within psychology and thinking about the relation of individuals and cultural forces comes within the social sciences. Admittedly, this is but one component of a reformation of university education, but, I think, one that is very important for making concrete what Maritain called for, especially in the section entitled "The Schools in Spiritual Life" within *Education at the Crossroads.*[7]

---

[7] Ibid., pp. 84–87.

John Poinsot:
On The Gift of Counsel

Romanus Cessario, O.P.

This essay examines the teaching of John Poinsot on the gift of the Holy Spirit called Counsel. In his treatment of the gift of Counsel, John Poinsot clearly exercises the role of a theologian. But the theological essay that he produces decisively demonstrates his philosophical genius. The academic conventions of seventeenth-century Spanish scholasticism adopted by Poinsot entailed a complete subordination to the work of Aquinas. But some 350 years after his death, we are in position to recognize how much Poinsot's own intelligence, manifest in his philosophical acumen, advanced his writing on Aquinas well beyond the status of a simple commentary. In this regard, Poinsot differs from the late medieval commentator John Capreolus (d. 1444) whose reputation rests principally on the merits of his organization of Aquinas's texts. In particular, Poinsot's discussion of the gift of Counsel displays a penetrating psychological analysis of the moral conscience.

Poinsot's treatise on the gifts occurs in his *Cursus Theologicus*, Disputatio XVIII, Article 5, where it is presented as commentary on Aquinas's *Summa Theologiae* Ia IIae, qq. 68–70.[1] In theological discourse, the gifts of

---

[1] The first edition of the treatise on the gifts of the Holy Spirit (Disputation XVIII) was published in 1645, one year after the death of Poinsot, by Didacus Ramirez as part of the 5th volume of Poinsot's *Cursus Theologicus*. In the Vivès edition, printed in Paris in 1885, the text of Disputation XVIII appears in vol. VI, pp. 655–665. All references to the texts of John Poinsot are from this edition, [and give the Disp., art., no. and (page no.)]. For the place of this treatise in the life of John Poinsot, see the well-annotated chronology established by John N. Deely in his interpretative arrangement of Poinsot's *Tractatus de Signis, The Semiotic of John Poinsot* (Berkeley, California: University of California Press, 1985), esp. pp. 443–444.

the Holy Spirit represent infused supernatural *habitus* of the soul that one can really differentiate from the Christian moral and theological virtues. As virtue-like *habitus,* moreover, the seven gifts form an ensemble of distinctive spiritual qualities that shape the life of the Christian believer. A discussion of Counsel, the gift that aids practical reasoning, allows Poinsot to explain how a gift exercises a direct formative influence on a person's moral comportment. It is this specific detail of Poinsot's general treatment that I want to focus on in this essay.

Poinsot begins his discussion of the gift of Counsel by distinguishing Counsel and the other traditional gifts of the Holy Spirit. The very name of the gift, observes Poinsot, suggests that Counsel represents a divine assistance that prompts the human person from within.[2] And he supports this contention by reference to St. Thomas's remark in the *Summa Theologiae* that the word counsel implies "the mind being moved to ponder under the influence of another's advising" (*motio mentis consiliata ab alio consiliante*).[3] It remains for Poinsot to show the distinctive operation of the gift of Counsel, distinguishing it from other divine movements so as to illumine the Church's practice in presenting Counsel as one of the seven gifts of the Holy Spirit.[4]

Demonstrating his creative use of Renaissance scholastic categories, Poinsot advances three arguments for establishing the conclusion that Counsel forms a distinct gift. First, he shows that one can distinguish this gift from the virtue of theological faith, from the gifts of Knowledge and Wisdom that respectively accompany faith and charity, and from the infused virtue of prudence. By establishing this distinction, Poinsot replies to those authors who hold the view that these infused *habitus* and higher movements are sufficient for directing the Christian moral life.

Secondly and as a result of the first argument, Poinsot affirms that one can identify a specific [formal] object for the gift of Counsel. Does this gift, he asks, embrace every sphere of rational human activity? Or does it concern only the regulation of those actions springing from human appetite—in short, what we call human behavior? Poinsot argues that Counsel is like the virtue of prudence which it principally aids. The gift of Counsel embraces all that pertains to the virtue of justice aided by the gift of Piety, to

---

[2] Disp. XVIII, art. 5, no. 1 (655): "Appellatur autem potius donum concilii, quam donum prudentiae ut magis per hoc insinuetur divina modo et instinctus. . . . "

[3] *Summa Theologiae* IIaIIae, q. 52, art. 2, ad 2: "per quod [consilium] potest significari motio mentis consiliatae ab alio consiliante."

[4] For the latest authoritative expression of this teaching, see the *Catechism of the Catholic Church*, nos. 1830–1831.

the virtue of fortitude aided by the gift of the same name, and to the virtue of temperance aided by the gift of Fear of the Lord. Counsel, in other words, directs the entire substance of the moral life.

Thirdly, Poinsot identifies a special act that belongs to the gift of Counsel. Indeed, some considerations suggest that there may not be a specific act that belongs exclusively to the gift of Counsel—the psychological landscape of the moral life being already sufficiently occupied. While Poinsot admits that Counsel possesses its own act, he also recognizes the difficulty in identifying it. Consider these quandaries: when a person is not sure that a particular inspiration comes from God, then he or she is compelled to follow the dictates of prudence, with the result that, properly speaking, the subsequent action belongs to the virtue of prudence. Or again, when a person claims to be sure about the authenticity of an interior movement, there exists the danger of promoting an anti-ecclesial individualism. Poinsot is thus challenged to give a specific definition to the act of counsel that does not risk promoting the spiritual hubris that he associates with the Protestant Reform of the 16th century.

In Article 5, which forms the equivalent of a modern chapter, Poinsot develops arguments demonstrating Counsel's specific character, its object, and its act. In addition, he aims to resolve the difficulties associated with each of his conclusions.

I. The Distinctiveness of Counsel

Poinsot's first line of inquiry aims to show how one should distinguish the gift of Counsel from other recognized endowments of the supernatural life. He begins by recounting the opinion of one of his contemporaries—a certain Gregory Martinez.[5] On the latter's account, Counsel differs from the infused virtue of prudence in the same way that a direct illumination differs from the exercise of discursive reasoning. Thus, prudence discovers "means proportioned to an end from the nature of the case,"[6] whereas the gift of Counsel enables the moral agent to consider better a "proportioned

---

[5] The Spanish Dominican Gregory Martinez (1575–1637), a noted theologian, preacher, and confessor, wrote a commentary on the *Summa Theologiae*; see his *Commentaria super IaIIae D. Thomae*, Bk II (Toledo, 1622), q. 68, art. 4, 2nd dubium.

[6] Disp. XVIII, art. 5, no. 5 (656): "virtus autem prudentiae discursu et inquisitione nititur. Et hoc inde confirmant, quia in prudentia quae est virtus respiciuntur media quae proportionem habent cum fine ex natura rei. . . . "

mean," through an exclusive reliance on the divine power.[7] But this dichotomous way of distinguishing virtue from gift, says Poinsot, clearly fails to take adequate account of the special character of the gifts of the Holy Spirit.

Poinsot undertakes a three-pronged rebuttal of the theory that Counsel is merely an instance of spiritual illumination. He first argues that the gifts of the Holy Spirit perfect human intelligence, and that they accomplish this goal without prejudice to the ordinary structures of human knowing. Secondly, Poinsot considers the parallel case of the infused knowledge of Christ. He recalls that even within the grace of the hypostatic union the human mind of Christ continues to function in a way that is recognizably human. Thirdly Poinsot appeals to ordinary human experience, which for the most part does not corroborate the supposition that persons receiving a special light from God thereby find human reasoning superfluous. Even those who are illumined and directed by the Holy Spirit do not thereby escape all work of discursive reflection. Moreover, it can occur that sudden bursts of inspiration befall even persons deprived of the gifts of the Holy Spirit.

Instead of distinguishing the gift of Counsel from the virtue of prudence by demarcating inspiration from discursive reasoning, Poinsot prefers to situate the gift within the full context of moral decision-making. But there still remains a difference between an infused virtue and a gift. In the case of Counsel, the gift regulates human action not within the limits set by human reasoning but rather according to the mode of God's own wisdom. Moreover, the human person's capacity to experience God makes this mode of the gift possible.

Counsel, writes Poinsot, works through "an intimate experience of divine realities that instruct the soul about everything necessary for salvation, without excluding the operation of discursive reasoning, the need for making inquiry, and the willingness to consult with other persons."[8] It should be emphatically stressed that Poinsot does not simply associate the illuminations of Counsel with what a person holds by the theological virtue of

---

[7] Ibid.: "Donum autem consilii non respicit medium proportionatum ex natura rei, sed ex divina potentia. . . . "

[8] Disp. XVIII, art. 5, no. 7 (657): "donum consilii dirigit ea quae agenda sunt non ex rationibus humanis præcise, sed ex divinis non præcise cognitis a fide, aut prophetia, qualiter potest esse in peccatore, sed ex affectu, et experientia divinorum interna, ex qua docetur, et inspiratur de omnibus necessariis ad salutem, etiam cum discursu, et inquisitione, aut consultatione aliorum, quia totum hoc inspiratur, et docetur a Spiritu. . . . "

faith or receives through prophecy; for, as he keenly observes, God communicates through unformed faith even to sinners and sometimes uses them as instruments of prophetic utterance.

Because John Poinsot considers himself to be engaged principally in a theological enterprise, we are not surprised to discover him resorting to the sacred Scriptures to show that his theological conclusion enjoys the confirmatory witness of divine revelation. Thus, Poinsot cites texts that he considers to be *loci* where the Bible speaks about Counsel as a special divine gift. First, there is the text from the 24th chapter of the book of Ecclesiasticus: "for her [wisdom's] thought is more abundant than the sea, and her counsel deeper than the great abyss."[9] Here, Poinsot points out how the sacred Scriptures emphasize that the human person needs to be moved by God, and indeed led by the Angel of Great Counsel who possesses wisdom more abundant than the sea and counsel deeper than the great abyss.

Poinsot next considers a text from a later chapter of the same book: the one devoted to the study of the law of the Most High "will give thanks to the Lord in prayer. He will direct his counsel and knowledge aright, and meditate on his secrets."[10] As a theologian with a profound awareness that the God of creation remains one and the same with the God of salvation, Poinsot's exegesis naturally leads to a broadening of his philosophical insight. The gift of Counsel, he concludes, reveals a new dimension of God's relationship with man, namely, that God touches the human person in the deepest interiority of conscience, the inner sanctuary of the self.

Poinsot then returns to his effort to identify the gift of Counsel as a special capacity of the moral life. He begins by explaining the difference between the way in which the virtue of prudence directs the moral agent and the way in which the gift of Counsel moves the believer. According to the Aristotelian account, the virtue of prudence cannot operate except that the person enjoy an affective connaturality for the end (*ex affectu ad finem*) as well as exercise a right judgment (*recta aestimatione*) about the end of human well-being. For Poinsot such adherence to the good ends of human flourishing forms the indispensable starting point for right judgment regarding the means to obtaining a virtuous end. Since Counsel supplies practical reasoning about the means to be chosen in order for the believer to reach beatitude, it operates in a similar way. The gift of Counsel evolves out of a special attachment to God that the person enjoys exclusively

---

[9] Sir. 24:29.
[10] Ibid., 39:6b, 7.

through the gift of divine grace; Poinsot even speaks about this union as mystical: *in mystico affectu, et unione ad Deum.*[11] Hence in this respect Counsel generically resembles the gifts of Knowledge and Wisdom which, though they aid human intelligence in grasping the propositions of faith, remain rooted and founded in the same source of connatural acquaintance with God.[12]

Counsel serves the perfection of the moral life in a world marked by human failure and even hardness to God's plans. So Poinsot suggests that the gift of Counsel is appropriately associated with the theological virtue of hope, whose act, hoping, includes a full reliance on the divine omnipotence and mercy. For the person whose counsel is conformed to the divine Counsel more readily recognizes the opportunities and means that are available only to those who acknowledge what is possible in light of God's omnipotence.

Theological hope, Poinsot argues, ensures that our counsels are limited neither to what human perspectives would consider the most expedient means to accomplish an end nor to what a person would consider within the limits of his or her own endurance. The persons who place their confidence in God's merciful omnipotence, or as some would put it, confide themselves to his omnipotent mercy, can overcome many obstacles. At the same time, such persons can ready themselves to sustain even extraordinary hardships, such as supporting death, sorrow, and other afflictions, holding riches in contempt, and following nakedly the naked Christ. In short they are readied to accomplish under the regulation of Counsel the works toward which the gifts of Fortitude, Piety and Fear prompt us.

In this theological argument Poinsot displays a profound psychological intuition concerning the important role that self-esteem rooted in hope plays in shaping a person's capacity for making virtuous choices. The notion of self-esteem might seem an overly modern concept to be found in the thought of Poinsot, but he arrives at an approximation of this contemporary psychological notion by distinguishing between formed and unformed theological hope. As I have said, those who exercise the virtue of hope judge human potential according to what they believe is possible with divine as-

---

[11] Disp. XVIII, art. 5, no. 10 (658): "Dabitur ergo donum consilii fundatum in mystico affectu, et unione ad Deum."

[12] Ibid.: "Si ergo datur pars speculativa affectiva, et mystica secundum cognitionem, et judicium fundatum in experimentali, et interno gustu Dei, et in quadam connaturalitate, et inviceratione ad divina, etiam pars practica poterit perfici mystice, et e{a}ffective ex eadem unione, et connaturalitate ad Deum, ex quo redditur habilior, et perfectior ad judicandum de agendis pars practica. . . . "

sistance, and not according to the weight of difficulty that a particular objective lays on human resources.

Poinsot holds that even sinners can hope, but in them the virtue is "dead" precisely because sinners, given that they stand outside the communion of charity, are blocked from personally experiencing the goodness and the power of God. In other words, sinners schizophrenically hope to obtain a good that they do not love. The just person, on the other hand, "is moved efficaciously" precisely on account of the personal experience of these divine qualities as fully operative in him or her. And such an experience, one must conclude, engenders a proper appreciation of one's self-worth. For, in Poinsot's view, grace decidedly perfects human nature.[13]

Given the foregoing justification for the existence of the gift of Counsel, Poinsot now turns to explain why this gift differs from the other endowments of the Christian life. As we have seen above, some theologians argue that the virtue of theological faith alone suffices to guarantee that the Christian believer remain steady in the practice of a good moral life. But the virtue of faith is about universal truths, such as those contained in the Creed or in the general instruction in morals that the Church from time to time fittingly sets forth. Since Poinsot realizes that judgments in the moral life are always about particular actions, he cannot accept the *sola fides* theory.

The gift of Counsel responds always to the here-and-now; it aims at particular actions by discerning and judging about the means that will best accomplish a certain end. Counsel guides authentically human operations in the very concrete circumstances that comprise the sphere of moral action. As Poinsot explains further on, the virtue of prudence works in this same domain insofar as virtuous activity falls under human regulations and is produced according to the human mode.

But as a gift, Counsel always remains concerned with what is beyond human rules, *id quod ultra humanas regulas est.*[14] In other words, Counsel represents an intervention in the practical intelligence that aids the moral conscience in making concrete choices. This distinction allows Poinsot to illuminate further the relationship of Counsel to the theological virtue of

---

[13] See Disp. XVIII, art. 5, no. 10 (658): "Sed tamen spes ista minus efficax est quando est informis, et in peccatore: sed quando est in justo qui experientiam habet de voluntate, et potentia Dead auxiliandum, et benignitatem ejus in se experitur, tunc efficaciter movetur, et tunc est spiritus, donumque consilii movens. . . . "

[14] Disp. XVIII, art. 5, no. 11 (659): "sed ad hoc ponitur virtus prudentiae quantum ad modum, et regulas humanas, et ad id quod ultra humanas regulas est, donum consilii."

faith by comparison with the way that prudence develops and particularizes synderesis, the *habitus* of the first principles of practical reason. Counsel, it is true, depends on faith, but the gift particularizes the judgments of faith to meet the requirements of moral action.

In the geography of the moral life, Counsel is situated among the gifts that aid the wayfarer to reach the goal of beatitude. To the saint who enjoys the beatific vision, the highest truth appears in its fullness. But as long as the believer remains here below, he or she must live according to the discipline of faith. This means that the believer enjoys epistemic surety about divine truth, but does not possess full evidence for what he or she holds to be true. Even when guided by the gift of Counsel, each human action of the believer participates in faith's lack of evidence. Still, because of the affective, experimental knowledge associated with the gift of Counsel, those who are moved by this gift do enjoy what Poinsot calls a "practical evidence" (*evidentiam practicam*).[15] This practical evidence helps the moral agent overcome the lack of evidential surety occasioned by faith. Reliance on this kind of evidence develops especially within a community that shares common convictions about what constitutes human well-being as well as shared views about the role of divine providence in human affairs.

The next line of inquiry further pursues the question whether there is need for a distinct gift of the Holy Spirit to serve the working of the practical intelligence. For some argue that the gifts that serve theological faith and charity, namely, Knowledge and Wisdom, should also suffice for directing the moral life. Poinsot admits, of course, that the gifts that aid the theological virtues of faith and charity do indirectly influence the practical order. Indeed, Christian faith teaches about both what is to be believed and what is to be accomplished—the *agenda*. But like faith itself, the gift of Knowledge helps the believer to enter into truths that are formulated in general terms.

Counsel is distinguished by its work of helping the Christian believer in "the [very] circumstances of an operation," as Poinsot says, "in the mode of choice, and not in the abstract."[16] Charity, aided by the gift of Wisdom, plays another role. As the supreme and architectonic virtue of the Christian life, charity and the gift of Wisdom transcend the distinction between the speculative and practical orders. St. Paul teaches this explicitly in I

---

[15] Disp. XVIII, art. 5, no. 13 (659): "ita prudentia de se petit evidentiam practicam fundatam in illa experimentali unione effectiva. . . . "
[16] Disp. XVIII, art. 5, no. 14 (660): "donum agens de ipsis in singulari, et de circumstantiis operationum modo arbitrio, et non scientifico."

Corinthians 13 when he writes that if we "understand all mysteries and knowledge" and if we give away all that we have, but have not love, we gain nothing.[17]

If Counsel is distinguished from the virtue of faith and from the gifts that assist it because of the concreteness that practical reasoning entails, how is the gift of Counsel to be distinguished from the virtue of prudence that it aids? Poinsot addresses this issue by distinguishing the mode of action that characterizes the gifts from the mode of the infused virtues. He articulates the quite subtle difference between grace working in a human mode and grace working in a divine mode. Obviously the most precise philosophical analysis is required for Poinsot to elucidate this crucial distinction.

His explanation runs as follows: Since the infused virtues constitute endowments of the supernatural life, they all contribute to the well-being of the Christian believer set upon the pursuit of eternal beatitude within the community of the Church. But the infused virtues do not enable a person to realize supernatural goods except in a human way (*nisi juxta modum humanum*), that is, in a way that accords with the common rules of virtue (*[juxta] communes regulas virtutum*).[18] In other words, the infused virtues enable a person to accomplish supernatural actions, including ecclesial actions such as the worship of God and sacramental reconciliation, but only as the result of judgments made in accord with the ordinary workings of human reason.

For Poinsot, then, there is nothing untoward about considering a human judgment that operates under the influence of divine grace. To put it another way, a human judgment can serve the purposes of the Christian life. Such a judgment in fact is made each time a person undertakes a specific activity on account of revealed truth, as happens when one frequents the sacraments or engages in other activities that depend upon revealed truth and grace.

As divine promptings, the gifts work according to another mode, a mode of divine inspiration. The gifts supply the moral agent with resources that enable him or her to step outside the limitations of rationality, so that the direction followed flows from a special divine instinct or prompting. The theologian attributes such promptings to the Holy Spirit on the basis of sa-

---

[17] 1 Cor. 13: 2–3.
[18] Disp. XVIII, art. 5, no. 15 (660): "prudentia etiam infusa . . . non cognoscit, nec attingit de istis agendis supernaturalibus, nisi juxta modum humanum, et communes regulas virtutum. . . . "

cred Scripture: "The wind blows where it chooses, and you hear the sound of it, but you do not know where it comes from or where it goes. So it is with everyone who is born of the Spirit."[19] But unlike his Dominican confrère Martinez, Poinsot does not interpret this text as one that justifies a completely charismatic account of the gifts, with the possible result that a person could claim exemption from following the established norms of nature or of the Church.

II. The Scope of Counsel

The second main line of inquiry centers on the object of Counsel. Poinsot considers the specific moral matter to which the gift of Counsel extends. As operational *habitus*, the gifts of the Holy Spirit of course are not constituted out of a determined kind of matter. In the case of an operational *habitus*, such as a virtue or a gift, the very activities that the *habitus* regulate are considered as the material cause—the *materia circa quam*, as the Scholastic authors would say.

The gift of Counsel concerns everything that falls under the purview of the behavioral virtues; in short, everything that involves human willing and affect. Because the gifts of the Holy Spirit operate among themselves in a certain harmony, Poinsot assigns as the material cause of Counsel every human action that is governed by the gifts of Piety, Fortitude, and Fear of the Lord. This means that the gift of Counsel per se fills up what is lacking in prudence and in the "common rules" that prudence seeks to supply for moral action. When Poinsot argues that Counsel per se directs works that surpass the common rules of morality, he is referring to moral conduct that surpasses the ordinary workings of human reason. As I have said, Christian theology considers such virtuous works the specific dominion of the gifts of the Holy Spirit.

Poinsot considers that a realistic view of human life compels one to take a broad view of Counsel's sphere of action, and he notes that Aquinas construes the working of Counsel in the broadest of terms. In *Summa Theologiae* IIa-IIae, q.52, a.4, Aquinas teaches that the gift of Counsel is at work in every action that moves a person further along towards accomplishing the end of human life, whether the action is strictly speaking necessary for obtaining the gift of eternal life or not. This perspective spurs Poinsot to reflect that Counsel can also guide good works that fall under the common rules of morality, including matters that pertain to the commandments, pro-

---

[19] John 3: 8.

vided that such works enjoy some special reference to the participated divine life. As proof of this, Poinsot asks us to reflect on the enormous difficulties that most people encounter when they try to submit every contingency of human life to the directive pull of the good ends of human existence. And this tension proves all the more acute, when one takes into account that, in the Christian view, every human being remains ultimately ordered to the one end of eternal beatitude.

Because of the weighty position that Counsel holds in the moral life, the Church teaches that every justified believer possesses the gift in some way. Poinsot, however, qualifies the received opinion by arguing that everyone who lives in the *communio* of divine charity does not exercise the gift in a most excellent degree. In making this qualification, he intends to establish that, while everyone who lives within the grace of the Church does manifest an *instinctus* for rectitude of life, only some persons outstandingly exhibit wise discretion and good judgment in every important moral choice. This *instinctus* or movement toward holiness takes the concrete form of placing earthly goods in their proper frame of reference, at least to the extent that a person does not allow the preoccupations of this world to obscure his or her vision of the highest excellence. Poinsot cites the *Moralia*, Gregory the Great's classic study of the virtuous life, which Poinsot recognizes as both anticipating and reflecting his own vision of Counsel.

> Each one of the elect still of the world in body, already rises in mind above the world; he deplores the bitterness of the exile that he tolerates, and rouses himself through the unceasing movement of love toward the sublime fatherland. [Whence] he discovers a salubrious counsel, namely, to despise the temporal world through which he passes. Then, as the knowledge of counsel which leads one to flee passing things develops in him the more, so also develops sorrow at not yet having attained those things that are lasting or eternal. . . . So the person who, with solicitude, fixes his spirit in life-giving counsel carefully and circumspectly reflects on himself in every action. And fearing lest an untoward end or [other] obstacle surprise him in the course of an action, he always begins with a soft tap, as if using the foot of his thought.[20]

---

[20] In Disp. XVIII, art. 5, no. 17 (661), John Poinsot in fact pieces together several sentences from Gregory the Great's *Moralia in Job*, I, chap. 25, no. 34 (*PL* 75: 542–543): "et unusquisque eorum adhuc in mundo corpore positus, mente jam extra mundum surgit, aerumnam exilii, quam tolerat, deplorat, et ad sublimem patriam incessantibus se amoris stimulis excitat. . . . invenit salubre consilium, temporale hoc despicere quod percurrit: et quo magis crescit consilii scientia, ut peritura deserat, eo augetur dolor, quod necdum ad mansura pertingat. . . . Nam qui solerter

The text continues to explain the need for special caution in the face of strong emotional pulls and tugs that can deter the workings of Counsel. Even though Pope Gregory's imaginative metaphor of testing the moral terrain aims to persuade the simple believer, Poinsot considers this patristic text as both an "elegant" testimony to an authentically Christian teaching on counsel and a profoundly realistic analysis of ethical action within the horizon of transcendence.

Yet if Counsel is a distinctive gift, then why do many persons who live within Christian community still seek counsel from other graced persons? This occurrence, Poinsot asserts, does not suggest that such persons are deprived of the gift of Counsel. Rather, the gift of Counsel itself moves a person to seek counsel from those persons whom God uses as secondary instruments, even for communicating the promptings of the Holy Spirit. Moreover, to seek counsel remains an ordinance of divine precept; and the gifts do aid the fulfillment of precepts. In the *Confessions*, St Augustine explains the supreme importance that the mature person attaches to taking counsel: "Your better servant is the one who is more ready to will what You speak to him than to hear from You what he himself wants."[21]

The theology of the gifts of the Holy Spirit cannot be used as a pretext for establishing an autonomous class of persons in whom God works in an exceptional way. Instead, the communion of the Church supposes an ordering of inferiors to superiors; this ecclesial *communio*, moreover, mirrors the choirs of angels, where we are told that the higher angels influence the lower ones. And so we observe that God encourages the holy ones of every age to seek counsel. In the New Testament, for example, Cornelius, who himself was the beneficiary of a revelation, was still told to seek counsel from the Apostle Peter,[22] and Paul, who even beheld Christ himself on the road to Damascus, was still instructed that he would be told what to do once he arrived in the city.[23]

---

in vitae consilio figit mentem, caute sese in omni actione circumspiciendo considerat; et ne ex re, quae agitur, repentinus finis adversusque subripiat, hunc prius molliter posito pede cogitationis palpat. . . . " Here, Gregory begins his moral or anagogical commentary on Job 1:1, "Vir erat in terra Hus, nomine Job." Earlier, Gregory gave the allegorical commentary on this first verse of the book of Job, explaining that Hus means "the Counsellor." See I, chap. 11, no. 15 (*PL* 75:533–534): "Hus vero [interpretatur] consiliator."

[21] *Confessionum* 10, chap. 26, 37: "Optimus minister tuus est, qui non magis intuetur hoc a te audire quod ipse uoluerit, sed potius hoc uelle quod a te audierit."

[22] See Acts 10:5ff.

[23] See Acts 9:6.

III. The Function of Counsel

The third major enquiry centers on the act of Counsel. Following Poinsot's method, if we can identify a determined field of activity associated with the gift of Counsel—its matter, if you will—then the gift must also possess its own specific act. Poinsot uses his examination of the act of Counsel to probe the certainty that it enjoys. Human experience, he says, proves that those who enjoy the gift of Counsel sometimes continue to experience doubts about what course of action they should follow.

What kind of certitude, then, does the Holy Spirit bestow with the gift of Counsel? According to St Paul, God "accomplishes all things according to the counsel of his will,"[24] and therefore the divine counsel can give no reason for a failure of resolve. But this does not mean that the gift of Counsel therefore takes away every doubt from the person who enjoys its help. Rather, the gift accomplishes its task by producing within us a kind of certitude and security, which at times comes from a private inspiration, and at other times, through the express teaching and example of others. Poinsot's analysis of how Counsel works reveals his balanced approach to human life as well as a certain psychological realism that complements his speculative achievement.

Lack of certitude manifests itself in two ways: first, incertitude arises when we recoil from a decision, asking ourselves whether we should do such and such or not; secondly, incertitude arises when we question whether a particular light of Counsel in fact comes from God. Poinsot estimates that some choices are such that no one who knows the truth of the Christian religion should find any positive cause to hesitate or doubt. Thus, the choice to suffer martyrdom rather than sin, or to enter a religious vocation, provide examples of indisputably good choices (although in the second example room is left for deliberation about particulars). Yet even in the case of unquestionably good choices, there exists the possibility that the acting person will experience a certain hesitancy, so that he or she requires the help of other persons. When this happens, however, there is no reason to doubt that the gift of Counsel is fully operative. St. Paul himself again provides an example of one who, though sure of his role as an apostle, went to seek the counsel of others, as he himself relates in Galatians.[25]

Poinsot discovers a divine pedagogical purpose in the indeterminacy that

---

[24] Eph 1:11.
[25] See Gal 2:1–10.

a person who enjoys the gift of Counsel may still experience. The hesitancy in the face of decision-making that compels a person to seek counsel offers the chance for both spiritual growth and human maturity. Insofar as we are moved to seek guidance from others, Counsel ensures that the believer is not left to his or her own devices. Isolation and particularity characterize those who rely exclusively on their own counsel, whereas the one who seeks counsel remains in solidarity with the whole ecclesial community. The Holy Spirit acts through a full range of secondary instruments so that individualism will not work against the good of the Body of Christ. Poinsot recognizes that the exercise of Counsel contributes to the building up of community in as much as those who are moved by the gift develop the *habitus* of human communication and mutual dependence.

Because Counsel always results in the execution of a good act, the gift can be considered as a sort of superior prudence. The gift of Counsel always helps us to realize in as perfect a way as possible actions that are in themselves intrinsically good. Counsel therefore moves us to seek discernment, especially the discernment of spirits that is encouraged by the New Testament.[26] Such discernment, argues Poinsot, does not subordinate Counsel to some other divine movement, but ministerially serves the gift. Because of this reliance on others, the gift of Counsel creates a prudential certitude in the one who acts according to the prompting of the Holy Spirit. Recall that prudential certitude results from a *habitus*-formed inclination to moral truth, and for that reason can be distinguished from the epistemic certitude of faith. In the moral order, many things remain obscure, but testing spirits results in a salutary humbling that only comes when one submits to another and thereby learns to cultivate a tested spirit—"un esprit éprouvé," as Raïssa Maritain translates this important phrase.[27]

Incertitude also arises in a person when one is not sure about the origin of a counsel. Poinsot next discusses the criteria for judging the authenticity of a given inspiration, especially the case of extraordinary counsels that sometimes are given to certain persons who, as a result of private revelations, are urged to act outside of the ordinary norms of Christian life. Citing cases where the Holy Spirit moves persons to perform acts that would not fall under ordinary human prudence, Poinsot recalls well-known cases from the Bible such as Samson's self-destruction and episodes from the lives of

[26] See 1 John 4 and 1 Thess 5.
[27] See *Les dons du Saint-Esprit*, traduction de Raïssa Maritain (Juvisy: Editions du Cerf, 1930), p. 202.

the saints recounting how certain martyrs actually thrust themselves onto the instruments of torture and death.

While it is true that the Holy Spirit remains free to inwardly inspire some persons with an assurance about what they should do, extraordinary examples such as these that seemingly go against the precepts of divine law cannot establish the norm. Whether such movements of the spirit come from God or not is often proved by their effects. In the final analysis, the Holy Spirit can be trusted to work ordinarily through examined counsel and communication with others. When, however, signs of emotional upset manifest themselves, then Poinsot suggests that God wants the person to devote further time to testing the spirit.

When a person openly claims to possess the spirit of God, especially when the inspiration affects some element of public teaching, the Church must take an active role in judging the authenticity of the affair. For less public matters, e.g. instructions or prophecies, it is always better to seek confirmation from several prudent persons who have not had the opportunity to consult among themselves. While there are cases both in the lives of the saints—Poinsot names St. Benedict, St. Catherine of Siena, St. Brigit, St. Vincent Ferrer, St. Francis da Paola—and even in the Old Testament where holy men and women appear to act on their own, the better course always leads to bringing the person into contact with the Church community. For in the Christian moral life, the experience of fruitful communication with other members of the community provides the indispensable starting point for moral development. To sum up, the gift of Counsel encourages a truly Christian sort of behavior, for it leads a person into an intimate union with Christ in the heart of the Church precisely through the experience of community.

IV. Poinsot's Achievement

Poinsot's *Treatise on the Gifts* forms a bridge between classical explanations of the moral life that view the human person as a free agent within a universe of divinely established purposes and ends and modern accounts of human agency that emphasize personal purposes and self-determination as the starting-point of moral evaluation. His work is distinguished by the delicacy and balance of its analysis. These qualities are especially evident in Poinsot's discussion of Counsel where he provides the classical clarification of the specifically mystical side of Christian moral life Poinsot takes great care to demonstrate that even when the Holy Spirit is fully at work in a soul, the person does not become the Christian equivalent of an ethical monad, but rather develops a full measure of human freedom through communion with others. Throughout his treatment of the gift of Counsel, Poinsot is able to acknowledge the importance of human subjectivity, but without slighting the normative character of divine truth for human conduct. This achievement surely merits him a distinctive place among philosophical theologians.

Learning as Recollection—
A Thomistic Approach to
Recovering Higher Education

Peter A. Redpath

Perhaps the two works of Jacques Maritain to which most of his students would be most inclined to look for a Maritainian philosophy of education are *Education at the Crossroads* and *The Education of Man.*[1] While such might be the case, I propose to turn to neither of these roads to education as the starting point for my present study. Instead, I shall turn to an earlier work of Maritain, namely, *The Dream of Descartes*,[2] as to a road not taken in either of the two former treatises, for the main principles of my reflections upon the problems in the state of current higher education in the United States—and for some suggested Thomistic remedies to these difficulties.

Among other things, a main reason I have chosen this approach is because, despite the fact that I consider these later works to be filled with all sorts of insights, it seems to me that both books neglect aspects of education in general and of higher education in particular which are not only sorely in need of reconsideration today but which were also recognized by Maritain as essentially neglected by the Modern turn in higher learning taken by Descartes in the seventeenth century. Specifically, that to which I am referring is Maritain's observation in the latter book about Descartes's

---

[1] Cf. Jacques Maritain, *Education at the Crossroads* (New Haven, Connecticut: Yale University Press, 1943) and *The Education of Man: The Educational Philosophy of Jacques Maritain*, Donald and Idella Gallagher, eds. (Garden City, New York: Doubleday and Company, Inc., 1962).

[2] Jacques Maritain, *The Dream of Descartes*, trans. Mabelle Andison (New York: Philosophical Library, 1944).

distrust of books and teachers, as well as of sensation, imagination, memory and intellectual abstraction apart from regulation by mathematics.[3] In my opinion, while contemporary college students suffer from a great deal of deficiencies, in particular what they suffer from is attention deficiency, dullness of imagination, weakness of memory, an almost total inability to think abstractly, and an overall inability to read a book. Furthermore, I think that a major reason that students find themselves in their present predicament lies in the Cartesian turn in learning that overthrew the classical faculty psychology of thinkers like Socrates, Plato, Aristotle and the Medieval and Renaissance scholastics as well as the *trivium* of liberal arts, and of theoretical sciences, and acts of intellectual abstraction as essential elements in the process of higher education.

Assuming that most would agree with me that the problems which I have identified are among the most serious ones confronting contemporary college students, let me suggest how I think we might use classical insights about learning to begin to reverse this ever-increasing decline in higher learning.

To begin with, I think it important that when we speak about learning we recognize we are, in some way, talking about adding to our knowledge; and that when we talk about knowledge what we are talking about is an activity by means of which human beings are able, at the very least, to distinguish, in a sensory way, the existence of one thing from the existence of another. While it might be the case that in dreams people might begin their knowing with clear and distinct ideas, for those of us who do philosophy as waking beings, it is essential to recognize that all knowing is an act not of a pure reason, but of an organic being, which originates with sensory contact with the existence of physical things.

This bare minimum of evident truth being admitted, I think we can all recognize that in order to go beyond this minimum of knowing, and to come to know with some sort of essential precision, as the great philosophers of antiquity generally recognized, what is needed is that human beings acquire experience, and that such experience presupposes the possession on the part of human beings of a faculty called a memory. Indeed, I think one of the most important discoveries of classical philosophy is the observation made by Socrates, Plato and Aristotle that it is the possession of a memory which makes any animal capable of learning.[4] The reason that

---

[3] Ibid., pp. 61–103.

[4] Socrates and Plato are well known for their identification of learning with recollection. In *Metaphysics* I.1 980a27–980b24, Aristotle stresses both the possession of memory and of *hearing* as necessary abilities for the teaching of animals.

this ancient observation is true is not only that a memory helps human beings to conserve the past so as to compare some previously sensed content to a presently sensed being but also to account for the existence of human habits.[5]

Habits, that is, only come into being through the conjoined action of the human memory and a particular faculty. For this reason, indeed, a person can only possess a habit for so long as a person *remembers* how to do something; and, furthermore, for this reason, primary education, or learning in its first beginnings, consists in inculcating the external and internal senses of a child with much memory.

That is, children are living organic beings who first come to know through the exercise of external sense faculties operating in conjunction with immaturely developed sense organs. What helps to bring these sense organs and their respective faculties to maturity is the healthy repetition of their own specific organic facultative acts. For this to occur, however, these external sense acts must be naturally inclined to take direction from the human memory, which puts these acts to masterful use by directing them in conjunction with the human imagination, the human intellect, the human will, and the human emotions. That is, as young human beings begin to repeat the performance of their natural, organic, facultative sense acts under the direction of their memory, they are imbedding these faculties and acts with mnemonic content (which, in its turn, is a kind of knowledge) through the help of emotion-laden images; and they are, thereby, simultaneously, bringing to these specific acts and respective faculties a greater mastery of operation by bringing to them a greater precision in act and also bringing to their respective organs a greater health and strength because these acts are becoming rightly ordered with greater precision by being performed under the habitual direction of knowledge.

Let me add that no human being remembers anything, or is able to put any sense organ to use in a conscious way, without the employment both of images and the human emotions—which only operate in response to the presence of images. For what enables a person to direct the senses is a command of the human intellect and the assent of the human will; and the human intellect cannot become active without the presence to it of an image, and the human will can only move the various human faculties

---

[5] For another study in which I examine the relation of memory, habits, and learning see my article "Saving the Academic Soul: the 'Fallacy of Misplaced Historicity,' the Wisdom of Socrates, Plato and Aristotle, and the *Via Media*," *Measure* 106 (May 1992): pp. 1; 8–11.

through its direction of the human emotions under the command of the intellect. Thus St. Thomas asserts:

> An image is the starting point of our knowledge, for it is that from which the operation of the intellect begins. . . . This is because images are related to the intellect as objects in which it sees, either through a perfect representation or through a negation. Consequently, when our knowledge of images is impeded, we must be completely incapable of knowing anything with our intellect even about divine things.[6]

And he adds both that, "emotion is a movement of the appetitive power in the imagination of good or evil";[7] and that:

> the sensitive appetite is subject to the will with respect to execution, which occurs through the motive power. In other animals motion results immediately from concupiscible and irascible appetition, just as a sheep, fearing the wolf, immediately flees, because the sheep is devoid of any superior appetite which might restrain it. But a human being is not immediately moved by irascible and concupiscible appetition; but awaits the command of the will, which is a superior appetite. Hence an inferior appetite is not sufficient to move unless a superior appetite consent.[8]

What is most important to realize from these above references to Aquinas is that not only is it possible for certain human faculties to exercise influence over others, but that when it comes to adding to one's knowledge, once this influence is accepted by a person's will and commanded by the intellect, the human imagination and the human memory play an essential role in all learning—whether it be higher or lower.

Thus, in the case of elementary and secondary learning, the young child and adolescent are primarily involved in gaining mastery over their external and internal sense faculties through the habituation of these faculties under the rational direction of sense memory and imagination, which themselves are in the process of maturing as they engage in exercising their direction over the other sense faculties. Furthermore, central to this process is the docility of the human imagination to take direction from the memory. The imagination, however, is flexible to the extent that it is fertile; and just as the external sense faculties are knowing faculties to the extent that they are capable of extracting sensible content from their contact with sensible

---

[6] St. Thomas Aquinas, *Commentary on the de Trinitate of Boethius*, q. 5, a. 2, ad 5, trans. Armand A. Maurer in *St. Thomas Aquinas: The Division and Methods of the Sciences* (Toronto: The Pontifical Institute of Mediaeval Studies, 1963), p. 71.

[7] St. Thomas Aquinas, *Summa Theologiae* IaIIae, q. 22, a. 3, sed contra.

[8] Ibid., Ia, q. 81, a. 3, c.

beings, so the imagination initiates its being as an actual knowing faculty to the extent that it is capable of extracting its own imaginable content from what is given to the external senses in external sense apprehension.

At first, however, these images are crude constructions; for the imagination itself has not been habituated to direct its activities with precision through the reasoned application of the human memory to the exercise of its own specific activity. As its visual, aural, tactile and other images become more and more precise, however, a person becomes capable of representing imaginable content in a more refined, uniform and contracted way. That is, a person begins to be able to represent images in a standardized way by means of hieroglyphs; and gives birth to the written and legible word. Following upon this, through a further contraction, uniformity and refinement of sensible images, human language arises to a level of imaginative abstraction in which a person becomes capable of using a phonetic alphabet to represent the content of the human imagination to the human memory and human intellect.[9]

The import of the above observations about the maturing of the human imagination is that since it is through the use of the human memory and the human emotions that the various sense and intellectual faculties eventually become capable of becoming habituated under the direction of the human intellect and will, it is through the development of the use of language that the content of the human imagination gains a uniformity and simplicity which enables it to prepare the human memory eventually to serve the human intellect in such a way as to raise intellectual activity to a level of highest human learning.

In order to understand how this occurs, it is necessary to recall, first of all that, for St. Thomas, a person is possessed not of one, but of two mnemonic faculties—a sensory one and an intellectual one. In addition, it is also helpful to recall that, for him, it is not the faculty which knows but the person who knows through the integrated action of various human faculties. Indeed, as Gilson has rightly noted, for St. Thomas a person senses with the human intellect and intellectualizes with the human senses.[10] If such be the case a person equally imagines with the intellect and intellectualizes with the imagination. Now, for St. Thomas, the sense faculties include a particular or estimative reason—the development of which is prin-

---

[9] Marshall McLuhan, *Understanding Media: The Extensions of Man* (New York: New American Library, 1964), pp. 81–90;145–50.

[10] Etienne Gilson, *Thomist Realism and the Critique of Knowledge*, trans. Mark A. Wauck (San Francisco: Ignatius Press, 1986), pp. 171–215.

cipally serviced by the other internal and external sense faculties—including the human memory and the human imagination. None of these faculties, however, either singly or in concert, is capable of developing human art, or, more generally, what we would call today "skill."

Yet it is through the use of skill, which involves employment, among other faculties, of both the human memory and the human imagination, that human beings raise the imaginable content of the mind to the level of linguistic uniformity; and are, thereby, provided with the primary tool through which human beings become capable of raising their intellects to a level of scientific habituation. The latter, however, requires not merely a refined and uniform content in the human imagination but also a mnemonic positioning and placement of this content in some sort of temporal and spatial order. That is to say, it is only as the human intellect begins to apprehend some sort of conceptual content in a mnemonically ordered way that human beings develop a habitual imaginative flexibility of phonetic language which enables them to think with a kind of intellectual abstraction needed to do the work of science.

To put all this in another way, one should recall that, for the Ancient Greeks, what today we call the "liberal arts" were first called "music"; and the Ancients so conceived of them because they were the daughters of Zeus and Memory. These arts, that is, were fine arts—arts which habituated not the body in the performance of servile work but the imaginative and mnemonic faculties of the human person in the service of human activities organized under direction of universal principles inspired either by the gods or by the natural inspiration of the human intellect.[11] As such, the liberal arts were and are principally and primarily language arts. Yet simply as language arts they require some association with arts of measurement, for all human knowledge begins with the sensible apprehension of physical beings. Physical beings, however, are not only diversified by quantity but sensible qualities are unintelligible apart from reference to quantity. Furthermore, the notion of quantity contains the notions of place and position.[12] Language arts, that is, cannot exist apart from mathematical arts. For the writer, the reader, the speaker, and the listener have to have a sense of measurement, order, due proportion, position, placement, geometrical line, surface, length, height, depth, breadth and so on just to be able to form an

[11] E.R. Curtius, *European Literature and The Latin Middle Ages*, trans. Willard R. Trask (New York: Pantheon Books, Bollingen Series 36, 1953), pp. 228–246.

[12] St. Thomas Aquinas, *Commentary on the de Trinitate of Boethius*, q. 5, a. 3, trans. Maurer. See especially Maurer's notes 33 and 35.

image in the form of a hieroglyph or of the refined line drawing of a phonetic letter.

Such arts are liberal, therefore, because they truly free the mind by providing it with essential tools by means of which it is enabled to do its work in a superior and excellent way. One of the reasons that this is so is because, as we mentioned above, and as noted by St. Thomas, the work of the intellect precisely as such begins with the imagination. That is to say, the human intellect becomes active as an intellect only when presented by its appropriate intelligible content; and this it receives not directly from external sensible being but from the content of the human imagination. Or, to put this all in another, and perhaps simpler, way, it is impossible for any human being to comprehend anything in an appropriately intellectual way unless a person can first imagine it in the *right* way. Intellectual abstraction from the human imagination, that is, is not a static act, nor is it simply one of intellectual apprehension. Rather, it is a dynamic act involving both apprehension and judgment of the intellect in the content of the imagination; and acts which are also involved in the abstraction of imaginable content from the content of external sense apprehension and judgment. This is so true that, as Stanley L. Jaki has so meticulously documented, it is precisely because so many cultures and civilizations have been unable dynamically to imagine the physical universe in a non-cyclical and non-deterministic fashion that they have been unable to make the sort of progress in physics that has been possible by people capable of imagining the universe to be the free creation of a creator God.[13]

Intellectual conceptualization and judgment, in short, involve intellectual abstraction. Such abstraction, however, never takes place apart from a corresponding kind of imagining. Indeed, it essentially involves it. For abstraction is abstraction from something. For appropriate imagining to take place, however, a person must have a rich imagination, and such an imagination cannot be developed without rich and flexible linguistic skills as well as precise intellectual apprehension and judging skills. It is for this reason, among others, that premature specialization kills the scientific intellect—for it stunts free play of the human imagination upon which depends not only the refinement of the imagination but also the very maturity of the human intellect in the direction of scientific activity.

To develop precision in intellectual conceptualization and science and wisdom in judgment, moreover, more is needed than simple flexibility of

---

[13] Cf. Stanley L. Jaki, *Science and Creation: From Eternal Cycles to an Oscillating Universe* (Edinburgh: Scottish Academic Press, 1986).

imagination and refinement of imaginable content. Beyond these, that is, is required a freedom and ability of intellect to consider its conceptual content in a universal fashion according to its different modes of imagining and of testing truth. For while all intellectual knowing has its initial beginning in an act of abstraction from the content of the human imagination, intellectual knowledge of any sort achieves its completion in an act of judgment. Consequently, while a knowledge of the qualitative features of physical things both begins and must be completed in an intellectual act verified in external sensation, the same is not the case with respect either to a knowledge of quantitative or metaphysical modes of being. For quantity is a property which is essentially subjectified in the substance of a thing, but is not so subjectified through a dependence upon quality. Thus, while the matter of a substance acts as the subject for its surface quantity, this surface quantity, in turn, acts as the subject for its color. Consequently, St. Thomas says, the notion of a quantity devoid of qualities is something as comprehensible to the human intellect as is the notion of a quantity which is not moving, but it is impossible to think about a qualified or moving substance without simultaneously thinking about some sort of figure or quantity so qualified.[14] Hence, while all knowing begins with some sort of sense stimulus and requires that the intellect work with images, it is the image upon which the human intellect depends for the principle of its intelligibility (rather than some act of external sensation) which determines where the act of intellection achieves its maturity and locus of verification. To conceptualize quantity the human intellect has no need to work with images which cannot be framed and considered apart from the imagining of sensible qualities any more than it has to think about one color or another when conceiving of justice or of God. As a result, the truth of an intellectual judgment about quantity is in no essential need of verification in conjunction with sensible qualities; and for this reason, intellectual judgments about mathematical beings, at times, need only to be verified by reference to their being in the imagination. As St. Thomas says:

> the knowledge we have through judgment in mathematics must terminate in the imagination and not in the senses, because mathematical judgment goes beyond sensory perception. Thus the judgment about a mathematical line is not always the same as that about a sensible line. For example, that a straight line touches a sphere at only one point is true of a an abstract line but not of a straight line in matter. . . . [15]

---

[14] St. Thomas Aquinas, *Commentary on the de Trinitate of Boethius*, q. 5, a. 3, trans. Maurer.

[15] Ibid., q. 6, a. 2

The import of this reference to the nature of human intellectual abstraction is, at the very least, twofold. For the truth of what St. Thomas says means that, as Jacques Maritain well understood, the acquisition of human science is a much more complicated affair than Descartes had ever dreamed. For this reason, any attempt to reduce the whole of science to one and the same mode of abstraction, imagining and method not only is doomed to failure but it is doomed to dull both the human intellect and the human imagination. For the achievement of human science is hard work, requiring a totally different way of putting the human memory to use than the way it is commonly used in primary and secondary education—one in which the human memory helps to elevate the intellect to an entirely new, habitual, abstract and specialized way of directing its own faculties in the acquisition of knowledge—namely, through the logical ordering of greater and greater abstract, and more than abstract, ideas and judgments. For the human memory to assist the intellect in this lofty work, however, what is needed are appropriate objects to be presented to the human imagination as food for abstract thought. Such objects, however, must progressively be further and further remote from immediate apprehension by perception through the external senses. For it is through the habitual abstraction of such transcendent notions that the intellect is able both to achieve its most completely intellectual activity but also its highest quality as an intellect. In short, nothing less than the disciplines of philosophy classically conceived and revealed theology (working through the handmaidens of liberal arts and exercised after the fashion of an Augustine, an Aquinas, a Maimonides, or a Maritain) is capable either of exercising intellectual activity according to its highest form of learning or of saving contemporary higher education from plunging into the abyss which it is currently confronting.

A Humble and Trembling Movement: Creative Intuition and Maritain's Philosophy of Education

Daniel McInerny

My theme in this essay concerns what Maritain calls the *dynamics* of education: i.e., "the inner vitality of the student's mind and the activity of the teacher."[1] It was due in part to its misunderstanding of these dynamics that Maritain saw modern education at a crossroads near the mid-point of this century. The misunderstanding, however, is as old as educational theory itself. Already in Plato's *Republic* we find the basic battle lines drawn. At the end of the allegory of the cave Socrates says to Glaucon that education is not what the professions of certain men assert it to be.[2] They proclaim to put knowledge into the soul that is not already in it, as though they were putting sight into blind eyes. Socrates' argument, by contrast, claims that the power to know already exists in the soul, as sight already exists in the eye, so that the role of education is foremost a liberation of the human person from the darkness of opinion into the light of knowledge.

While Maritain's Thomism rejects the precise Platonic formulation of this idea, it nevertheless agrees that the primary function of education is to be a cultivator of nature's ends rather than a purveyor of sophistical technique. To be sure, Maritain's philosophy of education replaces the Platonic idea of ready-made knowledge in the soul with an Aristotelian view of the soul as *tabula rasa*, ready to be fecundated, in Maritain's word, by sense perception and experience. Yet for Maritain as well as for Aristotle, the *tab-*

---

[1] Jacques Maritain, *Education at the Crossroads* (New Haven, Connecticut: Yale University Press, 1952), p. 29.
[2] *Republic* VII 510bff.

ula of the soul is not so *rasa* as to exclude a vital and active natural principle of knowledge. For this reason his preferred metaphor for the art of education is medicine. Just as medicine deals with a living being that already possesses inner vitality and the internal principle of health, so the art of education deals with a living being that already possesses the internal principle of knowledge and an inner vitality which seeks the truth. Moreover, as the doctor exerts real causality by imitating nature's ways and complementing her, so too the educator looks to imitate and complement the student's natural grasp of truth.

Across the spectrum of current educational debate attention has returned to the importance of this internal vital principle of learning. Contemporary educators and theorists are now focusing on how students' emotions and intuitions bear upon the dynamics of learning. The work of Harvard psychologist Howard Gardner, for example, is prominent in this regard, as is that of his Harvard colleague Daniel Goleman, whose recent bestseller argues the importance for education of what he and Gardner call "flow."[3] "Flow" is a moment of critical mass, comparable to what the athlete calls the "zone," in which mind, emotion and body are in total, unreflective sync. The resultant ecstasy, Goleman argues, should be the primary goal of all good methods of education.

It is easy to see how such a theory can devolve in practice, especially when placed at the service of a public policy like Outcome Based Education. Outcome Based Education, with its emphasis upon how the student feels about what he is doing, has been rightly criticized by many as being too soft on maintaining substantial curricula and standards of excellence. These critics assert that without a set of recognized standards American education is surely done for, and versions of this argument are popular now both from the Left and the Right. So far as it goes, of course, a list of standards, whether it be E.D. Hirsch's proposals or the Great Books advocated by Allan Bloom, is not a bad idea for American education at all levels. Maritain himself in *Education at the Crossroads* advocates a quite substantial curriculum for schools. But familiarity with the items on such a list could never be enough in itself to comprise the goal of education. What advocates of standards continually miss is the need for educational theory to grapple with foundational questions about human nature and its *telos*.[4] In their ef-

---

[3] Daniel Goleman, *Emotional Intelligence* (New York: Bantam Books, 1995).
[4] Cf. Curtis L. Hancock, "A Return to the Crossroads: A Maritainian View of the New Educational Reformers" in Peter A. Redpath, ed., *The Cultural Vision of Jacques Maritain* (American Maritain Association, 1990).

fort to avoid giving free rein to students' desires they commit the correlative error of disengaging learning from the *order* of learning, an error which Maritain terms *intellectualism*.

And not only does the error of intellectualism disregard the ends of the educational enterprise, it also tends to give short shrift to the proper affective element in learning. However much they may be misguided by behaviorist conceptions of the human person and inclusivist views of the human good, there is a germ of truth in what our contemporaries are saying about the need for teachers to direct attention to the individuality of the student and his inclinations. Consider in this regard some of Maritain's remarks from *Education at the Crossroads*. Of his three fundamental norms of education, the second of which advises teachers to "center attention on the inner depths of personality and its preconscious spiritual dynamism, in other words, to lay stress on inwardness and the internalization of the educational influence."[5] And how does Maritain propose to accomplish this? "By moving forward along the paths of spontaneous interest and natural curiosity . . . by causing the youth to trust and give expression to those spontaneous or noetic impulses of his own which seem fragile and bizarre, because they are not assured by any social sanction. . . ."[6] One can imagine a proponent of Outcome Based Education becoming enamored with such language taken out of its context. But what is its proper context within Maritain's philosophy of education? In what follows I would like to pursue this question, *first* by discerning what Maritain understands by the preconscious spiritual dynamism and to what extent this theory lends itself to a philosophy of education; and *second*, by determining how Maritain proposes to elicit this dynamism in students. I would then like to close by discussing how Maritain's philosophy of education avoids the pitfalls of voluntarism while salvaging what is best in the intellectualist's error.

Much of what Maritain has to say about the spiritual dynamism in question can be found in his writings on art, *Creative Intuition in Art and Poetry* foremost among them. This becomes less surprising when we realize that for Maritain the effort of all education is toward a great awakening of the inner resources and creativity, on the freeing of the student's intuitive power.[7] In *Creative Intuition* Maritain even refers to this preconscious spiritual dynamism as the musical unconscious, thus appropriating for Thomism the Platonic conception of the Muse. But what does Maritain

---

[5] Maritain, *Education at the Crossroads*, p. 39.
[6] Ibid., p. 43.
[7] Ibid.

mean here by preconscious and unconscious, and what could this spiritual undertow have to do with learning, which presumably occurs "above the surface," so to speak, on the level of conception, judgment and discursive argumentation?

First, in speaking of the spiritual preconscious or unconscious we must be clear that Maritain is referring to the preconscious life of the *intellect and will*, and not to that preconscious life of the irrational in man, the field of instincts, latent images, affective impulses, and sensual tendencies with which Freud was so interested.[8] The spiritual preconscious is described by Maritain as the field of the root life of the intellect and will, "the fathomless abyss of personal freedom and of personal thirst and striving for knowledge and seeing, grasping, and expressing. . . . "[9] I would especially note in this description Maritain's emphasis on the affective moment of the spiritual preconscious: its thirsting, striving, grasping. Maritain calls this dimension of spiritual activity *preconscious* because it occurs "beneath" the level of the intellect's explicit formations of concepts and judgments as well as the will's explicit choices. The correlation between education and poetic intuition is secured by Maritain's claim that this root life of reason's power is the well-spring "of knowledge and poetry, of love and truly human desires, hidden in the spiritual darkness of the intimate vitality of the soul."[10]

Maritain is led to posit such a preconscious, as he explains in *Creative Intuition*, by drawing forth certain implications latent in the Thomistic theory of knowledge. Without rehearsing all the elements of Maritain's theory, it is necessary to clarify two of its central components: (1) what Maritain calls the hidden activity of the *intellectus agens* or illuminating intellect; and (2) Maritain's identification of the intellect's preconscious activity or "creative intuition" with Aquinas's notion of affective connaturality.[11]

Maritain develops the first of these two components by first affirming that in our fully conscious grasp of truth, what we grasp, of course, is the world through the agency of concepts. The concepts themselves are not known except via a reflective turn upon the intellect and its operations. Yet, Maritain contends, even given the performance of such a reflective turn, much of the activity of the intellect, and especially of the illuminating intellect, evades the searchlight of reflection. Still hidden in darkness is the

---

[8] Ibid., p. 40.
[9] Ibid.
[10] Ibid., p. 41.
[11] See Jacques Maritain, *Creative Intuition in Art and Poetry* (New York: Meridian Books, 1957), chapter 4, esp. p. 87; and *The Situation of Poetry*, trans. Marshall Suther (New York: Philosophical Library, 1995), pp. 64ff.

ceaseless radiation of that intellectual sun which abstracts from phantasms the intelligible species and permeates every operation of our mind. Very often, too, the very images themselves from which the intelligible species are abstracted remain hidden or scarcely perceived in the process. As Maritain writes, though we may know often enough what we are thinking, we don't know *how* we are thinking. And before being formed and expressed in concepts and judgments,

> intellectual knowledge is at first a beginning of insight, still unformu-
> lated, which proceeds from the impact of the illuminating activity of
> the intellect on the world of images and emotions and which is but a
> humble and trembling movement, yet invaluable, toward an intelligible
> content to be grasped.[12]

We should remember as well that Maritain is following Aquinas in understanding the powers of the soul as emanating from its essence in an ontological procession from that which is naturally higher to that which is naturally lower. The imagination proceeds from the essence of the soul through the more perfect power of the intellect, and the external senses proceed from the essence of the soul through the imagination. The more perfect powers thus envelop the less perfect, and serve as their principles in two ways: first, as being their end; and second, as being the source of their existence. Accordingly, we should understand the life of reason as "an immense dynamism emanating from the very center of the Soul" that terminates in the powers of the external senses, and wraps up all lower powers into its own hidden spiritual life which is "stirred and activated by the light of the Illuminating Intellect."[13] Crucial here is the fact that all the soul's powers possess a common root, the still point of their emanation, which Maritain locates in the spiritual unconscious. Consequently, the hidden preconscious life of reason involves not only reason's activities, but also our loves and desires, our imaginative activities, and our emotions.

Here again we can recognize correlations between Maritain's philosophy of art and his philosophy of education. Earlier we noted Maritain's description of education as a great awakening of the inner resources of creativity. We have now seen Maritain locate these inner resources of creativity in man's spiritual preconscious. Readers of *Creative Intuition* will recognize the spiritual preconscious as the source of that intuition which is the lifeblood of poetic knowledge. Thus a reading of *Education at the Cross-*

---

[12] Maritain, *Education at the Crossroads*, p. 41.
[13] Maritain, *Creative Intuition in Art and Poetry*, pp. 78; 79.

roads makes clear that the lifeblood of academic knowledge consists in an intuition comparable to that of the creative artist. In *The Situation of Poetry*, Maritain more explicitly makes the analogy between creative intuition and learning I have been highlighting. He says here that the end of creative intuition is the work made, the poem, the picture, or the symphony, "which plays the role of the judgment in speculative knowledge."[14] So while we understand the activities of the creative artist and the student culminating in distinct ends—the one in the creative work, the other in speculative knowing—we should also understand them as commencing with a comparable intuition.

Moreover, as with the poet, all that the student discerns and divines in things, he "discerns and divines not as something other than himself, according to the law of speculative knowledge, but, on the contrary, as inseparable from himself and from his emotion, and in truth as identified with himself."[15] The intuition so important to learning is thus not primarily the work of explicit speculative knowledge. It certainly involves the intellect, but the intellect together with our affective inclinations and the dispositions of the will, indeed, *"as guided and shaped by them."*[16]

Explicit in this comment is the second of the two main components of Maritain's account of creative intuition: its identification with the Thomistic doctrine of affective connaturality.[17] For Aquinas, this doctrine is developed within discussions of the virtues of faith and prudence, where judgment is given on the basis of an affective grasp of a certain good. In regard to faith, for instance, the affective movement is embodied in the virtue of charity. In making this point Aquinas distinguishes between two kinds of judgments: those made according to the perfect use of reason (*secundum perfectum usum rationis*), and those based upon desire's connatural union

---

[14] Jacques Maritain, *The Situation of Poetry* (New York: Philosophical Library,), p. 64.

[15] Maritain, *Creative Intuition in Art and Poetry*, p. 83.

[16] Ibid., p. 85, emphasis added.

[17] Maritain distinguishes between four types of connatural knowledge in *The Situation of Poetry*, pp. 65–67, and sharply distinguishes the affective connatural knowing of the prudent person and mystic, on the one hand, and the affective connatural knowing which is creative intuition, on the other. Of this last he writes: "I mean . . . connaturality with reality according as reality comes to be buried in subjectivity itself in its quality of intellectually productive existence, and according as it is attained in its concrete and existential consonance with the subject *as subject*. This is poetic knowledge: radically factive or operative, since, being inseparable from the productivity of the spirit . . . and being unable nevertheless to issue in a concept *ad intra*, it can only issue in a work ad extra" (pp. 66–7).

with something (*propter connaturalitatem quamdam ad ea de quibus iam est iudicandum*).[18] The second sort of judgment, the judgment according to affective connaturality, is illustrated by an example involving the virtue of prudence: the prudent person rightly judges about matters pertaining to a virtue such as chastity, even though he lack the knowledge of this virtue through the perfect operation of reason, in large part because his *habitus* of chastity provides him with the measure of right action (*sed per quandam connaturalitatem ad ipsa recte iudicat de eis ille qui habet habitum castitatis*). A chaste person, in short, may not be able to provide a rigorous definition of chaste behavior, but he can correctly discern, directed as he is by the *habitus* of chastity itself, what to do in this or that set of circumstances.[19]

The two kinds of judgment—that according to the perfect use of reason and that according to affective connaturality—are to be analogously understood, an analogy based upon the sense in which each is an *adequatio* to things. The *adequatio* proper to the perfect use of reason is, as Aquinas argues, according to the mode of the knower, while that of affective connaturality is according to the soul's conformity with the mode of the thing as it is in itself. In the speculative knowing of matter-form composites, for example, we know things in the immaterial mode proper to intellection as forms are abstracted from their particular matter. But when we love, we become the other insofar as we let our desire be shaped by the other's own "existential" mode of being.[20] In one of Maritain's favorite phrases, taken from John of St. Thomas, *amor transit in conditionem objecti*.

It is important to keep in mind, however, that in conforming to things through the affections, through desire, we are still making judgments. Most properly speaking, of course, the term "judgment" refers to the speculative grasp of the necessary attributes of things at the level of universality. And in conforming to things through our affections we are not primarily engaged in abstracting universals, but in desiring things in all their particularity. Still, there is judgment in affective connaturality insofar as the intellect conforms itself to desire, and practical *truth* insofar as there is conformity

---

[18] *Summa Theologiae* IIaIIae, q. 45, a. 2.

[19] Cf. *Summa Theologiae* Ia, q. 1, a. 6, ad 3.

[20] A good discussion of this distinction, with a collation of the relevant texts in Aquinas, is found in Russell Hittinger, "When It Is More Excellent to Love than to Know: The Other Side of Thomistic 'Realism'," *The Proceedings of the American Catholic Philosophical Association* 57 (1983): pp. 171–179.

with right desire.[21] It is because the desire of the *prudens* is connatural with what is truly good for him that his desire can serve as *mensura* for the deliberations of practical reason. Similarly in the fine arts, and especially perhaps in poetry and narrative fiction, judgments are made insofar as we incline toward one side of a contradiction on account of the pleasing aspects of the writer's art. We become convinced that "To be or not to be" is the question just so far as the images, rhythms and metaphors of Hamlet's anxious soliloquy "move" us toward that conclusion.[22]

Yet for Maritain, creative intuition is hidden, preconscious. "It is not rational knowledge, knowledge through the conceptual, logical and discursive exercise of reason. But it is really and genuinely knowledge, though obscure and perhaps incapable of giving an account of itself."[23] It is difficult to square this claim with Aquinas's treatment of affective connaturality. For in the contexts in which Aquinas discusses this notion there is always some judgment, and hence some "conceptual, logical" exercise of reason, whether the context is that of faith, prudence, or the "judgments" of poetry.[24] Such judgments may indeed be incommunicable, as the judgments of prudence sometimes are.[25] In the cases of poetry and narrative art, they will depend upon some pleasing aspect for their conviction (as there is no necessity in Hamlet's consideration of suicide). But for all that, in the judgments of affective connaturality—at least as they are understood by

---

[21] See *Summa Theologiae* IaIIae, q. 57, a. 5, ad 3; and *In VI Ethicorum*, lect. 2, n.1130. Of course, as Aquinas explains at *In X Ethicorum*, VI, lect. 2, no. 1131, right desire is not an unmeasured measure, but is in turn measured by nature.

[22] See *In I Sententiarum*, prologus, a. 5, ad 3; *Summa Theologiae*, q. 101, a. 2, ad 2; and *In Libros Posteriorum Analyticorum*, proemium. It should not be forgotten, however, that the judgment of the particular which serves as the conclusion of practical and aesthetic reasoning is derived from a universal consideration, i.e. a major premise. At *In X Ethicorum*, VI, lect. II, no. 1132, Aquinas writes: "Dicendum est ergo, quod intellectus practicus principium quidem habet in universali consideratione, et secundum hoc est idem subjecto cum speculativo, sed terminatur ejus consideratio in particulari operabili. Unde Philosophus dict in tertio de Anima [III.11 434a16ff.], quod ratio universalis non movet sine particulari. Et secundum hoc, ratiocinativum ponitur diversa pars a scientfico." Cf. *In De anima*, III, lect. XVI, nos. 845–46.

[23] Maritain, *Creative Intuition in Art and Poetry*, p. 85.

[24] In this regard, see n.42 of Benedict Ashley's introduction to this volume, as well as Ralph McInerny, "Apropos of Art and Connaturality," reprinted in *Being and Predication* (Washington, D.C.: The Catholic University of America Press, 1986).

[25] The incommunicability of some practical judgments is a theme developed by Yves R. Simon. See his *Practical Knowledge*, ed. Robert J. Mulvaney (New York: Fordham University Press, 1991), pp. 23ff.

Aquinas—it is *the intellect*, fully conscious, working with concepts, which inclines toward one side of a contradiction.[26]

None of which implies, however, that every judgment of affective connaturality must be *clear*. While it would appear best, at least with respect to the philosophy of education, to prefer Aquinas's understanding of affective judgment to Maritain's extrapolation of it in his notion of creative intuition, what we can still learn from Maritain is that our approach to the truth should begin with an affective movement, a movement which will and must take the form of a vague assent based upon some enticing feature—hopefully, if the teacher has done his job, a genuine one—of the subject matter. At this level of knowing, the object is characterized, primarily, as either the good, the beautiful, or the noble (or some combination of same), and only secondarily as true in the speculative sense. For here there is not yet fully-articulated, philosophical knowledge. Still, one has grasped truth, that is, the truth in conformity with right appetite. A student beginning his study of the *Iliad*, for example, might be struck with the nobility of Achilles long before he understands what Homer has to say of the relationships between courage, honor, and death in that poem. In being swept up by Achilles's nobility the student joins, by a quasi-prudential, quasi-aesthetic syllogistic, his natural appreciation for great deeds (a kind of major term), with the character of Achilles (a kind of minor). Reading Homer, however, is doubtless much more than this. The limitations of the Homeric code of honor, the criticisms against it mustered by Plato and Aristotle, these are discriminations which are speculative in nature and go far beyond the student's original fascination for the poem. But again, what Maritain has to teach us, at least, is that the student's original cleaving to the object of knowledge through desire, thus bringing the object into his own subjectivity in something of a practical or aesthetic judgement, is the first indispensable movement in the pursuit of truth, a movement which will no doubt have to be renewed again and again throughout his inquiry. The right analogy to the student's situation is the judgment of faith. For here, too, we incline toward an object too high for our intellect—though this one necessarily beyond our grasp—by way of a judgment reposing on love.

But to be clear: the judgment of affective connaturality is only the awakening of the student's inclination to the truth. Its aim is a further connatu-

---

[26] It is true that these judgments are all concerned with singular existents, but for Aquinas singulars are only known through the intellect's "doubling-back" to the phantasm via its concepts. See *Summa Theologiae* Ia, q. 86, a. 1, c. and ad 2; and Aristotle, *De Anima* III.11 434a16–20.

rality, a properly intellectual connaturality whereby the intellect is proportioned to reality according to the intellect's speculative mode. Both the successful achievement of the original intuition as well as the bridge to speculative knowing are due in large part to the quality of the teacher's art.

I would now like briefly to focus on this part of the teacher's task, namely, on how Maritain proposes that teachers cultivate affective connatural knowing in students. In *Education at the Crossroads*, Maritain presents his proposal by way of a dichotomy between the notions of *pressure* and *aspiration*. By pressure Maritain means those educational methods based upon an atrophied rationalism he sees as ultimately derived from the Cartesian psychology of clear and distinct ideas.[27] On the one hand, such methods exert pressure on the *intellect* insofar as they present to students freeze-dried formulas of knowledge fit for memorization and regurgitation. On the other hand, they exert pressure on the *will* either by excessive, compulsory discipline or extraneous incentives which only motivate self-interest and competition. The result of such methods, Maritain concludes, is an internal world of the student's soul left either dormant or bewildered and rebellious.[28]

The art of the teacher should rather strive to awaken the *aspirations* proper to creative intuition. No technique, however impressive in its operations, can substitute for the teacher's obligation to liberate these aspirations in his students. In *Education at the Crossroads* Maritain suggests two guidelines according to which it can successfully be done.

The first comes down to a fundamental intellectual sympathy on the part of the teacher for the questions and difficulties the student confronts.[29] The teacher must keep in mind that the student's original affective grasp of the object, while a rich germ of intellectual life, is as yet inarticulate. It is a yearning that in attempting to articulate its object in concepts and arguments will often stammer and lapse into silence. Maritain warns, in a remark that must be sobering for any teacher, that "in fact any awkward gesture or rebuff or untimely advice on the part of the teacher can crush such timid sproutings and push them back into the shell of the unconscious."[30] For this reason the teacher must be especially attentive to encouraging the student's natural impulses as he engages an object of study; the teacher

---

[27] Maritain, *Education at the Crossroads*, pp. 39ff.
[28] Ibid., pp. 39–40.
[29] Ibid., p. 43.
[30] Ibid.

must learn to listen a great deal to the student's stammerings, so that he will keep speaking until the teacher's conceptual language becomes his own.

In regard to the presentation of the object of study itself, Maritain further suggests that in order to set the student's love for the truth free the teacher must offer to the student the same kind of fruit the creative artist desires, a fruit found more in sense experience, imagination, emotion and desire than in any purely intellectual object. In this Maritain follows Aristotle's teaching in the *Poetics* that all learning begins with imitation.[31] Imitation is by definition an inclination to form oneself to something else. While such a strategy is particularly appropriate for children, it is not exclusively so. Maritain does advise that before giving a youth the rules of good style, "let us tell him first never to write anything which does not seem to him really beautiful, whatever the result may be."[32] In *Creative Intuition* he quotes with approval the following statement of Marsten Morse:

> The first essential bond between mathematics and the arts is found in the fact that discovery in mathematics is not a matter of logic. It is rather the result of mysterious powers which no one understands, and in which the unconscious recognition of beauty must play an important part. Out of an infinity of designs a mathematician chooses one pattern for beauty's sake, and pulls it down to earth, no one knows how. Afterwards the logic of words and of forms sets the pattern right.[33]

Here we see that even for the adult armed with intellectual virtue it is often his affective connaturality that serves as his guide to the truth. It is thus the duty of teachers to practice setting before their students intelligible objects under the aspect of the beautiful, the good, and the noble, which the student, like the poet, can grasp as one with himself and his desire.[34]

Having indicated now in general terms how Maritain's notion of creative intuition can play an important role in the philosophy of education, and also, in rough outline, how Maritain thinks it should be cultivated. I would like to close by underscoring the essential difference between Maritain's concern with the individual student's affective connaturality and the ersatz version of this concern so prevalent in contemporary educational theory.

---

[31] See *Poetics* 4 1448b5ff.

[32] Maritain, *Education at the Crossroads*, p. 44.

[33] Maritain, *Creative Intuition in Art and Poetry*, p. 307, n. 21.

[34] In the interpretive essay attached to his translation of Plato's *Republic*, Allan Bloom speaks of Socrates's effort to lure Glaucon and Adeimantus into a philosophical discussion of justice by a way of an exercise designed to elicit their noble instincts, namely, the founding of a city, albeit a city in speech. See *The Republic of Plato*, trans. Allan Bloom (New York: Basic Books, Inc., 1968), p. 343.

What separates Maritain from our contemporaries is the distinction he makes, a Thomistic distinction, between the *individual* and the *person*. A man is a person according to the spiritual subsistence of his intellectual soul, while he is an individual according to the non-specific properties of signate matter. Even at the time of *Education at the Crossroads* educational philosophy was rife with forms of instruction which sought to liberate the student's inner dynamism for truth by an emphasis upon his *individual* inclinations; and for Maritain, such emphasis could only result in a disordinate letting loose of those tendencies which are present in the student solely by virtue of matter and heredity.[35] Maritain claims that educators who fail to make the distinction between individuality and personality

> mistakenly believe they are providing man with the freedom of expansion and autonomy to which personality aspires while at the same time they deny the value of all discipline and asceticism, as well as the necessary striving toward self-perfection. As a result, instead of fulfilling himself, man disperses himself and disintegrates.[36]

It may be that for a teacher to inspire a given student's desire for a particular subject matter he must pay attention to one or other aspect of the student's individuality. This is simply good pedagogy. But if the attention paid to individuality devolves into a glorification of the student's material ego, teachers who engage in it must be regarded as engaged in an elaborate form of pandering, at bottom no different than that sophistical pandering which Socrates and Plato were so determined to combat.

For Maritain, the right way to liberate the inner dynamism of the student is to liberate the student's personality—his spiritual nature—from all that is selfishly individual. This liberation should not be equated with a false, despotic conception in which all sentiment, inclination and particular talent is rooted out for the sake of a standardized conception of what a human being ought to be. Rather, this liberation seeks to guide the student's natural desire for the truth out of the inarticulateness of affective knowing, and show the way toward conceptual truth. This freeing of the personality is a constant endeavor for man, involving of course a lifetime of study and action.

---

[35] Maritain, *Education at the Crossroads*, p. 34.
[36] Ibid., p. 35.

Great Books Business Education

Ernest S. Pierucci

This paper suggests that the opportunity for the synthesis of liberal and professional education urged by Maritain may already be here in a compelling way. I propose that the development of modern business activity as the application of knowledge to knowledge demands the cultivation of the natural intelligence through the kind of great books education outlined by Maritain.

Students of the forces shaping the future of business have for some time asserted that we are entering an era in which knowledge is the principle business resource. In his 1993 book *Post-Capitalist Society*, Peter Drucker, one of the most widely read and influential contemporary management theorists, provides a useful analysis of this trend. Drucker describes the phenomena that are leading to the emergence of the knowledge society and the transformation of business into essentially the application of knowledge to knowledge. In this context, Drucker addresses the kind of education the business manager will require. While I believe that he falls short of an adequate understanding of contemporary management education, he points the way to the heart of the issue.

Drucker understands knowledge as a utility that proves itself in transitive action, i.e., in results outside the person. He explicitly rejects knowledge as self-development or self-knowledge. Drucker discerns three stages of development of business, each stage caused by a shift in the meaning of knowledge.

The Industrial Revolution found its genesis in the *Encyclopedia* of the French Enlightenment, wherein traditional crafts were abstracted into methodologies, i.e., technes. These technes ultimately became disciplines, e.g. engineering, and thus, according to Drucker, a plurality of distinct and equal "knowledges."

The Productivity Revolution began in the late nineteenth century and crested during the Second World War. Its principal representative was Frederick Taylor, who reduced labor to elementary steps and thereby allowed unskilled workers to perform the tasks necessary to make the increasingly sophisticated products of modern society.

The Management Revolution is the current stage of business development. Drucker describes the Management Revolution as follows:

> The traditional "factors of production"—land (i.e. natural resources), labor and capital—have become secondary. They can be obtained and obtained easily, provided there is knowledge. And knowledge in this new sense means knowledge as utility, knowledge as a means to obtain social and economic results. . . . These developments, whether desirable or not, are responses to an irreversible change: *knowledge is now being applied to knowledge.* This is the third and perhaps the ultimate step in the transformation of knowledge. Supplying knowledge to produce this result is, in effect, what we mean by management. But knowledge is now also being applied systematically and purposefully to decide what new knowledge is needed, whether it is feasible, and what has to be done to make knowledge effective. It is being applied, in other words, to systematic innovation.[1]

Complementing this understanding is Drucker's view of the business organization. An organization is a human group composed of specialists. Its function is to make knowledges productive. However, systematic innovation requires the organization be designed to allow knowledge specialists to pursue their work as deeply and intricately as possible.

Drucker recognizes that knowledges, as utilities, are sterile in themselves. Specialists pursuing ever more detailed exploration of their particular fields cannot make knowledge productive. The productivity of knowledge requires that the various knowledges pursued within an organization be, in Drucker's term, "welded" together to produce a marketable product or service.

On this account, the management of the organization faces two critical questions. First, what must the manager know and do to bring together the work of specialists to fulfill the business organization's mission? Second, since the continuously deepening knowledge the organization needs is available only through persons, how does the manager attract, motivate and retain highly qualified, knowledgeable workers?

---

[1] Peter F. Drucker, *Post-Capitalist Society* (New York: Harper Business, 1994), p. 42.

These developments produce, according to Drucker, the critical need to reexamine what it means to be an educated person and, more specifically, the educational requirements of business managers. The definition of the educated person is the central issue in the transition from the post-capitalist society to the knowledge society.

Drucker sees higher education divided essentially in two groups. On one hand, he places the deconstructionists, post-Marxists, radical feminists, and others, who argue that there can be no such thing as a universally educated person. Drucker describes their opposition as the "Humanists" who still hold to the possibility of the universally educated person. He writes,

> The Humanist critics demand a return to the nineteenth century, to the "liberal arts," the "classics". . . . They do not, so far, repeat the assertion made by Robert Hutchins and Mortimer Adler fifty years ago at the University of Chicago that "knowledge" in its entirety consists of a hundred "Great Books." But they are in direct line of descent from the Hutchins-Adler "Return to Pre-Modernity."[2]

Drucker rejects both camps: the deconstructionists *et alia* because they have abandoned any hope for the universally educated person, the Humanists because their view of the liberal arts spurns integration with technes, the new knowledges, and because they offer only a bridge to the past, continuing to see liberal education as a social ornament.

What education is needed for the knowledge society? In order to make knowledge productive, managers must know how to relate knowledge to knowledge; therefore, management education aimed at producing simply another specialist will fail. As Drucker proposes,

> We neither need nor will get "polymaths" who are at home in the many knowledges; in fact we will probably become even more specialized. But we do need—and what will define the educated person in the knowledge society—is the ability to *understand* the various knowledges. What is each one about? What is it trying to do? What are its central concerns and theories? What major new insights has it produced? What are its important areas of ignorance, its problems, its challenges?[3]

At this point, Drucker's vision of the education of the business manager meets Maritain's understanding of the development of the natural intelligence through great books education. If Drucker is correct about the new role of knowledge in business, then I propose that Maritain's view of great

---

[2] Ibid., pp. 211–12.
[3] Ibid., p. 217.

books education is an essential and animating element of business management education. This assertion will come into focus if we look at the ways
in which Maritain's view of great books education differs from that of Mortimer J. Adler.

Adler and Maritain agree on many fundamental issues of educational
philosophy, including the central importance of the great books program.
However, Maritain's view departs from Adler's in two ways. First, Maritain
understands that the nature of the person requires liberal education to engage transitive action and business. He advocates an explicit synthesis between liberal and business education at the undergraduate level. Adler, on
the other hand, draws an absolute and unyielding line between vocational
education and liberal education. Second, while Adler asserts that undergraduate great books education should be concerned with the development
of the essential means to knowledge and nothing more, Maritain understands undergraduate great books education to be essentially concerned
with the development of the natural intelligence. This implies not only the
grasping of the means of education, but also a real, intuitive grasping of the
beauty and meaning of the disciplines. These two distinctions establish the
basis for the relevance of great books education to contemporary business
management education.

Maritain understands the unchanging mission of education to be the formation of man as man. He seeks "an integral education for an integral humanism."[4] Education should account for and unify all that is proper to the
human being. For Maritain work is proper to the human person and directed
toward freedom.[5] He advocates the subjective dimension of labor and in
this regard his understanding of labor is a precursor of that expressed in the
encyclical *On Human Work*.[6]

In *Education at the Crossroads*, Maritain called for education that over-
comes "cleavage between work or useful activity and the blossoming of
spiritual life and disinterested joy in knowledge and beauty."[7] Maritain did

[4] Jacques Maritain, *Education at the Crossroads* (New Haven, Connecticut: Yale
University Press, 1943), p. 88.

[5] Jacques Maritain, *The Education of Man*, eds. Donald and Idella Gallagher
(Notre Dame, Indiana: University of Notre Dame Press, 1962), p. 150.

[6] John Paul II, *On Human Work* (Boston: St. Paul Books & Media, 1981). Cf.
Jacques Maritain, "Convocation Address" in *Academic Convocation Commemorat-
ing the Tercentenary of the Birth of St. John Baptist de la Salle* (New York: Manhattan College, 1951), pp. 148–151.

[7] Maritain, *Education at the Crossroads*, p. 89.

not view liberal education as merely a social ornament for the leisure classes. In his address on the occasion of the tercentenary of the birth of St. John Baptist de La Salle, Maritain asserted that the synthesis of vocational and liberal education was implicit in the Christian Brothers' education of the working class poor of seventeenth and eighteenth-century France.

Adler, by contrast, is not shy about asserting the Aristotelian dichotomy between liberal and servile arts:

> I hope I step on nobody's toes too hard when I say, as I must say, that
> . . . it is an absolute misuse of school to include any vocational training
> at all.[8]

Perhaps Drucker has good reason to believe that the Hutchins-Adler line of descent turns its back on business; however, it should be clear that Maritain asserts a vital relationship between the world of business and liberal education.

Maritain does not view liberal education as simply an exercise of the mind preliminary to, and in the service of, a practical education. Any notion that a student should, for example, take two years of general requirements and then—perhaps having become more clever or having acquired useful mathematical or rhetorical skills—get on with a business major, misses the significance of "integration" and "synthesis."[9]

The integration or synthesis between liberal education and business education is shaped by Maritain's notion of the hierarchy of values. In every system of education there is a conscious or unconscious hierarchy of values that gives direction to the education process. For the Thomist, knowledge and love of what is eternal are superior to knowledge and love of what is temporal. However, an inextricable part of that principle is that whatever is eternal will "embrace and quicken" what is temporal.[10] Maritain puts the point this way:

> [I]t must be said that knowledge is contemplative in nature, and that
> education, in its final and highest achievements, tends to develop the
> contemplative capacity of the human mind. It does so neither in order
> to have the mind come to a stop in the act of knowing and contemplat-
> ing, nor in order to make knowledge and contemplation subservient to

---

[8] Mortimer J. Adler, *Reforming Education,* ed. Geraldine Van Doren (New York: MacMillan Publishing Co., Inc., 1988), p. 105.

[9] Here I rely upon Michael J. Naughton and Thomas Bausch, "The Integrity of an Undergraduate Catholic School of Management: Four Integrating Characteristics," unpublished manuscript.

[10] Maritain, *The Education of Man,* p. 53.

action, but in order that once man has reached a stage where the harmony of his inner energies has been brought to full completion, his action on the world and on the human community, and his creative power at the service of his fellow—men, may overflow from his contemplative contact with reality—both with the visible and invisible realities in the midst of which he lives and moves.[11]

Effective transitive action, work and its management, follow upon and arise from the contemplation of creation. Work is a response to reality.

This leads to Maritain's second point of departure from Adler and back to another look at Drucker's definition of the knowledge society's educated person.

In his 1941 essay "The Order of Learning," Adler argued that the great books program is the best means to achieve the ends of Catholic education. He asserted that at the undergraduate level the liberal arts of reading, listening, speaking, observing and measuring, the indispensable means to the attainment of the intellectual virtues, are all that should be taught. Represented by the great books, the subject matter becomes the means by which the student learns the arts. The great books are like bones on which the student sharpens his intellectual teeth. The books must be tough, not the predigested mush of text books. In the end, the quality of the education is measured by looking at the effect on the student's teeth, not the effect on the bone.[12]

In *Education at the Crossroads*, Maritain made a detailed analysis of the order of learning. Taking up the metaphor of the puppy (the student) chewing on a bone (the great books), he commented,

> To bring the metaphor to completion, it should be added that this large bone is a marrow bone, and that not only do the puppy's teeth have to grow sharper, but his living substance also has to feed itself on the valuable marrow. . . . The reason why college education must embrace *all liberal arts*, as required for all, is precisely the fact that it is only concerned with the comprehension thereof by the youth's *natural* intelligence, progressing in this way toward the *habitus* or virtues. . . . [E]ducation in the liberal arts is not only an education in the practical and "artistic" rules of good thinking . . . (that is to say, an attainment of indispensable *means*), it is also and mainly an education in knowledge and insight, and in a real grasping of truth and beauty (that is to say, an attainment—proportionate to the universe of thought of the youth—of

---

[11] Ibid., p. 54.
[12] Adler, *Reforming Education*, pp. 176–191.

the ends of the intellectual effort which are the various subject matters).[13]

Maritain argued that the distinction between natural intelligence and the intellectual virtues must be maintained in order to have effective undergraduate liberal education. Once the threshold of virtue is crossed, knowledge becomes necessarily particularized. Universal knowledge, the capacity to integrate knowledge and understand the relationship between disciplines, is only possible at the level of natural intelligence. The object of undergraduate education is not the possession of the intellectual virtues as such. The development of the natural intelligence allows the student to grasp the object, nature and scope, and the particular species of beauty each of the sciences and arts discloses to us.[14] Thus Drucker's definition of the educated person is met.

The development of the natural intelligence according to a firmly established hierarchy of values is essential for the formation of the human person. Maritain insisted that unity and integration are necessary to unlock the power of intuitive grasping, the genuine and living fire of the natural intelligence. This permits the student to remain the master of the material offered to him or her and to develop as a free and responsible person even in a world of hyper-specialization. Any undergraduate education that passes over the development of the natural intelligence and attempts the immediate development of particularized knowledge will produce, in Maritain's view, a "learned intellectual dwarf."[15] Neither the polymath nor the intellectual dwarf is properly equipped to pursue the application of knowledge to knowledge.

In "Thomist Views on Education," Maritain sketched the organization of an undergraduate college to fulfill the goals of liberal education in accordance with the hierarchy of values. It should be essentially concerned with the development of the natural intelligence and also allow the student to take the first steps toward the acquisition of the intellectual skills proper to the student's intended occupation. A core of liberal arts, explicitly including physics, natural sciences and mathematics, would be taught based on "the ways and methods" of the great books program.[16] In addition, "institutes of

[13] Maritain, *Education at the Crossroads*, pp. 70–71.
[14] Maritain, *The Education of Man*, p. 71.
[15] Ibid., p. 95.
[16] Ibid., pp. 73–74.

oriented humanities" would permit students to study the beginnings of their intended occupations, in vital relationship to the great books core. One of the institutes Maritain proposed is for the education of businesspersons.[17] Therefore, accounting, marketing, finance—the nuts and bolts of business—would still be taught. However, all the faculty, including the business faculty, would be primarily engaged in the development of the natural intelligence through the great books core. In this way, undergraduate business management education can develop students' natural capacity to integrate knowledge and assist them in understanding how business skills might serve that integration.

This vision of undergraduate education presents a radical challenge to American colleges. But what are the alternatives? Drucker's reliance on the rationalist and utilitarian traditions does not point the way to a resolution of the two challenges he claims management will face in the knowledge society. Those traditions have devolved into deconstruction and other forms of postmodern ideology, and thus provide no basis for the integration and synthesis of knowledge. The refusal to see knowledge as self-development presents an insidious obstruction to the attraction and retention of genuinely knowledgeable workers. If their work is not understood as self-development, then personal policies will be based on the instrumentalization of the intimate human act of knowing, and, therefore, on an ever deeper alienation of the person from work. Maritain's understanding of business education allows us to perceive the business organization as a community of persons. This opens up the possibility of the application of knowledge to knowledge in a world of hyper-specialization as well as the introduction of personnel policies based on the unified life of the worker. It also provides, for example, a basis for a comprehension of the relationship between business and the common good that moves beyond the sterile chess board of stakeholder analysis.

An examination of the role of the natural intelligence in the education of contemporary business managers should revitalize the great books program in American higher education.

---

[17] Ibid., p. 73.

Arts in Conflict

Michael W. Strasser

In 1941, after Jacques Maritain had concluded his Aquinas Lecture on the "Problem of Evil" at Marquette University, a naive youth approached the philosopher to ask him a question unrelated to his lecture. The young person introduced himself as a student of liberal arts at that university and explained that he was advised by the director of those lectures to pose his question to Maritain himself. The question was the following: how is it possible to convince one's parents, who, while intelligent, have had no more than an elementary education, that it is good to study the liberal arts?

Maritain gave the young questioner his complete attention. Then he said: "Young man, that is a very difficult question."

I submit that it has always been difficult and that it is to this very day. Why should anyone spend so much time and money in studying the liberal arts? Why should a person labor over the ancient Greek and Latin languages, English Literature, European history, mathematics and philosophy, when he desires most of all to become a physician? The answer given in all the books the young man could find on the liberal arts was that these were the subjects that made up the necessary background for all professional studies. This answer was completely unintelligible to his parents.

So let the question be posed again: What does this expression "liberal arts" mean? What is so good about them? And, in any case, who needs them?

Most college graduates would consider the first question absurd. Without hesitation, they would say something like this: English, History, Biology, Economics, and German—exactly the subjects they had studied as undergraduates. But since, at some excellent universities, many undergraduates never study half of the subjects just mentioned, the question, "What are the liberal arts?," does not appear absurd. Besides, has any teacher of liberal arts ever found a consensus among his colleagues on the answer to this question?

I. Ancient Origins: Plato and Aristotle

If we look at two great ancient Greek educators, Plato and Aristotle, we learn what education meant to them; "the liberal arts started with the Greeks, and, as so often, it was the Romans who gave them a canonized form."[1]

"The one great thing—or instead of great let us call it sufficient" thing for the citizens of a republic is "their education and nurture (*paideia* and *trophe*)," says Plato; if the city is "good in the full sense of the word it will be wise, brave, sober and just."[2] These virtues are for the soul what health is for the body.[3] Also, the guardians, or philosophical leaders of that city, will always have their eyes fixed on "the most true" (*alethestaton*) as they frame laws that are beautiful, just and good. This turning of the mind from a day whose light is darkness to the true day is in Shorey's translation a "conversion" (*peristrophe*).[4]

For Plato, the educational process, for both boys and girls, begins with music (which includes literature) and gymnastics in their simplest forms. Music will also include learning to play the lyre and cithara. Gymnastics include dancing and military exercises for both sexes. These studies should occupy the years ten to thirteen.[5]

For a select few, the above subjects should be followed by the study of arithmetic, geometry and astronomy.[6]

The last formal studies will be given to philosophy ("dialectic") for five years. The consummation of this education will be fifteen years of public service. These guardians of the republic will retire at the age of fifty, and

---

[1] B.L. Ullman, "Geometry in the Medieval Quadrivium," in *Studi di Bibliografia e di Storia: In Onore di Tammaro de Marinis*, vol. 4 (Verona, 1964), p. 263.

[2] *Republic* IV 423e–427e. Translations of the *Republic*, with some few changes, are those of Paul Shorey, reprinted in *The Collected Dialogues of Plato*, eds. Edith Hamilton and Huntington Cairns (New York: Bollingen Foundation, 1963).

[3] Ibid., 444c.

[4] Ibid., VI 484d. Cf. *Republic* vii 521c. On this topic see my article, "The Desire for God and the Love of Learning: A Sketch of Plato and Aristotle" *Florilegium*, vol. 8 (Ottawa: Carleton University, 1986), pp. 23–39; and Gustave Bardy, *La conversion au christianisme durant les premiers siècles* (Paris: Aubier, 1949).

[5] *Laws* VII 809e. Translations from the *Laws* are taken from that of A.E. Taylor, reprinted in *The Collected Dialogues of Plato*, eds. Hamilton and Cairns.

[6] Ibid., VII 817e. Cf. *Republic* VII 525a–531e.

will spend the rest of their lives "devoting the greater part of their time to the study of philosophy."[7]

For Aristotle, "there are two periods of life with reference to which education has to be divided, from seven to the age of puberty, and onwards to the age of twenty-one."[8]

Aristotle in his day spoke of education as it was actually practiced much as we might speak of it in our own day:

> That education should be regulated by law and should be an affair of state is not to be denied, but what should be the character of this public education, and how young persons should be educated, are questions which remain to be considered. As things are, there is disagreement about the subjects. For mankind are by no means agreed about the things to be taught, whether we look to virtue or to the best life. Neither is it clear whether education is more concerned with intellectual or with moral virtue. The existing practice is perplexing; no one knows on what principle we should proceed—should the useful in life, or should virtue, or should higher knowledge, be the aim of our training; all three questions have been entertained. Again, about the means there is no agreement; for different person, starting with different ideas about the nature of virtue, naturally disagree about the practice of it.[9]

The word "virtue" (*aretē*) for Plato and Aristotle always means *excellence*. However, Aristotle does indicate some of his educational preferences:

> There can be no doubt that children should be taught those useful things which are really necessary, but not all useful things; for occupations are divided into liberal and illiberal; and to young children should be imparted only such kinds of knowledge as will be useful to them without vulgarizing them. And any occupation, art, or science, which makes the body or soul or mind of the freeman less fit for the practice or exercise of virtue, is vulgar. . . . There are also some liberal arts quite proper for a freeman to acquire, but only in a certain degree, and if he attend to them too closely, in order to attain perfection in them, the same evil effects will follow . . .
>
> The customary branches of education are in number four; they are: (1) reading and writing, (2) gymnastic exercises, (3) music, to which is sometimes added (4) drawing. Of these, reading and writing and drawing are regarded as useful for the purposes of life in a variety of ways, and gymnastic exercises are thought to infuse courage.[10]

[7] *Republic* VII 532a–540b.
[8] *Politics* VII 17 1336b38–40.
[9] Ibid., VIII 2 1337a33–b4.
[10] Ibid., 1337b4–27.

The importance of moral training seems to be the same for Aristotle as it is for Plato: "We ought to have been brought up in a particular way from our very youth as Plato says[11] so as both to delight in and to be pained by the things that we ought; for this is the right education."[12]

To Aristotle, the most puzzling of these subjects is music; for he does not see it as necessary or even useful in the way that the other subjects are. "There remains, then, the use of music for intellectual enjoyment in leisure."[13] After discussing at length the various rhythms and modes of music he settles upon the Dorian as being the most temperate and therefore the most suitable for young people. "Thus it is clear that education should be based upon three principles—the mean, the possible, the becoming, these three."[14] And, as Thomas More likes to say: the mean is hard to find.

So far, we have seen nothing of mathematics in the Aristotelian curriculum. However, when we look at "that one of the mathematical sciences which is most akin to philosophy—namely astronomy,"[15] we see his appreciation for mathematics since astronomy was the highest branch of ancient mathematics, presupposing knowledge of arithmetic and geometry. Yet this must be qualified because, like optics and harmonics, astronomy is one of the more physical of the branches of mathematics.[16] Also, when Aristotle refers to astronomy as that branch of mathematics "most akin to philosophy," the word "philosophy" must here signify first philosophy, not only because this is said in his work on that subject (the *Metaphysics*), but for two other reasons as well: (1) astronomy is a branch of mathematics which itself is, for Aristotle, one of the three types of theoretical philosophy; and (2) astronomy is needed to discover how many prime movers are required to cause the eternal movement of the animated heavenly bodies.[17]

We have sketched the ideal curricula of Plato and Aristotle for two reasons. First, because the origins of important matters are intrinsically fascinating; we cannot forget the popularity of Isidore *Etymologies* or *Origins* in medieval times. But, secondly, because a principle conduit of the liberal arts to the Middle Ages was the *Marriage of Philology and Mercury* by Martianus Capella, described by his twentieth-century translator as a

---

[11] *Laws* I 635ff. Cf. *Republic* III 401e–402a.
[12] *Nicomachean Ethics* II.3 1104b9–13.
[13] *Politics* VIII.3 1338a20.
[14] Ibid., VIII.7 1342b33.
[15] *Metaphysics* XII.8 1073b4.
[16] See *Physics* II.2 194a7–12.
[17] On this point see Joseph Owens, *A History of Ancient Western Philosophy* (New York: Appleton-Century-Crofts, Inc., 1959), p. 333.

"philosopher's curriculum."[18] Why does Stahl name it that? The short answer to this question is that while present usage of the term "philosophy" is restricted to logic, philosophy of nature, metaphysics, philosophy of knowledge, ethics and political philosophy, in antiquity it also included all the branches of mathematics as well as rhetoric and literary criticism and all the sciences that investigate natural phenomena.[19]

It is important to notice that Aristotle sees reading, writing, drawing, gymnastic exercises and moral training as "useful" subjects; therefore the *distinction* of liberal and useful arts should not in practice be made a *separation*. Also, Aristotle's addition of drawing and no doubt, some of his physical studies makes a *different curriculum* from that of Plato.

Why these differences? (1) Individual people differ: Plato was a follower not only of Socrates but also of Pythagoras; Aristotle as Plato's student had probably studied mathematics at the Academy but before that he was the son of his *physician* father. (2) Also, because it is neither possible that *all* subjects could be included in a curriculum for all students (it would take too long for the students to do anything with their lives besides studying); nor would it be possible to assemble an adequate faculty since, echoing Albertus Magnus, *other sciences* of the future are still waiting to be born.

II. A Fifth-Century Tradition: Martianus Capella

We know that the most important sources of the liberal arts are those ancient Greek giants, Plato and Aristotle in the fifth and fourth centuries B.C. We also know that Varro and Vitruvius included the theory of architecture and medicine among the liberal arts in the first century B.C.; also that Martianus Capella omitted both those studies in his famous fifth-century A.D. *The Marriage of Philology and Mercury*, because they were too "mundane."[20] Nevertheless, Thomas Aquinas in the thirteenth century seems to

---

[18] *The Marriage of Philosophy and Mercury*, trans. William Harris Stahl in *Martianus Capella and the Seven Liberal Arts* (New York: Columbia University Press, 1971), p. 91.

[19] Owens, *A History of Ancient Western Philosophy*, p. vi.

[20] "Since these ladies (Medicine and Architecture) are concerned with mortal subjects and their skill lies in mundane matters, and they have nothing in common with the celestial deities, it will not be inappropriate to disdain and reject them." *Martianus Capella and the Seven Liberal Arts*, vol. 2, *The Marriage of Philosophy and Mercury*, trans. William Harris Stahl and Richard Johnson with E.L. Burge (New York: Columbia University, 197), p. 346. Hereafter this work will be referred to as *Martianus*.

consider them as possible candidates for re-admission to the list of liberal arts since each of them is a kind of wisdom in its own field.[21]

For Martianus, Mercury symbolized eloquence and Philology learning; the former represented persuasive speech; the latter the trivium (grammar, logic and rhetoric) and the quadrivium (arithmetic, geometry, music and astronomy). Together, writes W.H. Stahl, these subjects "constituted the only academic curriculum familiar to the Roman world."[22]

A brief description of Martianus's work, "one of the most popular books of Western Europe for nearly a thousand years,"[23] may be useful. We omit the first two books on the betrothal and marriage of the principles.

"Grammar" in antiquity always included the study of literature.[24] However, the chapter of Martianus devoted to this subject is unremarkable. It is doubtful that anyone teaching Latin grammar today would find it useful.

Martianus's treatment of "Dialectic" is substantially the formal logic of Aristotle's *Prior Analytics*. In writing his "Rhetoric," Martianus borrows from a variety of ancient sources but most of all from Cicero's *De Inventione*.[25] In any case, it is to the contemporary reader the most interesting and charming part of the entire work.

We should also notice that there is in antiquity no Latin version of the geometry in Euclid's *Elements*; that work does not appear until it is translated from Arabic into Latin in the twelfth century by Adelard of Bath.[26]

What is it then that Martianus calls "geometry?" Stahl describes it as a "mathematical geography."[27] For the most part, it gives the measurements of various places in the then-known world and their distances from each other; in short, it is the work of Roman surveyors (*agrimensores*).

The second book in Martianus' account of the quadrivium is on "Arithmetic." The first dozen pages are devoted to "arithmology" or "numerology" or number symbolism. This part of his treatment seems to derive from the *Introduction to Arithmetic* of Nicomachus of Gerasa (about 100 A.D.); it is thought to have originated with the early Pythagoreans and to have lasted until the late Middle Ages.[28] As the translator rightly says, this "be-

---

[21] *Summa Theologiae* IIaIIae, q. 45, a. 1.

[22] *Martianus*, vol. 1, p. 25.

[23] Ibid., p. 21.

[24] Ibid., p. 100.

[25] Ibid., p. 118.

[26] See Ullman, "Geometry in the Medieval Qudarivium," pp. 264; 273.

[27] *Martianus*, vol.1, p. 46.

[28] Ibid., p. 44.

comes for us tedious reading."[29] The other ultimate source is Euclid's *Elements*. The balance of the work is confined to the ratios of odd and even numbers by way of addition, subtraction, multiplication and division, though he also discusses prime and incomposite numbers. At this point the translator says: "Readers may wish to skip over the remainder of Martianus' account which makes dull reading."[30] He could have said this as a footnote to the first sentence of this entire "arithmetic."

Book viii on "Astronomy" is less daunting than the contemporary non-historian might have thought. Granted, many constellations and signs of the zodiac appear strange to him. Even more strange to the twentieth-century reader is the geocentric view of the universe; yet, there is one exception to this. Martianus reports that Venus and Mercury do no travel about the earth; they encircle the sun. Copernicus himself is said to have been impressed with this; but, Stahl says, other popular handbooks had already made this statement.[31] Most surprising is Stahl's judgment that "Astronomy makes the best presentation of the quadrivium bridesmaids, perhaps of all the seven bridesmaids."[32]

Strangest of all, "music," or "harmony" in Stahl's translation, has nothing to do with learning to sing or to play an instrument. After his first dozen pages of introduction, Martianus describes the mathematics of music; it is similar to the first five books of Augustine's *De Musica*, written about the same time as Martianus's *Marriage of Philology and Mercury*. No doubt it is intelligible to any musicologist who has specialized in early medieval music. But for the present purpose, its most notable contribution is Martianus' description of the liberal arts in his last paragraph as "encyclopedic arts."[33]

Few if any historians of the Middle Ages praise the work of Martianus. At best, they say nothing about him apart from giving his name and a bibliography for him.[34]

Any person today who has taught three or four of Martianus' liberal arts, e.g. Latin grammar, Aristotelian formal logic, or high school mathematics and science must be grateful to the successors of Martianus who have de-

---

[29] Ibid., p. 152.

[30] Ibid., p. 164.

[31] Ibid., vol.2, p. 333.

[32] Ibid., vol.1, p. 201.

[33] Ibid., vol.2, p. 381.

[34] See Etienne Gilson, *A History of Christian Philosophy in the Middle Ages* (New York: Random House, 1955), pp. 95; 601–602.

veloped the liberal arts so far beyond their condition in the fifth century A.D. Even Christopher Dawson refers to the fifth century as a "dark age."[35]

However, to say anything more about the history of any of Martianus's seven liberal arts would be rash since today those very histories have become specialties of numerous scholars over and above those who practice these arts or sciences themselves. For example, when working on the history of Archimedes we consult the works of Marshall Clagett; in medieval science we look to Pearl Kibre and Charles Homer Haskins; for Copernicus and Kepler we return to A. Wolf and Alexander Koyre; for Galileo, Stillman Drake and William Wallace; for the entire history of science, Pierre Duhem, A.C. Crombie and George Sarton. None of these historians is considered to be a scientist; they are thought of as humanists. We have already sampled two such historians, Stahl and Ullman, in their accounts of the devolution of the liberal arts.

III. Modern Reflections: Jacques Maritain

Jacques Maritain taught so many human beings in the twentieth century that it is appropriate to conclude our discussion with a few words about him. Besides, Thomas Aquinas, Maritain's main source, lived centuries before Copernicus and therefore could say little about the sciences which were to be pursued during the "scientific revolution" of the seventeenth century; but we today cannot ignore them. We cannot even imagine a curriculum of liberal arts that does not include some of them, e.g., biology, chemistry, physics and at least one branch of higher mathematics which is for modern scientists the indispensable instrument with which they daily practice their science.

We must also applaud Maritain's suggestion that we include the *history* of science in our liberal arts curriculum. Such a history is like the work of the ancient Thucydides or the modern Etienne Gilson; that is, it is not science in the modern sense of that term. Hence Marshall Clagett, the historian of Archimedes, works in the "Institute for Research in the *Humanities*" at the University of Wisconsin. On the contrary, our modern sciences concentrate on that spectrum of facts which are the latest to be discovered in their field; that is, a modern scientist, *as a scientist*, does not seem to need history. At the same time, those students who do not plan on becoming scientists will find the *history* of a science to be something they can under-

---

[35] "St. Augustine and His Age" in T.F.B., ed. *A Monument to Saint Augustine*, (London: Sheed & Ward, 1945), p. 32.

stand; in this way, it becomes an approach to what, taken in itself, might be simply beyond their native talent.[36]

Secondly, Maritain thinks that we today should not require "dead" languages of all our undergraduates in liberal arts programs. How many of them will ever use sufficient Hebrew, Greek or Latin after they leave their formal schooling? All one has to do is look around at one's larger family to know that the majority of them have not had the time for such things, nor will they, nor need they. As Maritain puts it, those who go on to graduate studies in literature, philosophy or history can learn these things as needed.[37] This was already apparent to John Locke in the eighteenth century; Locke was educated as a physician, a Christian, and one who had learned enough Greek to teach it at Oxford University. But he also tutored enough young men to learn what was necessary and what was not. John Locke may have been the most commonsensical of all the British Empiricists.

Thirdly, Maritain, who had read authors from the ancient Aristotle to the modern Emile Zola, reminds us that in teaching young people in an introductory curriculum of liberal arts we should not require *too many authors*. More important than a large number of such writers is the student's being led to *savor* the beauty and the truth of *some* of them. This takes much reading and re-reading. But, joy in the truth and beauty of such teachers is the one incentive that will draw young people to move themselves to further study. Especially for children who have for one reason or another acquired a distaste for learning, the delight in coming to know can lead them to study for the sheer love of seeing with their minds throughout their lives.[38]

Without this *disinterestedness* in knowing what we ought to know[39], we cannot appreciate the great-souled energy of mind in Socrates of Athens. Aristotle never met Plato's Socrates in person; but he did know from Plato himself the kind of man that Socrates was. Aristotle devotes all of Book iv, chapter 3 of the *Nicomachean Ethics* to what must be a portrait of the man who was Plato's spiritual father. Aristotle is discussing the virtues concerned with honor; the first virtue he mentions is, in Greek, *megalopsychia*. W.D. Ross translates this word as "pride;" M. Ostwald and H.G. Apostle

---

[36] See Jacques Maritain, *The Education of Man*, eds. Donald and Idella Gallagher (New York: Doubleday and Co., Inc., 1962), pp. 18; 71.

[37] Jacques Maritain, *Education at the Crossroads* (New Haven, Connecticut: Yale University Press, 1943), p. 69; and *The Education of Man*, p. 90.

[38] Maritain, *The Education of Man*, pp. 72–79.

[39] Ibid., p. 47.

translate it as "high-mindedness;" only H. Rackham expresses it as "great-ness-of-soul" which is an exact, literal translation of Aristotle.[40] To see how closely Aristotle's view of moral virtue is to the Socratic identification of virtue and knowledge, read Aristotle: "A good man (they think)[41], since he lives with his mind fixed on what is noble, will submit to argument, while a bad man, whose desire is for pleasure, is corrected by pain like a beast of burden."[42]

The liberal arts may be seeing the morning of a new day. Some presidents of community colleges are now proposing them for everyone.[43] What is more, this American dream is now being dreamed by the people of Russia also and those of Nigeria and those of England. Just a few years ago Donald and Idella Gallagher said this was not *utopian*. Indeed it is not, if the word is translated as "no-where."[44] But the liberal arts are utopian if they are understood to mean good-place, reasonable-place, happy-place. Thomas More knew a good pun when he saw one. *That is the point.* Liberal arts are not needed for our survival. They are needed for our *well-being.*

Also, they are needed for our survival if "survival" means our survival as a democracy; as Maritain translates that name of which we are so proud, "government of the people, by the people and for the people."[45] Yet, if our pollsters could return to Athens as it was in 399 B.C. to ask men and women on the street what they thought of this question, just about as many might vote for universal access to a college education as against it. After all, Socrates himself was surprised at the large number of people voting for his release at the same time that a majority voted for his condemnation. As Maritain puts it: democracy "demands primarily liberal education for all." Why? Because the "common man" must "be capable of judgment about the good of the people."[46]

But why is that enrichment of the mind, known as a liberal education, still so rare? One of Maritain's students may have answered that question when he said: "education is really the divine schooling of human existence."[47] This reminds us of the fact that we learn from a teacher by listen-

---

[40] See *Nicomachean Ethics* IV.3 1123a4–1125a35.
[41] Cf. *Laws* IV 722dff.
[42] *Nicomachean Ethics* X.9 1180a9–11.
[43] See *Pittsburgh Post-Gazette*, 21 March 1995, section B, p. 2.
[44] Maritain, *The Education of Man*, p. 147.
[45] Maritain, *Education at the Crossroads*, pp. 19–20.
[46] Ibid.
[47] Anton C. Pegis, "St. Thomas Aquinas," in Lee C. Deighton, ed.-in-chief, *Encyclopedia of Education*, vol. 1 (New York: Macmillan Publishing Co., Inc., 1971), pp. 250–257.

ing to him *only when we want to*: that is to say, we believe for the sake of knowing[48]—but no one can make us believe if we do not choose to.

Education is at a crossroad in every generation. Why? Because *knowledge is a personal possession*. This means that unless one has it in himself, or as a part of himself, such a person literally does not know what he is missing. This is the way it is with all spiritual things; they are *known* in the full sense of that word only when received.[49] They are invisible; or, they are visible only from within to the person who has one.

Consequently, the endless debates of the 1960's between the presidents of universities, deans of liberal arts and sciences, the members of the faculties of such colleges and their students. What had been taken for granted for so many years was now called into question. The question of the liberal arts was not only difficult to answer, it was *impossible to demonstrate* the value of such disciplines to anyone who did not already possess at least one of them.

The incommunicability of prudence is clear enough for it is a kind of wisdom. But that this is also true of all the other intellectual virtues is not obvious. No doubt the arts and sciences can be taught; after all they are being taught every day around the world. What we are saying is *they are teachable but not otherwise communicable*. Apparently, teaching is an extraordinary kind of communication.

Most mysterious of all is the fact known to such towers of wisdom as Archimedes and Ignatius of Loyola, but, it seems, to few others: that the only way to prove to oneself or to another that one knows a subject is *actually to teach it to someone else*. That is why in the thirteenth century A.D., and apparently not much longer than that, a university degree was granted only to those students who, having done their formal studies, were recognized now to teach them to beginners under the strict supervision of senior professors. This was simply an extension of the practice followed by earlier guilds (or trade-unions) of carpenters and physicians.[50]

[48] Maritain, *Education at the Crossroads*, p. 26. See also St. Augustine, *De Magistro*. XI.38.

[49] St. Thomas Aquinas, *Commentary on the Gospel of St. John*, chap. 4, lesson 2, trans. J.A. Weisheipl and F.R. Larcher (Albany, New York: Magi Books, 1980).

[50] A recent report on this medieval seriousness regarding the reciprocity of learning and teaching is in "Saint Thomas Aquinas and Education" in Torsten Husen and T. Nevil Postlethwaite, eds.-in-chief, *The International Encyclopedia of Education*, 2nd edition, vol. 9 (New York: Pergamon, 1994), p. 1523. A longer account of the social and inseparable connection of learning and teaching is in my "Educational Philosophy of the First Universities," in Douglas Radcliff-Umstead, ed., *The University World* (Pittsburgh, Pennsylvania: University of Pittsburgh Press, 1972), pp. 1–23.

What are the results of our investigation? All human beings need the liberal arts because they are liberating arts. They deliver us from *ignorance*, from prejudice and from pure self-interest.[51]

Also, as John Dewey puts it, a well-rounded education shows a person access to a virtual infinity of occupational options. And for Maritain, every citizen in a democracy needs what Martianus called the "encyclopedic arts" because every citizen must be prepared to make good judgments about the welfare of all, the *common good*. For Aquinas, it seems that everyone needs the "speculative arts" simply because they are perfections of human nature. They mold or shape us *as humans*. Is it possible that every man could benefit from a "philosopher's curriculum"?

It is not only possible. It may even be actual. Does not every parent— and of course we only mean those worthy of the name—wish to leave good things for their children? And is not education and nurture "the one, great, sufficient thing" as Plato said? Plato even calls a counselor of young people a "foster father."[52] A liberal education may be mankind's *patrimony* to its youth.

What good is conflict over the continuance of the liberal arts tradition? Like the imminence of death, conflict marvelously concentrates the mind. Also, like "the good fight" of which Paul speaks, it can be the "moral equivalent of war" that William James dreamt of. Finally, if we make war only so that we may have peace, as Aristotle puts it, then all of us must relish such a conflict. Long live the liberal arts!

[51] See Plato, *Republic* VII 486a.
[52] *Laws* VII 809b.

The Freshmen Seminar:
A History of the Western University

Walter Raubicheck

I would like to discuss a new approach to the freshman year curriculum which would feature a course in the history of the Western university, a course which could also be combined with a Great Books program for our most academically prepared students. I would also like to demonstrate how Maritain's ideas about education have helped me to conceptualize such a course.

The Freshman Year Experience is a popular term today for programs of advisement, orientation and academic support directed at the incoming freshman. Such programs have developed rapidly over the last ten or fifteen years as enrollments have declined and statistics show that the highest drop-out rate occurs during and immediately after the freshman year. Nationally about one in every four students who enters a college or university will not return to that institution the next Fall. As a result, the Freshman Year Experience has become an important field of research and academic innovation as our colleges and universities strive to retain the students they have admitted. Although academic preparedness certainly plays a role in a freshman student's success or failure, many other factors are involved, including financial concerns, clarity about personal and career goals, alienation from the new and unfamiliar environment of the world of higher education, etc. Gone are the days when at orientation an administrator could proudly direct each student to look at the persons sitting to his right and left and then announce that one of them would not be back next year. Now we are trying to support each student as he or she comes to our campuses for his or her first and probably most difficult year of higher education.

One of the most recent developments in first-year programming is the University 101 course, a freshman seminar that assists students in making the difficult transition from high school to college. Topics covered in such a course include study skills, test taking skills, time management skills, stress management skills, as well as issues such as diversity, interpersonal relationships, and major and career choice. Such courses—which usually run for one semester, which in some schools are required but which in others are optional, and which often, but not always, carry academic credit—have successfully increased both the freshman-sophomore retention rate as well as enhanced the academic performance of students at many colleges and universities. Advisement is thus provided to these students through the organized, efficient method of a course.

Many University 101 courses are unified by certain themes, such as identity formation and goals clarification. The theme that has always appealed to me the most is the history of the university concept. Some colleges do use it as one of the components of the University 101 course. For example, California State University begins its University 101 reader with an essay by Robert O. Bucholz entitled "Be True to Your Medieval University Tradition" which is a breezy but informative look at student life and the typical curriculum of the medieval university and which makes comparisons to its modern counterpart. Here is a sampling of the essay's approach:

> Aristotle presented medieval European scholars with a new way of looking at the world, one which emphasized reason and observation over faith. This methodology—and all of the new information which it was to bring—would have to be reconciled with the old Biblical world-view. The medieval response to this challenge was to invent the university. In our own day, the computer revolution promises a similar knowledge explosion. We, too, will have to get used to new ways of acquiring, storing, and retrieving unprecedented amounts of information—if we are to reconcile it with what we already know.[1]

The reader also contains essays on the history of academic freedom and tenure, free speech in the university, stress management, etc.

The course I have in mind would begin with a study of the rise of the medieval universities in Europe in order to investigate the meaning and history of higher education as well as more specific topics such as the origin of the various degrees and rituals (wearing of gowns, commencement, etc.) and the relationship of the university to society (town/gown issues). Then

[1] Robert O. Burcholz, "Be True to your Medieval University Tradition," in Sharon L. Olson, ed., *The University in Your Future*, Long Beach, California: California State University Press, 1994), p. 12.

the history of the university in the United States would be studied: the original religion-affiliated institutions, Jefferson's innovations at the University of Virginia, the land-grant and other state universities, and the modern college and university. The student will then be able to locate his/her particular college or university in its historical and cultural context and clarify how the goals and values of his/her school relate to the tradition of the Western university. Once this identification is accomplished—or while it is being accomplished—students will be introduced to the usual University 101 type information and advisement, but now from a richer perspective. Such an approach also insures academic validity for the course.

For example, students would be able to see the pedagogical relationship between the core curriculum that they are beginning to follow in their freshman year and the medieval trivium and quadrivium that prepared students for advanced study in medicine, law, or theology. They would also learn the origin and meaning of the various degrees—bachelor's, master's, doctorate—and thus understand how they as students relate to their medieval counterparts. For first generation college students in particular such an awareness can be particularly beneficial and inspiring. And depending on whether their institution is private or public, religious or secular, a study of the history of the university will demonstrate to freshmen the essential similarities and differences between the mission of their institution and that of the surrounding colleges and universities in any part of the country. Hopefully a real comprehension of the school's mission will help each student to clarify his/her own mission as a student and as an adult.

To be sure, a course such as this one is susceptible to attack for a Western and patriarchal bias. I will suggest that in the history of the university course that I have in mind the entrance of women into higher education in the late nineteenth and early twentieth centuries should be a strong focus of the latter part of the course, as well as the developments in our own century that have caused women to become the majority of today's undergraduate population.

All high school graduates, even if their SAT scores and high school averages are impressive, usually find the freshman year to be the most challenging on personal, social and academic levels. Learning better test-taking and note-taking skills, as well as managing time more effectively, can be a tremendous advantage for many honors students who needed to do little work in high school to succeed but are having difficulty navigating the collegiate waters with the same facility. And such students, as much as any others, need to develop interpersonal skills and clarify personal goals. Certainly all University 101 courses try to integrate students into the university community in all its social and cultural dimensions. However, as a former University 101 administrator and teacher, I have come to understand that the more academically-prepared students need to attain these transitional skills in a theoretical context that complements the "case study" and "active learner" approach of most freshman seminars. Otherwise they tend to reject the course or treat it as an unnecessary burden, thereby losing its potentially vital effects.

It seems to me that students who are highly qualified when they enter college would benefit the most from a course that combines the history of the university component with the traditional Great Books course that has long been established at Columbia, St. John's College, the University of Chicago, and other institutions. As Maritain says, studying the classic texts "feeds the mind with the sense and knowledge of natural virtues, of honor and pity, of the dignity of man and of the spirit, the greatness of human destiny, the entanglements of good and evil, the *caritas humani generis* Such reading, more than any course in natural ethics, conveys to the youth the moral experience of mankind."[2] In combining these two approaches to the freshman seminar, we can connect the great thinkers of the Western world to the rise and development of the university itself. For example, studying Plato and Aristotle in the context of the Academy and the Lyceum would reveal to our students the social and historical background of Greek philosophy without relativizing the truths contained in the texts themselves. Plotinus can be better appreciated as a teacher and thinker when he is seen against the background of the intellectual ferment at the schools in Alexandria. Studying the great Scholastics such as Aquinas and Bonaventure will be even more rewarding when a student understands the positions of these thinkers at the University of Paris, and the way the University of Paris related to the other new European universities and to the church and the state. Students will be able to see not only how they developed out of monastic schools, but how a center of learning such as the University of Paris, in Josef Pieper's words, "touted itself as a new Athens." Pieper's feeling is that this continuity—from Plato to Thomas Aquinas, let us say—is not an unhistorical construction, and that the notion of the *translatio studii*, the transplantation of the Platonic Academy to the city of the paradigmatic university, is not a mere fiction."[3]

[2] Jacques Maritain, *Education at the Crossroads* (New Haven, Connecticut: Yale University Press, 1943), p. 69.
[3] Josef Pieper, *Guide to Thomas Aquinas* (Notre Dame, Indiana: University of Notre Dame Press, 1962), p. 63.

In other words, the development of Western thought will be taught in the context of how that thought was transmitted from one generation to the next, and of the institutions of learning that were created to facilitate that transition, just as our students are learning about their own institution and are being introduced to the great ideas through the faculty of that institution. A year-long course such as this one is an excellent way to help our students begin a true education, the kind that Maritain defines as "[guiding] man in the evolving dynamism through which he shapes himself as a human person—armed with knowledge, strength of judgment, and moral virtues—while at the same time conveying to him the spiritual heritage of the nation and the civilization in which he is involved, and preserving in this way the century-old achievements of generations."[4]

Moral virtues, of course, are controversial in the contemporary atmosphere of relativism. However, even in our secular colleges and universities, the usual list of the objectives of the core course experience or the institution's mission statement includes an ethical dimension, even though our course catalogues are usually rather vague in explaining precisely how such an ethical education will take place. This vagueness has contributed to the "Can Ethics Be Taught?" debate. The lack of interdisciplinary and/or cross-disciplinary approaches is an obstacle here: how can moral development take place when the ideas and information learned in introductory psychology and sociology courses, for example, are presented by faculty who are jealously guarding the primacy of their disciplines? I have always believed that the freshman seminar is an excellent site for such ethical discussion and for revealing the connections among the disciplines.

Maritain has been particularly helpful to me in thinking about the ethical dimensions of such a course. He insists that direct education of the will should occur in other educational spheres (i.e., the Church) or in extra-educational spheres. What the college and university can do is exert indirect action on the will by "keeping sight, above all, of the development and uprightness of speculative and practical reason. School and college education has indeed its own world, which essentially consists of the dignity and achievements of knowledge and intellect, that is, of the human being's root faculty. And of this world itself that knowledge which is wisdom is the ultimate goal."[5]

[4] Maritain, *Education at the Crossroads*, p. 10.
[5] Ibid., p. 28.

Thus the knowledge of the great books, seen as storehouses of speculative and practical wisdom, will produce the intellectual basis for the development of character. And indeed, despite the typical obsession with political correctness of many University 101 courses—ethical development sometimes seems to be equated with appreciation of ethnic and racial diversity—it remains true that most University 101 programs are concerned with practical problems of moral choice faced by most college freshmen, choices involving sex, academic integrity, drugs and alcohol, etc. By studying Plato and Shakespeare, and then discussing moral choice in the context of these great writers, students will gain the intellectual grounding they need to inform their own wills as they move from late adolescence into young adulthood. The goal of such a University 101 course would thus be to introduce freshmen to the world of the college or university in such a way that the practical problems of the transition from high school to college can be addressed from the perspective of "the best that has ben known and thought" as Matthew Arnold put it, and in the context of the great tradition of the Western university.

What would such a course look like? In the first semester students would read about Socrates, Plato, and the establishment of the Academy, as well as study an early dialogue such as the *Crito* and a later one such as the *Republic*. This would be followed by an examination of the Lyceum and a reading of Aristotle's *Nicomachean Ethics*. Students would thus learn about the Socratic method, exactly who were the followers of Socrates and who were the followers of the Sophists, and which class of young men actually studied at the schools in Athens, at the same time that the major ideas of Plato and Aristotle would be compared and contrasted. Then the Socratic method can be looked at as a method of teaching in the twentieth century classroom; the role of the philosopher in Plato's ideal republic can be discussed in its relation to the meaning of the word "philosopher" in our own culture and institutions of higher learning; and Aristotle's discussion of the moral and intellectual virtues can be applied to both the content of the student's college curriculum and his or her own decisions that will have to be made regarding social relationships, responsible sexual decisions, and the dangers of substance abuse. This pattern of studying the institution and the ideas promulgated there that were directly related to classic texts would continue through the medieval and modern universities. For American students a particularly interesting topic would be the intellectual connection between Jefferson's republican idealism as reflected in the Declaration of Independence and the mission of the University of Virginia.

Ultimately, I hope that this interdisciplinary freshman course will open up the world of knowledge and virtue to our incoming students in a way that is both traditional and innovative, demanding and inspiring. My highest expectations would be that either of the two courses I have described here—the freshman seminar based on the history of the University and a more advanced version that is combined with the Great Books—will fulfill Maritain's prescription that education should provide a student with "the foundations of real wisdom, and with a universal and articulate comprehension of human achievements in science and culture, before he enters upon the definite and limited tasks of adult life in the civil community, and even while he is preparing himself for these tasks through a specialized, technical, or vocational training."[6] For much of Western history the foundations of real wisdom, the direct training of the intellect with an indirect influence on the will, have been laid in the universities, and these Freshman seminars will show our students how this process has continued into our own time, and, hopefully, how he or she can become an active part of the process.

[6] Ibid., p. 48.

Education for Politics:
Knowing, Responsibility, and Cultural Development

Henk E.S. Woldring

Introduction: Political Culture

The matter which I want to discuss is political responsibility regarding cultural development, a subject which is part of the study of "political culture." The concept of "political culture" stands for ideas citizens have about what ought to happen in a political system (according to norms and values), what probably will happen (expectations), what is desirable and worth striving for (interests and goals), and fundamental views on political phenomena (worldviews). Empirical research about the ideas citizens have on these questions is the task of political scientists. However, the fundamental worldview orientations of people are philosophically most interesting, and these will be my topic in what follows.

Almond and Verba distinguish three kinds of fundamental orientations: a) "cognitive orientation," that is, knowledge of and belief about political phenomena; b) "affective orientation," or feelings about these phenomena; and c) "evaluative orientation," judgments and opinions about these phenomena.[1] In short, we can summarize these orientations in three questions: *What* political phenomena does a person discuss? *Why* does a person like or dislike certain phenomena? *How* does she/he judge certain political phenomena.

The political phenomenon I shall discuss is the responsibility of the state for cultural development. I shall compare the philosophical theories of the Thomist philosopher Jacques Maritain (1882–1973) and the Calvinist

---

[1] G.A. Almond and S. Verba, *The Civic Culture: Political Attitudes and Democracy in Five Nations* (Princeton, New Jersey: Princeton University Press, 1963), p. 15.

philosopher Herman Dooyeweerd (1894–1977) on this subject. My central question is: "What cognitive, affective and evaluative orientations do Maritain and Dooyeweerd have concerning the responsibility of the state in relation to cultural development?" *First*, I shall discuss Maritain's philosophy of political society in relationship to the state and his theory of "degeneration and revitalization" in cultural development. *Second*, I shall discuss Dooyeweerd's philosophy of the state in relationship to the political society, and his theory of "differentiation and integration" in cultural development. *Third*, I shall compare their "cognitive," "affective" and "evaluative orientations."

The Political Society and the State

In our time the concepts "state" and "political society" are often used synonymously. However, Maritain made a distinction between these two, and considered the state as a part of political society. In Maritain's view the political society is by its nature the most perfect society (*"societas perfecta"*).[2] He argues that political society should promote the "common good" of the entire nation, in which everyone has the economic right to labor and property, and also possesses civic and political rights, and cultural participatory rights.[3] As such the "common good" is the most general goal of political society. Therefore, the "common good" as a general goal should not be confused with concrete goals of the government's policy in, for example, the fields of education, social security, or public health care. The "common good" is also a normative idea by which the effects of government's policy can be judged.[4] As a general goal and as a normative idea the "common good" refers to what is "common *to the whole and the parts.*"[5] According to Maritain, this last phrase presupposes a just distribu-

---

[2] Jacques Maritain, *Man and the State* (Chicago: The University of Chicago Press, 1951), p. 10.

[3] Ibid., p. 54.

[4] T.R. Rourke and C.E. Cochran, "The Common Good and Economic Justice: Reflections on the Thought of Yves R. Simon," *The Review of Politics* 54 (1991): pp. 231–252; and Ralph McInerny, *Art and Prudence: Studies in the Thought of Jacques Maritain* (Notre Dame, Indiana: University of Notre Dame Press, 1988), pp. 87–91.

[5] Jacques Maritain, *Christianity and Democracy and The Rights of Man and Natural Law*, with an introduction by Donald Gallagher (San Francisco: Ignatius Press, 1986), p. 94. Cf. C.P. O'Donnell, "Maritain and the Future of Democratic Authority" in Peter Redpath, ed., *From Twilight to Dawn: The Cultural Vision of Jacques Maritain* (Notre Dame, Indiana: American Maritain Association/University of Notre Dame Press, 1990), pp. 74–76; and Yves R. Simon, *The Tradition of Natural Law* (New York: Fordham University Press, 1992), p. 90, and *A General Theory of Authority* (Notre Dame, Indiana: University of Notre Dame Press, 1980), pp. 28–29.

tion of material and immaterial goods that can be achieved by justice. Therefore, Maritain uses "justice" and the "common good" as equivalents. In any case, the "common good" is not the sum of "particular goods," as liberals often argue, nor the interest of the community to which citizens are subordinated, but a normative idea: "integrity of life, the good and righteous human life of the multitude."[6]

According to Maritain, political society is a superior unity that comprises families and other social institutions, a unity that gives the greatest possible autonomy to these institutions. In this context "autonomy" means that every social institution governs itself, and carries out its duties according to its own competency and responsibility. As such, the true political society is characterized by a social pluralism in which all social institutions contribute to the vitality of political society.[7]

The State as an Instrument

As a part of political society, the state has, in particular, the task of maintaining laws, of promoting public order and public interest. As such, the state is the totality of institutions which can wield power and force, and which at the same time serves the interests of citizens. In view of these particular tasks, Maritain characterized the state as a superior part of political society: superior, that is, in relationship to other parts of political society.[8] However, in this hierarchical social order the state should acknowledge the autonomy of other social institutions, though it can, if it is in the public interest, provide assistance subsidiarily if these "lower" social institutions cannot achieve their tasks.[9]

The state possesses political authority but it does not have this authority of its own right. The state has this authority by virtue of the political soci-

---

[6] Ibid., pp. 95–96.

[7] Maritain, *Man and the State*, pp. 9–12. Cf. Yves R. Simon, *Philosophy of Democratic Government* (Notre Dame, Indiana: University of Notre Dame Press, 1993), p. 15; *A General Theory of Authority*, pp. 137–139; and David T. Koyzis, Yves R. Simon's Contribution to A Structural Political Pluralism" in Michael D. Torre, ed., *Freedom in the Modern World: Jacques Maritain, Yves R. Simon, Mortimer J. Adler* (Notre Dame, Indiana: American Maritain Association/University of Notre Dame Press, 1989), pp. 138–139.

[8] Ibid., pp. 12–13.

[9] Cf. John P. Hittinger, "Jacques Maritain and Yves R. Simon's Use of Thomas Aquinas in Their Defense of Liberal Democracy," in David Gallagher, ed., *Thomas Aquinas and His Legacy* (Washington, D.C.: The Catholic University of America Press, 1994), pp. 149–172.

ety to which it is subordinate; it wields this authority in service of the "common good." So, Maritain did not mark his position only in relationship to liberalism but also in relationship to collectivism. According to Maritain, in our time we are not confronted with a subsidiary state but with an "absorbing" state which controls political society[10]— a situation that he criticizes: "The State is not a kind of collective superman."[11]

Maritain characterized his theory of the state as an "instrumentalistic" one, in order to make the political significance of the state as clear as possible. The state is not a goal in itself but a means to promote the "common good," including the achievement of social justice, economic improvement, and self-protection against totalitarian threats.

Instrument of Justice

Maritain's view is not meant to disqualify the state. He recognizes that laws for employment and labor are necessary for achieving the "common good." He characterizes the modern state as a "juridical machine," with its laws, its power, its discipline and organization of the social and economic life as "part of normal progress." However, Maritain affirms that a degeneration of this progress could occur if the state becomes identified with political society. In that case, one could speak of an "absorbing," and perhaps even totalitarian, state, that not only from a political point of view has supervision on the "common good," but organizes and controls economics, science and other social sectors. In totalitarian states progress is suffocated but in democratic states it contains risks, in particular risks of social justice.[12] Therefore, the state should promote decentralization and depoliticize social life, in order to enforce a pluriform society.

So, the task of the state is to promote the "common good" of the multitude or social justice; that is, the betterment of the material conditions of human life and the improvement of moral and spiritual capacities. In short, Maritain holds that "the political task is essentially a task of civilization and culture, of helping man to conquer his genuine freedom of expansion or autonomy."[13] Although the task of politicians is always embedded in a given culture, they also have the task of transcending the given culture, of forming culture. Insofar as the state can achieve this task of civilization and

---

[10] Maritain, *Man and the State*, pp. 14–15.

[11] Ibid., p. 13.

[12] Ibid., pp. 19–20.

[13] Ibid., p. 55. Cf. Maritain, *Christianity and Democracy and The Rights of Man and Natural Law*, p. 126.

culture, Maritain speaks of growth and progress. He adds: "Maybe man will not become better. At least his state of life will become better. The structures of human life and humanity's conscience will progress."[14] Still, Maritain also speaks of regression and degradation of culture.

Degradation and Revitalization

Maritain pays particular attention to ideas of progress and regression in regard to democracy. In relation to these phenomena he discusses the "consciousness of self" (*"prise de conscience"*), that is, "the growth in awareness of an offended and humiliated human dignity."[15] This growth in awareness appears as a historical gain; it means the rise toward liberty and personality. For Maritain, all forms of progress of the modern age, of art, of science, of philosophy, also of politics, exhibit this growth of awareness.

There is a movement of progression in societies themselves evolving in history. According to Maritain, this movement depends upon "the double law of the degradation and revitalization of the energy of history, or of the mass of human activity upon which the movement of history depends."[16] This means that while the wear and tear of time and mental passivity degrade the moral energy of human beings. Creative forces which are so characteristic of the spirit of human dignity and liberty and which normally find their application in the efforts of the few (who are destined to be sacrificed), constantly revitalize the quality of this energy. Thus, a political society advances thanks to the vitalization of moral energy springing from this spirit and liberty. This means that progress will not take place by itself but by the ascent of consciousness that is linked to a superior level of organization: a civilized community. This community cannot be achieved by external forces and compulsion but only by the progress of moral consciousness and relationships of justice and brotherhood or civic friendship.[17] Justice and brotherhood are the "essential foundations" of this community or political society which, in particular, should be promoted by the state.[18]

---

[14] Maritain, *Christianity and Democracy and The Rights of Man and Natural Law*, p. 127.

[15] Jacques Maritain, *Integral Humanism* (Notre Dame, Indiana: University of Notre Dame Press, 1973), p. 231. Maritain, *Christianity and Democracy and The Rights of Man and Natural Law*, pp. 36–37.

[16] Maritain, *Christianity and Democracy and The Rights of Man and Natural Law*, p. 113.

[17] Ibid., pp. 114–115; 118.

[18] Ibid., p. 121.

However, at the time of World War II Maritain was prompted to ask this embarrassing question: "What is the reason for the failure of modern democracies to realize democracy?" During this war, when many people were victims of a demonic ideology and of the totalitarian Nazi regime, Maritain wrote his book on democracy. For him the main question was not how to win the war, but how to win the peace. His purpose was to indicate a direction in which he believed we would have to proceed: "In any event it [World War II] will not be truly won until the concrete outline for a new spiritual and social world will have its appearance in history."[19] He did not believe that these things could be done easily, or that the internal conflicts would be surmounted without trouble. He continues: "Public opinion has understood that in order to escape from the base frivolity and the infamous weakness of politicians who were not all bad, but whose inner life was dust, we must exact from our leaders moral consistency, the strength of one who acts on principles and not honesty alone, but virtue."[20]

This mission can be achieved only by great political vigilance activated by a process of education.[21] This political vigilance and process of education should be activated, in turn, by the authority and the right of the rulers.[22] But what happens when the political leaders have become morally bankrupt? Then it is time "to call upon the moral and spiritual reserves of the people, of common humanity—the last reserves of civilization. And these moral and spiritual reserves are not a tool in the hands of those with authority; they are the very power, and the source of initiative, of men cognizant of their personal dignity and their responsibility."[23]

An important reason for the failure of the modern democracies to realize democracy was "the fact that this realization inevitably demanded accomplishment in the social as well as in the political order, and that this demand was not complied with."[24] Yet political and social democracy are not merely manners of organizing society. First and foremost they designate a general philosophy of human and political life and a state of mind, in which human dignity and the right of the person are the "essential bases." Therefore, according to Maritain, the principal reason for the failure of modern democracies is a spiritual one: "This form and this ideal of common life,

---

[19] Ibid., p. 76.
[20] Ibid., p. 78.
[21] Ibid., p. 26.
[22] Ibid., pp. 41–42.
[23] Ibid., p. 64.
[24] Ibid., p. 19.

which we call 'democracy,' springs in its essentials from the inspiration of the Gospel and cannot subsist without it."[25]

Maritain summarized the meaning of the Gospel for democracy and for its revitalization: the unity of the human race, the natural equality of all men, the inalienable dignity of human beings, of labor, and of the poor, compassion with the weak and the suffering, the inviolability of conscience, and viewing every human being as our neighbor. These characteristics are the basis of his ideal of "personalistic democracy." By virtue of the "hidden work" of the evangelical inspiration, secular political philosophical theories contain ideas of inalienable rights of the person, e.g. equality, the government as representative of the multitude, political rights of the people whose consent is implied by any political regime, relations of justice and the legal order at the base of society, the ideal of fraternity, and promotion of the "common good" of the multitude.[26]

Structure of the State

Dooyeweerd distinguishes clearly between the structure of the state and the structure of other social institutions. As he puts it, the state is an organization that is based on a monopolist "power of the sword" (judicial, police and military power) over a certain territorial cultural area. But since the state is qualified as a community of public law the use of power should be regulated by law.[27] Therefore, according to Dooyeweerd, the state should be considered as a community that is historically founded (upon power), and juridically qualified, that is, law should be its principal function.

For Dooyeweerd, the state is a juridically organized community of citizens and government. This means that the public interest, not particular interests, should dominate, and, at the same time, the interests of individual citizens and social institutions should be served. Therefore Dooyeweerd holds: "The internal political activity of the State should always be guided by the idea of public social justice."[28]

According to Dooyeweerd, "public social justice," the qualifying characteristic of the state, should be distinguished from the goals of the state. A government can have many goals, for example, to create employment, to

[25] Ibid., pp. 19–20.
[26] Ibid., pp. 34–41; 57–59.
[27] Herman Dooyeweerd, *A New Critique of Theoretical Thought*, vol. 3 (Amsterdam: The Presbyterian and Reformed Publishing Co., 1957), pp. 412–414.
[28] Ibid., p. 446.

cut down the expenses of health care, but in realizing these goals the criterion of "public social justice" should be decisive.

Dooyeweerd thus rejects a restrictive idea of law as a characteristic of the state, because in his view law is a normative aspect of reality (based upon the "divine creation order"), interwoven with other aspects, for example, with the aesthetic and the ethical. Insight into the connection of these aspects can deepen the understanding of the juridical aspect. This means that law can be deepened in an aesthetic direction: in achieving a balance and harmony of interests. Law can also be realized in a moral direction, by harmonizing private interests into a promotion of the public interest.

We have seen that Dooyeweerd defines the state as a juridically organized community. Although he sometimes used words such as "state" and "political society" as synonyms, he also distinguished the two concepts.[29] Identifying the two concepts is, according to him, a result of a totalitarian idea of the state.[30] However, his distinction between the political society and the state differs from that of Maritain. Dooyeweerd does not speak of the state as a part of the political society or as an "instrument of justice." He is particularly interested in the structural analysis of the state as a community *sui generis* which is distinguished from the differentiated social institutions within the territory of the state which comprise political society.

Other Competencies

Dooyeweerd also discusses the competencies of these various social institutions. His theory of the variety of spheres of competency is founded on the neo-Calvinist principle of "sphere-sovereignty," understood as an utterance of God's "creation order." Based on this principle, family, school, industry, church and state are considered as realities *sui generis* that should be distinguished according to their own nature. He acknowledges that God is the absolute sovereign to whom all other forms of authority are subordinated. This acknowledgment means that no social institution can be self-sufficient or can have an absolute power, and that no institution derives its sovereignty and competency from another institution. It also means that human beings should never be considered as being

---

[29] Contra David T. Koyzis, "Toward a Christian Democratic Pluralism: A Comparative Study of Neothomist and Calvinist Political Theories" (Ph.D. diss., University of Notre Dame, 1986), p. 357.

[30] Dooyeweerd, *A New Critique of Theoretical Thought*, pp. 433, 446.

absorbed by, or as parts of any culture, social community or tradition, unless by force. Dooyeweerd speaks of a political society in which differentiated social institutions, although interwoven with each other, exist with their own competencies and responsibilities. In opposition to Maritain, Dooyeweerd does not consider the social order as a hierarchical one in which the state is the highest part and other institutions are lower parts. Rather, he sees their relationship as "horizontal." However, though all social institutions exist within the territory of the state and fall under the jurisdiction of the state, these institutions retain their own nature and should achieve their own competency (within the bounds of law). Moreover, the distinctive nature (or qualification) of the state can be a means to oppose both liberal and "absorbing" state visions.

Concerning the horizontal and vertical ordering of society, one more nuance must be noted. I have already pointed out that Maritain acknowledges a hierarchical order of political society but that social institutions are *primarily* characterized by autonomy. If a social institution falls short in achieving its own tasks, the state may then act *subsidiarily*. The criterion by which to judge when and how the state should act in this way depends on the "common good" of the political society.

Although Dooyeweerd starts from the idea of "sphere-sovereignty" and from a horizontal ordering of society, he also acknowledges the idea of subsidiarity. He admits that the qualifying function of the state requires an active role by the government. With an appeal to "public social justice" the government is empowered (by virtue of a judgement of the law-court) to deprive parents of parental rights, to put citizens in prison, and to make regulations for industries in order to protect the natural environment or the interests of consumers. Although we discover influences of different philosophical traditions in the thought of Maritain and Dooyeweerd, the differences between their visions of the social order in relationship to political practice are, in my judgment, only differences of accent.

Differentiation and Integration

Regarding progress Dooyeweerd pays particular attention to processes of social differentiation. In his view there is a fundamental difference between differentiated and undifferentiated societies. In undifferentiated societies there is no room for the freedom of human actions and for the formation of distinctive life spheres according to their own nature. The entire life of the members of such a society is enclosed within the bonds of kinship, tribe, church or dictatorship. In these societies tradition exercises an absolute power. Human beings cannot transcend the existing tradition.[31]

For Dooyeweerd, the process of cultural development always takes place in historical continuity. This means that cultural development is impossible without tradition. In his discussion of tradition Dooyeweerd does not mean to refer to conservatives who simply want to stick to the status quo, but rather to the embodiment of a communal heritage acquired by the passing generations. Tradition, in other words, is a communal and conserving power binding the past to the present. However, a dynamic culture does not vegetate upon its tradition but rather unfolds it. In this way new forms come from old ones, and in new phenomena old ones are always present. Tradition, therefore, is not the old-fashioned and unprofitable; for progress and renewal have a rightful place within it. On the other hand, not everything that is announced as a renewal contributes to true cultural progress. In retrospect it may be considered as conservative, reactionary or even as degenerative.[32]

For Dooyeweerd cultural development in the sense of progress is made possible when the inner nature of the different spheres of human society can freely unfold. In this context he speaks of "the progressive course of the opened development of culture." He argues that "cultural development as progress" can be realized by the double law: the "normative principle of cultural integration and differentiation." This means that the process of differentiation has its counterpart in the process of integration. The process of "opening" or "disclosure" of undifferentiated cultures produces new contacts with other cultural groups, new relationships and new forms of cooperation in art, scientific research, commerce and religion. The modern state is also an example of integration: the central government has carefully to weigh the various private interests against each other and against the public interest. Ultimately, private interests should be harmonized and integrated in the public interest under the idea of "public social justice."[33] So, at the same time, Dooyeweerd discusses the state as an example of differentiation

---

[31] Dooyeweerd, *A New Critique of Theoretical Thought*, vol. 2 (Amsterdam: The Presbyterian and Reformed Publishing Co., 1955), pp. 346–368. See Dooyeweerd, *Roots of Western Culture: Pagan, Secular and Christian Options* (Toronto: Wedge, 1979), pp. 74–75.

[32] Ibid., pp. 242–243; Cf. Dooyeweerd, *Roots*, pp. 71–72.

[33] Dooyeweerd, *A New Critique of Theoretical Thought*, vol. 3, pp. 260–262; 446; 488; 491.

and in regard to its responsibility regarding cultural development: "The State may promote the interests of science and the fine arts, education, public health, trade, agriculture and industry, popular morality, and so on."[34]

According to Dooyeweerd, the ultimate reason for cultural development, in particular the promotion of differentiation and integration, is that such activity is based on God's "creation order." God gives humanity the cultural mandate to subdue the earth and to have dominion over it. This means that humanity has the calling to bring to realization the possibilities and potentials present in creation. Yet, does this cultural mandate imply that people should strive for differentiation and integration?

Of course, everyone will judge positively the fact that human beings and social institutions can achieve freedom and responsibility according to their own nature. However, compared with Western societies, people in less differentiated societies live differently. They have their own division of labor and other social tasks, and they may be happy, perhaps even happier than many people in Western countries who have a hurried existence and suffer from a murderous competition. Indeed, human beings in less differentiated societies have other ideas of freedom and responsibility, but their cultures cannot be characterized as necessarily being of a lower level than other cultures. Dooyeweerd criticizes these undifferentiated societies because of the compelling forces of tradition and morality which hinder possiblilities of cultural development. To the extent that these compelling powers exist, they should be criticized. However, in Western culture, characterized in many respects by processes of differentiation and integration, the compelling powers of capitalistic world-economy are evident. Dooyeweerd would certainly agree with criticism of the dominance of the capitalistic world-economy. He would acknowledge that capitalism degenerates human life and social institutions in many respects.

However, in discussing the "norm" of cultural development by processes of differentiation and integration, Dooyeweerd seems to be a typical Western philosopher. He defends, for example, differentiation and integration as they arose in Western societies after the French and the Industrial Revolution. How could this differentiation and integration have taken place in Western culture? In his criticism of Dooyeweerd, Nicholas Wolterstorff argues that this question can only be answered by studying the rise of the capitalist world-economy. Although Dooyeweerd does not acknowledge

[34] Ibid., pp. 445–446.

this cause of differentiation and integration, he appears to be beholden to it.[35]

Dooyeweerd's philosophy, moreover, contains speculative ideas of "creation order" which have dangerous implications. He defends "principles of the creation order" which are no principles at all. For instance, he upholds economic inequality as a "divine order" that finds expression in relationships of property and authority between employers and employees (who committ themselves to earning only their wages). By this argument he rejects economic shared control by employees and their participation in the profits of industry.[36] Another example is his idea of democracy as a mere political form of government. He rejects any idea of "social democracy" that could be applied to other social institutions, as this would level all differences of the internal structures of human relationships.[37]

Conclusions

Let us go back to the distinction I made earlier between "cognitive," "affective" and "evaluative orientations." The "cognitive orientation" of Maritain and Dooyeweerd concerns the same political phenomena. Both discuss the responsibility of the state regarding cultural development, and both hold that this development is determined by a "historic law." In relationship to this law they discuss problems of progress and regression of cultural development. Both discuss the relationship between the state and a pluriform society.

Maritain's and Dooyeweerd's "affective orientations" are partly the same. Both judge the state as important for realizing justice in society because they hold a normative view of the task of the state. Both defend a pluralist society consisting of "autonomous institutions" as realities *sui generis* in opposition to totalitarian and liberal views of the state. However, an important difference between Maritain and Dooyeweerd is their view of democracy. Maritain considers democracy as an important instrument for governing the state. Moreover, he defends "social democracy," that is, the pursuit of democracy in other social institutions. For Maritain, this "social democracy" implies an ac-

---

[35] Nicholas P. Wolterstorff, *Until Justice and Peace Embrace* (Grand Rapids, Michigan: Eerdmans, 1983), p. 59.

[36] Dooyeweerd, "Medezeggenschap der arbeiders in de bedrijven" ("Shared Control of Employers in Industries"), in *Antirevolutionaire Staatkunde*, vol. 1 (1924–25): pp. 291–306; and "Tweeërlei kritiek: Om de principiële zijde van het vraagstuk der medezeggenschap" ("Twofold Criticism of the Principal Aspect of the Problem of Shared Control") in *Antirevolutionaire Staatkunde*, vol. 2 (1926): pp. 1–21.

[37] Dooyeweerd, *A New Critique of Theoretical Thought*, vol. 3, p. 479.

knowledgement of the dignity of human beings that should be achieved in all social institutions. Dooyeweerd, for his part, rejects "social democracy" because he regards democracy only as a political form of government that cannot be applied to other non-political institutions.

Maritain's and Dooyeweerd's "evaluative orientations" are quite different. I shall discuss four differences.

First, Maritain makes a distinction between the political society as a community that is characterized by promoting the "common good," and the state as the necessary instrument of justice of the political society. Dooyeweerd regards the state not as an instrument but as a community *sui generis* that is characterized by "public social justice."

Second, both Maritain and Dooyeweerd defend a pluralist society consisting of "autonomous" institutions. However, they produce different justifications for it. Maritain maintains a hierarchical view of society: the political society is the most perfect society, and the variety of social institutions in it are considered as the parts which should achieve the greatest possible autonomy. Dooyeweerd maintains a horizontal view of society in which all institutions achieve their "sphere sovereignty" according to their own qualifying characteristics. However, as I have indicated, in political practice these different views are only differences of accent.

Third, both philosophers acknowledge that human beings should not be considered as parts of the state and of other social institutions. Maritain, therefore, affirms a "personalistic democracy," and seeks to renew the "basic values of democracy" (human dignity, brotherhood, justice, "common good," etc.). For this reason Maritain values the spiritual base of democracy, moral strength (particlarly in politicians) and the education of democratic values. Dooyeweerd does not discuss these issues. For in his view democracy is an "instrument" only suitable for governing the state.

Fourth, both Maritain and Dooyeweerd value the responsibility of the state in respect to cultural development. Both hold that cultural development is determined by a "historic law." Relative to this law they discuss problems of progress and regression. However, they have different interpretations of this "historic law." Maritain speaks of the double law of "degradation and revitalization," while Dooyeweerd speaks of the double law of "differentiation and integration." In relationship to the "double law of degradation and revitalization" Maritain discusses, on the one hand, that the wear and tear of time and mental passivity degrade the moral energy of human beings, and, on the other hand, that moral creativity is characteristic of the spirit of human dignity and liberty which vitalizes moral energy. When this vitalization occurs by the ascent of consciousness, linked to a superior level of organization of the political society and other institutions, and characterized by relations of justice and brotherhood, then Maritain speaks of "cultural progress." He would certainly agree with the "historic law" of differentiation and integration as put forth by Dooyeweerd because he also defends the "autonomy" of social institutions. Therefore, like Dooyeweerd, Maritain rejects both a liberal and a totalitarian state, and defends a pluralist society. In other words, differentiation and integration are presupposed in his discussion of the "law of degeneration and revitalization."

However, Maritain does not stop with the law of "differentiation and integration." He finds it necessary to consider concrete social and political situations in order to judge whether the above moral characteristics are achieved. In his view these characteristics should be constantly revitalized. Thus, he not only discusses the structures of social institutions but, in particular, he pays attention to the moral quality of the politicians and other participants of these institutions.

Maritain would certainly hold that the historic law of "differentiation and integration" could not serve as an adequate criterion of cultural progress. He would not deny Dooyeweerd's idea that the modern state is an example of both integration and differentiation because it has to weigh carefully the various private interests against each other, and to integrate these interests in the public interest. However, he would not judge this idea of integration, as such, as progress. He would seek to determine this by asking the question of how this process of integration should be achieved morally. The answer to this question would determine whether this integration could be valued as progress or not.

So, however important it may be to distinguish social institutions according to their own nature, as Dooyeweerd held, more important is the question: "Are these institutions performing well in practice?" Dooyeweerd would probably answer the criticism that he analyzed "normative principles" of social relationships by saying that human beings have the responsibility to realize these principles in practice. In some sense Maritain could agree with this answer. However, Maritain would certainly conclude that a social and political philosophy should not only be "principle-oriented" but also "praxis-oriented."[38] Moreover, he would stress that a social and political philosophy should be responsible for misuse that could be prevented by an elaboration of basic values of "personalistic democracy" and social democracy. Dooyeweerd fails to verify his ideas of differentiation and integration by these values.

[38] See Wolterstorff, *Until Justice and Peace Embrace*, pp. 170–173.

The Multiconfusion of
Multiculturalism

J. Meric Pessagno

As I understand it, culture signifies the amalgam of values, moral, literary and aesthetic, encapsulated in one or more closely related languages, the expression of the historically developed views of a people, whether they be ethnically homo- or heterogeneous. We Americans are the neatest, if not the only example of the latter, while most of the rest of the world exemplifies the former.

I have been unable to locate with certitude the time and place of the first use of term "multiculturalism." Despite this failure, though, one may comment on the linguistic formation of the term, viz., the addition of the abstract ending -ism to the adjectival from cultural. This formation is not without significance, for, if I am correct, it explains why mutliculturalists are more interested in systems of description than in culture itself. Hence the close logical connection between the rise of multiculturalism and the phenomenon of political correctness in speech. For, in both cases, what is important is the verbal formation by itself, apart from any intent of the speaker.

As with any system, multiculturalism is built on certain suppositions. The strength and the truth value of the system rest therefore on the strength and the truth value of the suppositions. I find that multiculturalism, as it has developed and expressed itself, on both the national and the university scenes, is the global expression of three separate, but related theses, whose truth and accuracy will determine its truth and accuracy.

The first thesis is that, up to this point, American universities have either ignored or downgraded the study of any culture other than that of Western Europe. As anyone in the field can testify, to the degree that the study of non-European cultures has been neglected, the principal cause has been the

241

lack of student interest which has produced a low level of financial support in the normal budget. Only when external events have intervened has money gone into these cultural areas. Thus the Vietnam War produced a windfall in the funding of East Asian studies, and, to a lesser degree, the oil crisis of 1973 increased funding to Arabic and Islamic studies. In this first thesis we find, then, what will become the distinguishing feature of multiculturalist analysis: the melding together of the true and the false, and most often of all, a proper phenomenological observation, whose existence is then explained in what one may charitably say is some fanciful causality. In this case, for example, the neglect of concern for non-European cultures is laid to a conspiracy that simply does not exist and never has. The sadly more realistic causality of student non-interest, often combined with student laziness in the study of foreign languages, is conveniently ignored, perhaps because it is too prosaic.

The second thesis is perhaps the one that lies at the heart of the multiculturalist creed. One may state it as follows: All cultures are equal, and it is not possible to say that any one culture is superior to any other one. Because of this position, one finds in the writings of multiculturalists a jungle of references to disparate cultures, invoking their authority on any given question with little or no differentiation. Hence, too, their justification for running down traditional central characters in history and substituting for them obscure characters whose chief claim for attention is often either their gender or their color and little else. This second thesis embodies a very particular philosophical position, namely, the exclusion of culture in whatever form from the realm of rational judgment.

But why does the judgment occur and even persist that one culture is superior to another? The multiculturalist response is sure and certain: A dominant culture is only dominant insofar as its followers are able to suppress other cultures. These are heady assertions indeed and deserve our most serious examination.

Why does multiculturalism insist on the equality of all cultures? For two reasons, I believe. First, that no culture be offended by being told that in the scheme of things it is less important than another. Second, because it confuses the intrinsic and extrinsic value of a given culture.

A culture's intrinsic value signifies what that culture engenders in the life, the individual life of one who possesses it. Presuming that all cultures in some way speak of the true, the beautiful, values and standards, to the individual who holds that culture, in this sense all cultures are equal, for each supplies to one who embraces it a framework for individual judgment and action. So, for example, the aesthetics of beauty for an African can only validly grow from an African culture and in this respect cannot be judged inferior to that of another culture. In this intrinsic, individual sense, then, all cultures are equal. But, and it is indeed a big but, in terms of extrinsic value, i.e., their societal effect, all cultures are not equal, and it would be both perverse and silly to claim they are. Let us be specific. For whatever reasons, and they will be many, complex and, to some degree, obscure, the societal effect of European culture has led historically to an economic, political and scientific superiority that must lead one to conclude that this European culture in these respects is superior to other cultures. Note, I did not say morally better or more humane. These categories constitute matters of quite separate judgment. But no rational person can question that the distinguishing marks of Western culture—rational investigation and consequential application—has made it preeminent among world cultures. And it is this self-evident preeminence of Western culture that leads us to consider the thesis of multiculturalism: that cultural superiority is only achieved by political suppression of rival cultures. Once again, in this assertion, as in others, we have a combination of truth and falsehood. Yes, it is true that political suppression of the conquered culture has often taken place in history. But there are counter-examples as well. So, Rome which conquered Greece militarily was, as Horace gracefully put it, conquered culturally by the conquered land. The Islamic Empire strove at first to segregate itself religiously and culturally from the people it conquered. But the lure of social and economic advantage overwhelmed the planned and preferred segregation of the Arab conquerors. More recently we have the Austro-Hungarian Empire, which might serve as a multiculturalist model; Vienna imposed fashion, cooking and style, while leaving intact indigenous cultures. In short, the multiculturalist analysis of the relationship between culture and politics is simplistic and far too sweeping in its assertion of the political nature of culture. No people lack some form of politics. That their culture is proportionate to their political power is less than certain. One may perhaps offer the Mongols as an historical case. In their sweep across the lands of Islam they conquered and destroyed well, but that was the limit of their achievement.

What is significant in these observations is that it is history herself which refutes the theses of multiculturalism. How then shall one believe that multiculturalism represents a proper historical attitude for this country to take at this or any other instant in our tumultuous story? Even more to the point, how can multiculturalism offer such a flawed historical analysis, so flawed that it well-nigh refutes itself? Because multiculturalism sees culture as the way to and claim on political power. Their position is neatly circular: political power imposes culture which, in turn, produces more and greater political power. Granted their logic, their reasoning is impeccable. But who is it that becomes powerful through the *application* of their reasoning? Those groups who by their prior political failure, color, gender or sexual preference, for too often they will claim these as the reasons for their failure, were kept out of the ruling circle. Hence the exaltation in the curriculum and at scholarly conventions of history from the loser's point of view, not that we may be broadened by such consideration, but in order to uncover a mythical historical conspiracy that will prove that the vanquished ought to have been the victors. We have here something close to Nietzsche's demand for a transvaluation of values. Multiculturalism has meant in practice the substitution of one extreme for another. If one is male, white, of European origin, heterosexual, one is at best an insensitive bigot who must be trained to value diversity. If one is female, of color, non-European (it is difficult here to place Hispanics), gay, lesbian or bi-sexual, one is now in the "in" group, beyond criticism and so beyond truth which is dependent on such criticism. What started as perhaps a demand for balance, tolerance and reasonable protection of diversity has in practice become the exaltation of endless excuses for any lapses. So the strange and pitiful spectacle of Maya Angelou's charge of racism against the game show "Jeopardy" because it has too few non-white contestants.

Yet behind the absurdity of seeing racism in everything, which is as mad as seeing it in nothing, and using it to explain every defeat and disappointment, there is a certain Alice in Wonderland logic supplied by the theses of multiculturalism. Since culture is a function of political power, any and all cultural failings may be assigned to varying degrees of political suppression, for otherwise all cultures would be equal. Hence the whole concept of personal responsibility is endangered. For the multiculturalist the emphasis is more on the group than the person and to the group is transferred the major responsibility, at least for failure. This attitude explains, I believe, why black writers who attack Jews in statements both outlandish and dangerous will yet maintain that neither they not their statements are anti-Jewish. They are simply the proper analysis of political exploitation, which led to economic exploitation upon which white, Jewish success has been built. That facts do not justify such analysis means nothing, for, as in all -isms, it is the -ism that is the sole, valid interpreter of the true meaning of the facts, not the other way around. And this attitude, in turn, helps to explain why, if a Jew wrote the same of blacks, it would be proof of his racism. Things mean what I want them to mean. It is this dogmatic certitude that makes debate with the multiculturalist so difficult a task, for any criticism of multiculturalism can only—by multiculturalism's own standards—spring from racism or sexism or both. Given, then, the evil source of the criticism, any weapon used against it is justified, even if the limits of fairness must stretched or totally disregarded. That is why to be accused of racism or sexism in the context of multiculturalism is already to be guilty as charged. There can be no more innocent until proven guilty because any delay in announcing the guilt of the accused is equivalent to comforting the enemy and conspiring with him. If it is felt that this statement is somewhat exaggerated, may I invite you to peruse available records of what has happened to opponents of multiculturalism on the university level, whether they be faculty or students. Indeed, among several characteristics that mark multiculturalism as a new and different phenomenon is the attempt to silence student criticism thereof and not simply that of the faculty.

It would be appropriate, I believe, to give credit now to the book that really brought some degree of popular attention to the question of multiculturalism and its peculiar vision of America. I refer to Richard Bernstein's *Dictatorship of Virtue*, published by Knopf in 1994. I must note that, while rich in anecdotal material, this work has an analytic flaw that weakens the author's critique of what he sees as multiculturalism. The author sees in this -ism an example of what an analyst of the French Revolution has called *dérapage*, which Bernstein understands in the sense of slipping, giving the reader the idea that multiculturalism strayed, for reasons unknown, from a noble idea and so landed in its present mess. But this is not, I believe, what the French analyst meant when he described the Terror as a *dérapage* from the ideals of *liberté, égalité, fraternité*. Rather, the word is to be understood in its quite normal figurative sense of a *changement non controlé*, an act of change that is not controlled. It is this meaning which more accurately portrays the true nature of multiculturalism. First, it was a change. In its case a massive one. From a cry to cherish, respect, and, if need be, protect diversity, which term seems to be the historical precursor of multiculturalism, there arose a new shout—that diversity is itself the *summum bonum*, that to attempt to stress the need for unity is but a cover for the discredited "melting pot" idea of an America that is no more. May I here offer a comment. Multiculturalism exhibits a profound historical ignorance of what the "melting pot" really was. Quite apart from any individual acts of prejudice and bigotry, the aim of the melting pot philosophy was to reconfigure the public persona of the immigrant, i.e., to see to it that the language of his public discourse would be at least an approximation of standard English and that his public political philosophy would be in conformity with the American Constitution. What a person did, spoke, thought or cooked at home was of no interest to the melting pot idea. Contrary to this idea of the necessity of some public unity, multiculturalism, at least in its extreme, would splinter the linguistic unity of the nation, depriving us of this vital link of communication among ethnically diverse people. This is truly a *changement*. Indeed, it is a revolution. And an uncontrolled one. For those who might have controlled the excesses of multicultural zeal, frightened that they would be called bigots or worse, essentially abandoned the field to those whose aim was a new segregationsim which has led on most campuses to the existence of ethnic, cultural clubs whose principal purpose seems to be that we associate with our own kind. So, in place of the idea of a university as a place which empowers one to overcome parochial divisions, multiculturalism cements and glorifies these divisions, essentially destroying the unity of the university. It steadfastly clings to its fundamental confusion that to be divided is the essence of being diverse. The damage already done on the university level by this unchecked, unchallenged and uncontrolled -ism is now rapidly descending into the texts and techniques of American high schools where even more damage will be wrought.

Nothing of multiculturalism has anything to do with virtue or its imposition. For virtue, first of all, stands in the middle. Multiculturalism is but another expression of the extreme. Virtue likewise emphasizes doing good, while multiculturalism centers on feeling good, even if the good feeling must be based on encouraging absurdities such as the anti-historical myth that all of Greek philosophy was stolen from Africa and turning Columbus from saint into sinner, when neither title is historically accurate. Mr. Bernstein is inaccurate, therefore, when he conceives of multiculturalism as a dictatorship of virtue. Multiculturalism is concerned neither with virtue, education or intellect. Unabashedly it is a pure power play, for, true to itself, culture is but an arm of politics and politics is but the route to power.

What should be deduced from this analysis of multiculturalism and its multiconfusion? Primarily that there is little, if any, academic content in it. It is rather solganeering which takes place in academia and under the cover of its pietistic slogans masks a fundamentally anti-intellectual attitude. One must hope that academics and administrators will at last muster the courage to shout that the emperor has no clothes, or, more apropos of our topic, that multiculturalism has no culture.

Latin American Democracies
at the Crossroads

Mario Ramos-Reyes

It is man who is in bankruptcy. Man who is, before all, a moral being; today [some people] intend him to be an exclusively economic being. A philosophical and spiritual formation is more urgent than an economic formation.

—Edurado Frei Montalva

Politics demands the presence of men capable of working for ideals, with honesty and devotion.

—Rafael Caldera

"Revolution" and "rebellion" have been more common political terms than "democracy" and "stability" in Latin America. Since Independence, the continent has been disrupted by *coups d'etat*, rebellions, and revolts many times. Indeed, Latin American political history since the nineteenth century has been polarized by two seemingly irreconcilable ideologies. The conservatives, supporters of the privileges of the Catholic Church, the army, and the landed oligarchy, have claimed to be the natural heirs of Spain. The liberals, defenders of the rights of individuals, the secularization of society, and the idea of liberal democracy, have espoused the ideals of endless progress and modernization.

This rivalry demonstrates that an essential problem for Latin America is the search for a modernizing ideology which can unite its Hispanic Catholic tradition with the ideal of republicanism and democracy. The apparent "schizophrenia" between Catholic conservatism and anticlerical democracy has been a persistent conflict in Latin America's modern history, particularly from the 1830's to the 1920's.

In the 1930's, however, Jacques Maritain's *Integral Humanism* inspired a new political model for Latin Americans. The New Christendom was democratic and Catholic at the same time. Maritain was critical of the individualism and secularism of modernity, yet he did not propose either a return to Medieval Christendom or the rejection of democratic values. His new approach, as the Uruguayan historian Alberto Methol Ferre suggests, incorporated "within Thomism the modern subjectivity, democracy and criticism toward capitalism."[1]

From the early thirties until 1968 (the year of the Third Conference of Bishops of Latin America in Medellin, Colombia), Latin American Catholicism in general was markedly influenced by Maritain's political thought. This period, which became known as the era of the "New Christendom," was characterized by attempts to establish a new, distinctively Christian civilization. The influence of Maritain's political philosophy reached its peak in the 1960's when two Maritainistas–Eduardo Frei in Chile (1964) and Rafael Caldera in Venezuela (1969)—won presidential elections.

This decade was also a time of fateful political confrontations. The most extreme elements of the Latin American Left opted for violent solutions. Some priests and members of lay associations. concluding that Catholics and Marxists shared the same goals, joined "guerrilla" movements.[2] In other cases, reactionary and dictatorial military governments toppled long-standing democracies. Authoritarian "revolutions"—such as the military governments established in Brazil (1964), Chile (1973), Uruguay (1975), and Argentina (1976)—implemented the so-called "Doctrine of National Security" to defend the values of "Christian Western Civilization." Polariziation between authoritarian militarism from the left and from the right seemed to replace the old dichotomy between liberals and conservatives. Both leftist and rightist approaches to solving Latin American economic and social problems were mockeries of a true Christian humanism. Unfortunately, after 1968, Maritain's approach, as Alceu Amoroso Lima gloomily

---

[1] "Y en relacion a la historia, *Humanismo Integral* donde busca recuperar dentro del tomismo la subjetividad moderna, la democracia y la critica al capitalismo. Esto acaece durante la Gran Depresion, en la tumultuosa deacda de los 30." Alberto Methol Ferre, "El Resurgimento Catolico Latinoamericano" ("The Resurgence of Latin American Catholicism") in *Religion y Cultura* (Bogota, Columbia: Consejo Episcopal Latinoamericano, 1981), p. 103.

[2] The late sixties and early seventies witnessed the cases of "Christian Socialism" of the priests Camilo Torres Restrepo in Colombia and Carlos Mugica in Argentina. Both were killed by military forces.

said, "play[ed] no role except among . . . sequestered and powerless forces."[3]

During the early eighties and nineties, however, Latin American countries, one after another, recovered their political liberties. In 1983, after decades of political repression and instability, Argentina elected a president, Raul Alfonsin. Similarly, the 1985 election of Jose Sarney in Brazil and the election of Patricio Alwyn in Chile ended military dictatorships that had stood for twenty and seventeen years, respectively. In Paraguay, the first free elections in four decades were held in 1989 after a bloody *coup d'etat* led by Andres Rodriguez deposed the thirty-eight year old Stroessner dictatorship. The fall of Communism in Eastern Europe in 1989 contributed to the consolidation of these new democratic regimes.

Today, all Latin American countries (with the exception of Cuba) are democracies. It must be noted, however, that these new regimes are mere formal political democracies. Not only is the military threat still alive— many of them are only "tutelaged democracies" (*democracias tuteladas*)— but they are going through severe political and social tensions. The process of democratization appears to have led to political instability.[4]

Unfortunately, this democratization process came in the middle of one of the worst financial and economic crises since the thirties. To solve this crisis, new economic policies of privatization, with a reduced role for the state in economic and social policies, have been implemented. An emergent "laissez faire" neo-liberalism is rampant even in those countries where parties which historically have been "pro-workers and pro-peasants" are in power, such as the Mexican PRI, Argentinean Peronism, the Paraguayan

---

[3] "In Peru and Bolivia, the local "Christian Democratic Parties" support these political movements of the military forces of the "left." Of a left, moreover, as anticommunist as the right. Whereas in Brazil and Argentina, the "Christian Democratic Parties" are dissolved; and its members or sympathizers, are accommodated to the military regimes; are exiled; or are leading, in the tolerated opposition, a patient and difficult struggle." Alceu Amoroso Lima, "Personal Testimony: On the Influence of Maritain in Latin America," *The New Scholasticism* 46 (Winter 1972): p. 83.

[4] Paraguay and Peru are typical examples of these new democracies in that, though they are governed by civilian presidents, they are "guided" by the military. The Venezuelan democracy, one of the most solid in the continent, has also been threatened by the military over the past two years. Even in Chile, where the influence of the Christian Democratic Party is determinative, the military still retains the "last word." Although General Augusto Pinochet resigned the presidency and allowed the elections of Patricio Alwyn and Eduardo Frei's son, he has reserved for himself the post of "commander in chief" of the armed forces.

Colorado Party, and even the Chilean and Venezuelan Christian Democratic Parties. Retaking the individualistic Latin American liberal tradition (which dominated from the 1850's until the 1920's), the new regimes defend the idea that the common good is but the sum of individual private interests and satisfactions. In general, these policies have resulted in significant economic growth, a controlled rate of inflation, and a flow of international investment.

At the same time, however, these economic policies have made a tremendous impact on the Latin American cultural ethos. These new "utilitarian" democracies emphasize the role of government as a neutral rule maker which encourages private initiative. They do not take the cultural and moral dimensions of a democratic system into account. Quite the contrary, consistent with their emphasis on individual freedom, these new regimes have advocated a sort of laissez faire, where almost anything goes in the moral and cultural arena. A new, radical and individualistic "morality" has emerged in the political landscape and some unpleasant consequences are being felt: a loss of the sense of social justice (the unemployment rate has risen visibly and the gap between rich and poor has widened), a lack of civil citizenship, increasing fraud, and above all, widespread corruption.

In this context, the new generation has been introduced to a moral relativism which comes from post-industrialized countries with a post-modern culture: the culture of rock videos, violent films, sexual license, and the cultivation of desire, along with the innovation of the right to choose (abortion) and even the temptation of euthanasia. Along with political liberties and free market economy, this self-centered moral outlook (new to the Latin American ethos) is one of the three most important characteristics of the new democracies; and where it increases, the role of government as a moral leader is diminished. Any concept of the common good which can diminish individual freedom is seen not only as a threat to political liberties but as a reactionary assault from the right.

The culture and political system are so consumed by a positivistic and materialistic mentality that the formation of humanistic leaders is inhibited. It would seem that technology, free trade, and economic individualism have revived the problematic of the 1930's: the need for a new moral political leadership, a new revival of a politics of Christian inspiration. The theologian Oscar Rodriguez Madariga recently pointed out the lack of true leaders. Overwhelmed by lack of resources, the continuing process of secularization, a culture of consumerism, and the invasion of Protestant fundamentalist sects, the Church "seems to have exhausted its resources to a degree and so we must find a new missionary impetus."[5]

Within this context doubts remain as to whether these new democracies will survive. Are they a viable model for the survival and growth of the Latin American Catholic cultural tradition? And if they are not, what would an alternative political model look like at this crossroads? I have already suggested that, although the flourishing of these new democratic regimes is encouraging, their major challenges are not economic but rather moral and cultural. In what follows I shall argue that the key to transforming these systems into "integral" democracies is a return to their historical roots. And I believe that Jacques Maritain's political philosophy is the most important part of these roots. A "renaissance" can only occur, however, if Maritain's legacy is interpreted first and foremost as an educational and cultural heritage and not as exclusively political.[6]

Jacques Maritain was, as his disciple and friend Yves R. Simon pointed out, a "nonspecialized philosopher." He wrote with the same intellectual rigor about the different branches of philosophy from metaphysics to aesthetics. Although it was his political writings that gave him international recognition, particularly in Latin America, Maritain felt himself to be neither a politician nor an ideologue of any particular group. Rather, he hoped to be considered a philosopher who inspired and illuminated the world of politics, and who was interested in democracy as the most suitable form of government for Christians.

In the early thirties, the imagination and intelligence of Latin American intellectuals and politicians were challenged by a crisis that rocked the liberal capitalist democracies as a result of the Great Depression. In that period, the political thought of the Social Christians joined the Latin American Catholic tradition with universal ideals of modernity. For them, the problematic of the democratic crisis was clear: it was the decline of a cul-

---

[5] Oscar Rodriguez Madariga, "A Church of Silence?," interview by Andrea Tornielli, *30 Days* 3 (1995): p. 25.

[6] This is also the opinion of Professor Edward Lynch. But he seems to attribute the Christian Democrats' failure mainly to the "wrong" public policies they established, such as stateism. "Having spent most of the 1960's and 1970's finding one reason after another to increase state economic power, Christian Democrats faced the new challenges of the 1980's liberalism without any coherent ideological basis for response. Squeezed between more radical statists and the rising liberals, the movement threatened to disappear altogether. . . . If Christian Democracy has a future, it lies in rediscovering the potency of the philosophy that gave it birth." Edward Lynch, *Latin America's Christian Democratic Parties: A Political Economy* (Westport, Connecticut: Praeguer, 1993), p. xvii.

ture, the breakdown of a moral order. In order to provide a solid intellectual foundation to their new organizations and their countries' political systems, these young Catholic militants decided to adopt and, above all, to adapt the political thought of the French philosopher Jacques Maritain.

These Latin Americans—among whom were the Brazilian Alceu Amoroso Lima (1893–1973), the Chilean Eduardo Frei Montalva (1911–1981), the Venezuelan Rafeal Caldera (b. 1922), and later the Paraguayan Secundino Nunez (b. 1920)—believed that Maritain's political thought was the most useful intellectual tool for "healing the schizophrenia" between liberals and conservatives, and creating a Latin American democratic thought without rejecting the Catholic tradition. These young politicians proposed an alternative political project to overcome the critical situation of unemployment, fear of reactionary *coups d'etat*, and the emergence of extreme nationalism. They felt that a new revolutionary political attitude should be established, to lead to the spiritual and moral transformation of their societies. The political structure would change afterwards.

The decade of the thirties was a defining political moment for Latin American intellectuals. For many secular anti-liberals, the ideological alternatives were Italian Fascism, German Nazism, or Russian Marxism. For Catholics, however, the choice seemed to be more difficult. The conservative majority leaned toward *criollas* forms of Fascism, influenced mainly by the Falangist movement of the Spaniard Jose Antonio Primo de Rivera. Those Catholics who wished for a democratic alternative without resorting to an ideological extreme saw Maritain's ideas as a possible third alternative.[7] The Brazilian thinker and writer Alceu Amoroso Lima interpreted Maritain's philosophy as a new dawn for Latin America. He saw Maritain as a "link between the elite and the people, in the sense of the revolutionary future, and also as a rallying-point between the past and the present, in the sense of a traditional equilibrium."[8]

Maritain visited Brazil in 1936 and spent a short time in the capitol, Rio

---

[7] "From Europe the influence of Jacques Maritain began to excite the dream of a "New Christendom" for Latin America, and particularly as a result of Maritain's philosophy, Christian Action emerged as a significant force. Christian Democracy was a reaction to the rightist propensity of the Spanish Fascist government of Francisco Franco, who came to power in 1936, the year when the Christian spirits divided in a germinal way, a division that would be accentuated during the time of the Second Vatican Council." Enrique Dussel, *A History of the Church in Latin America: Colonialism to Liberation (1492–1979)*, trans. and rev. Alan Neely (Grand Rapids, Michigan: Eerdmans, 1981), p. 107.

[8] Amoroso Lima, "Testimony: On the Influence of Maritain in Latin America," p. 75.

de Janeiro. There, he was introduced as a member of the Brazilian Academy of Letters by Amoroso Lima himself, and gave a lecture on "Action and Contemplation" at the Dom Vital Center; this later became a chapter of his book, *A Question of Conscience*. After visiting Brazil and Uruguay, Maritain went on to Argentina, arriving in Buenos Aires on August 14, 1936. Invited by the "Cursos de Cultura Catolica" and the journal *Sur*, he lectured for two months, until October 16, and was later named Honorary Professor. Some of those attending Maritain's lectures were nationalists identified with the Old Spanish Catholic tradition, who claimed to represent the most genuine form of Catholicism and the depository of the national conscience. But there were others who held Maritain's pro-democratic positions. Nevertheless, the philosopher was seen by most people, friends and foes alike, as the most important thinker of the Europan Thomistic renaissance.

But Rafael Caldera and Eduardo Frei represented the highest points of Maritain's influence in Latin America. Maritain was the intellectual mentor of both of these founding fathers of the Christian Democratic movement. A careful reading of their political writings indicates a clear "Maritainian" character. The apparent success of totalitarian ideas, Caldera explained, "confirmed that the democratic ideal is suffering a tremendous crisis in Europe. The fascist fashion and the Communist fashion try to divide the political camp, as the most valorous brigades of the new generations. At that moment, it seemed impossible to think in a democratic formula to solve problems."[9]

Despite this apparent impossibility, Caldera rejected any authoritarian solution. Unlike other Latin American thinkers, secular and Catholic, he favored a democratic formula based on a cultural—Christian—revival. In pursuing this, he immersed himself in the study of Latin American reality through the "lens" of Don Andres Bello.[10] The young Caldera looked at the

---

[9] "[L]a idea democratica esta padeciendo en Europa una crisis tremenda. La moda fascista y la moda communista tratan de dividirse el campo, como las brigadas mas aguerridas de las nuevas generaciones. En aquel momento parece imposible pensar en la formula democratica como la solucion de los problemas de esos paises y del mundo." Rafael Caldera, *Especificidad de la Democracia Cristiana* (Caracas, Venezuela: Editorial Dimensions, 1987), p. 45.

[10] The Venezuelan Andres Bello (1781–1865) was one of the most brilliant Latin American intellectuals during the first half of the nineteenth century. Heavily influenced by Jeremy Bentham's utilitarianism, he was the ambassador of Latin American pro-independence groups in London during the 1820's. His talents covered many fields. He was the author of the Chilean Civil Code and a study of classical Spanish grammar—*and* the founder of the University of Chile. For information about Bello, and the Chilean Generation of 1842, see Harold Eugene Davis, *Latin American Thought: An Historical Introduction* (Baton Rouge, Louisiana: Louisiana State University Press, 1972), pp. 80–87.

great Venezuelan thinker as a role model, that is, as a "synthesis man"—"a true spiritual epitome of Latin America"—a man who could join philosophy and political reality.[11] Bello's openness to the world, his ability to join universal ideas and regional political circumstances, appealed to Caldera. Bello believed in political freedom and self-determination; he did not reject European philosophical traditions.[12] "Imitate the spirit, but not the total product of European culture," he would often say. Caldera would follow this advice during his lifetime by being revolutionary without rejecting the value of tradition. His political ideas sprung from two poles; an inherited European Social Christianity which came from Jacques Maritain, as well as from Luigi Sturzo, L.J. Lebret, and Emmanuel Mounier, and the Latin American context.

Caldera believed that the impact of the Russian revolution on the Eurpoean continent, with the consequent expansion of communist ideas as well as the spread of Fascism in Italy and Germany, showed the impotence and moral emptiness of Western liberal democracies. It was on a trip to the United States, in New York, during the summer of 1942, that the young Caldera met Maritain for the first time. The French philosopher made a tremendous impact on the Venezuelan deputy. Caldera saw Maritain as a "coherent thinker who opened clear and definite paths in the middle of the thick fog."[13] Moreover, he was a political theorist for whom "the concept of democracy is not constrained within its formal mechanism but springs from the dignity of the human being and transforms people into an organic entity, true models of their own destiny."[14]

As the leader of the Christian Democratic Party, COPEI, Caldera was one of the builders of the Venezuelan democracy in the late fifties and early sixties, following General Perez Gimenez's dictatorship.[15] After his first

[11] Rafael Tomas Caldera, "Introduccion General," in *Ideario: La Democracia Cristiana en America Latina* (Barcelona: Ariel, 1970), p. 3.
[12] Rafael Caldera, *Derecho del Trabajo*, vol. 1, 2nd ed. (Buenos Aires: Editorial Ateneo, 1960), pp. 19–20.
[13] Caldera, "Personal Testimony," p. 13.
[14] Ibid.
[15] "In the 1958 Pact of Punto Fijo, AD [Democratic Action Party] and COPEI [Christian Democratic Party] were joined by the Democratic Republican Union (URD) of Juvito Villalba in pledging civic collaboration as the means of nurturing the fledgling democratic system. . . . Only the persuasiveness and moral authority of the two principal founders of the democratic system, [Romulo] Betancourt and [Rafael] Caldera, discouraged a military seizure of power." John D. Martz, "Venezuela, Colombia, and Ecuador," in Jan Kippers Black, ed., *Latin America, Its Problems and Its Promise: A Multidisciplinary Introduction* (Boulder, Colorado: Westview Press, 1991), pp. 438–39.

presidency of the Republic (1969–1973), Caldera, as an elder statesman, was chosen for a second time as president of the Venezuelan people in 1994.

The example of the Chilean President Eduardo Frei is no less striking. Frei met Maritain in Paris in 1934, and was at once impressed by Maritain's revolutionary idea of integral humanism. From then on, Frei became a faithful political echo of Maritain's teachings in Chile. After Frei became President of Chile in 1964, he was called, by Maritain himself, one of the few truly revolutionary men, and the best example of putting a Social Christian agenda into practice. In 1965, Maritain wrote that President Frei's tenure in Chile was,

> the first time in centuries that an authentic and real Christian politics has been established. . . . Personally I have very good friends in Latin America, especially in Uruguay (Esther de Caceres), and in Brazil (Amoroso Lima), but it is only in Chile that I see a positive accomplishment inspired by a profound political philosophy very conscious of itself, of its principles and its ends.[16]

The concept of a crisis of civilization was the starting point of Frei's political thought. The Chilean believed that any political crisis is basically a "spiritual" crisis, a breakdown of the human soul, a cultural and anthropological failure. This was Frei's assessment of the thirties. If there is a crisis of Western civilization today, the Chilean affirmed in 1934, it is because the idea of man behind this civilization has failed or his image has become obscure, tarnished, unintelligible.[17]

---

[16] "Es la primera vez, desde hace siglos, que se ve surgir en la historia, una politica autentica y realmente cristiana. . . . Personalmente tengo muy buenos amigos in America Latina, especialmente en Uruguay (Esther de Caceres) y en Brazil (Amoroso Lima), pero es unicamente en Chile donde veo una realizacion positiva procedente de una inspiracion sufficientemente profunda y animada por una filosofia politica muy consciente de si misma, de sus principios y de sus fines." The complete letter that Jacques Maritain wrote to Professor Gregorio Peces-Barba, in which he explains some aspects of his thought as well as his apparent influence in Latin America, can be found in Gregorio Peces-Barba, *Persona, Sociedad, Estado* (Madrid: Edicusa, 1972), pp. 312–16.

[17] It is interesting to notice that this diagnosis of Europe's decline was not only pointed out by Maritain and his Latin American disciples Frei and Caldera, but it was also a widespread assumption among European thinkers themselves. From *The Decline of the West* (1918) by the German Oswald Spengler, to *The Revolt of the Masses* (1930) by the Spaniard Jose Ortega y Gasset, the message was the same: liberal democracy was a system incapable of achieving socioeconomic progress and political stability. The various thinkers' proposed solutions, however, differed substantially.

The idea of man to which Frei referred was the Enlightenment anthropology. Frei believed the Enlightenment project had converted human beings into mere economic and material units with an illusive idea of progress. It was a naturalistic and, in some cases, materialistic anthropology. In his view, the separation of man from God brought about by the pride of Enlightenment thinkers led not only to a loss of religious sentiments but also to selfish individualism, social injustice, and ultimately totalitarianism.[18] Maritain analyzed the weaknesses of liberal democracy and the rise of totalitarianism in Europe as the results of a crisis of intelligence inaugurated by the modern anthropocentric humanism propagated by the Enlightenment. Frei did the same with Latin America.

Caldera and Frei's have been the most formidable attempts to create the theoretical basis for—and the practice of—a Latin American Social Christian thought grounded in a cultural and moral awakening. Their political philosophy begins with cultural ethics, nurtured by Christina principles, and builds up to the political and economic system.[19]

Another example has been Paraguay where Maritain's ideas influenced a generation of young intellectuals who established the Social Christian movement in 1960 and, five years later, transformed it into the Christian Democratic Party. One of the mentors of this generation, Professor Secundino Nunez, had been the most articulate Latin American exponent of Maritain's ideas. Through his lectures in the Catholic University in 1960, as well as through articles and books, he has labored to popularize Social Christian ideas for more than forty years. In 1989, after the overthrow of Alfredo Stroessner, Nunez became the first Christian Democratic presidential candidate in Paraguayan history. Today, Professor Nunez is a senator representing a third political force, the "National Encounter."[20]

Like the crisis of the new Latin American democracies today, the political crisis of liberal democracies in the thirties was a cultural crisis, a problem that had concrete ideological roots. It was rooted in the heritage of the nineteenth-century liberal positivism—so pervasive in countries such as Brazil, Paraguay and Venezuela—which had crippled the democratic spirit.

---

[18] Oscar Pinochet de la Barra, *El Pensamiento de Eduardo Frei* (Santiago de Chile: Editorial Aconcagua, 1983), p. 25.

[19] Caldera, *Ideario*, p. 3.

[20] The Paraguayan Christian Democratic Party was declared illegal by Stroessner's dictatorship. From its founding in 1965 until the fall of the dictatorship in 1989, the party was viewed as subversive and an "agent" of Moscow; its leaders were persecuted and many of them arrested, tortured and killed.

Out of this diagnosis Social Christian Maritainistas tried to rehumanize the world of Latin American politics by providing a reasonable moral foundation for democracy, a task that today again seems to be necessary.

One aspect is clearly reiterative: the real danger is cultural and moral, not economic. Although a democratic system strengthens political liberties and the free market economy, it will eventually fail if it neglects culture. That is why the goal of the 1930's Maritainistas must be revived today: to develop a sound personalistic political philosophy which can be an alternative both to authoritarianism (the politics of strong men: *caudillismo*) and to secular individualism. And the means to achieve this, I believe, is an educational process of the sort that Maritain hoped for: the conquest of individual and spiritual freedom; the liberation of the human person "through knowledge and wisdom, good will and love."[21]

Thus, an "integral education" which can reestablish the value of communities in order to rebuild intermediate institutions (family, unions) is the way to defend the social fabric from the aggressive adversary culture. Working against this humanistic approach will be the ideology that, as Maritain already warned in the early forties, considers "technical" education the only means to democratic progress. "The present war creates an immense need for technology and technical training," Maritain wrote in 1943, and then added, "it would be an irremediable mistake not to return to the primacy and integrity of liberal education." I would argue the same of today's new Latin American democracies. There, too, "the educational system and the state have to provide the future citizens not only with treasure of skills, knowledge, and wisdom—liberal education for all—but also with a genuine and reasoned-out belief in the common democratic charter, such as is required for the very unity of the body politic."[22]

This educational and cultural project must avoid two extreme attitudes: anti-intellectualism and a spirit of corporativism. First, the tendency toward anti-intellectualism, which has clear populist overtones, is suspicious of any educational reform which may enhance the perfection of intellectual and ethical virtues. It assumes that any education in the virtues is aristocratic rather than democratic, seeking only to establish the government of a tiny elite. Secondly, the spirit of corporativism, which has long been part of Latin American culture, is dangerous because it dismisses any effort at personal growth as individualistic and selfish.

---

[21] Jacques Maritain, *Education at the Crossroads* (New Haven, Connecticut: Yale University Press, 1943), p. 11.

[22] Jacques Maritain, *Man and the State* (Chicago: The University of Chicago Press, 1951), p. 120.

The historical evolution of the New Christendom in Latin America passed through five main stages between 1936 and 1968. First came the moment of the intellectual formation of the leaders. Young Catholics were taught about the social principles of the Catholic Teachings, and how to put these principles into practice. That was the task, primarily, of Catholic Action. Then, after these young men became social activists, they abandoned Catholic Action and joined political parties, generally conservative ones, which were believed to be the only ones which could provide a truly Catholic political view. Next, the Social Christian views of these leaders collided with the old, conservative Catholic practices. They realized that these parties were obsolete in the changing times, and decided to establish new political institutions. Thus, in the following stage, the Social Christian leaders founded Christian Democratic parties, and tried to become political players in each country. Some of them accomplished their dream, and seized political power. And, finally, due to diverse circumstances, internal and external, these Christian Democratic parties started losing influence, and the New Christendom as a model went into decline. Do we have to start all over again?

I believe that a renewed Christian politics in the upcoming third millennium should not be "official" and "clerical." This model of Christian political groups, whether they are formed by Christian Democratic political parties or by liberationist theological groups, is exhausted. Instead, I would rather support the participation of individual Christians in the public arena. This approach would allow Christian values to be introduced within different political parties regardless of their Christian "confessionality." Today, even political parties of Christian inspiration in Latin America have become prisoners of corruption and ambition, combatants in a Machiavellian struggle for power—something that Maritain totally rejected. The only way to change this "style" is to replace the "power politics" cultural climate that made it possible.

As Maritain pointed out, in this reconstruction of the social fabric, three components will be unavoidable: the recreation of a sound Christian humanistic philosophy, the building of a renewed Christendom, democratic and pluralistic, and the establishment of a new educational commonwealth. After the restless political experimentation of the 1960's and the harsh and inhumane politics of the 1970's, these new democracies need to find a firm foundation: the rediscovery of ancient truths, the reassertion of fundamental values, and, above all, the redefinition of what is good and what is evil, in absolute and not merely relative terms. In this task, Maritain's Christian humanism may provide a viable political alternative.

Truth Values and Cultural Pluralism

Charles R. Dechert

The past 50 years have witnessed a revolution in human affairs, a "change of phase" inaugurating a global community unprecedented in numbers and extent, literally encompassing all men and the earth's entire surface. There is a sense of expectation, the emergence of a global culture and society to be characterized by new interaction patterns that will replace the interstate system created at Westphalia and the political and ideological "cold war" following World War II that ended with the collapse of Leninism, a temporary American global hegemony and widespread weakening of the older mechanisms of social control.

Historically the major cultures and their attendant civilizations have largely been tied to the shared *Weltanschauung* and values provided by a shared religion. Some element of the transcendent, a reality beyond and giving meaning to sensory perception and experience, has been called upon to validate, authenticate, and ultimately to sanction human institutions and human behavior (both individual and corporate). In more primitive societies the civic and religious cultures fuse; the gods of the vanquished are destroyed or incorporated into the victor's pantheon. Defeated Israel's continued devotion to a transcendent yet personal God, Yahweh, marked a universalization of the notion of deity and provided a basis for continued group identity in exile—and ultimately in diaspora while this universalized, transcendent yet personal God became the foundation of the societies emerging from Greco-Roman, Syrian and Irano-Arabic antecedents. The Indic-Buddhist, Sinic, and pre-Columbian American societies developed identifiable civilizations whose integrity was assured for millennia by the relative physical, intellectual and spiritual isolation of these major cultural components of the human family.

Five hundred years ago, with maritime technology, industrial production, printing, and the breakup of Western Christendom there emerged the forces leading to the ecumenical society, the "one world" coming into being in our lifetime. Sheer power, the ability effectively to assert directed will, emerged in Western Europe in new combinations that submerged the Western Hemisphere and over the centuries imposed a colonial hegemony over Africa, the Middle East, Asia, and the Pacific. The centralized, rationalized, bureaucratic state, disciplined military forces with a new weapons technology and logistic support, commerce, banking and credit—all combined to create the systemic interdependencies that would result in global unity. The products, technologies and institutions of Western society proved extremely attractive; they not only compelled, they seduced. Building upon the systematized knowledge of antiquity, Western Christendom institutionalized the preservation, extension and diffusion of learning in the cathedral schools, in monastic and courtly libraries, and above all in the universities with faculties dedicated to Medicine, Law, Theology, the Liberal Arts and Natural Philosophy. Experimental methods took root, particularly in the knowledge based craft guilds (including the fine arts), mining and civil engineering. These eventually also found a home in the modern university.

Knowledge and skill complemented and enhanced the dynamism of modernity, and were made self-aware, systematized and taught in the universities. With the development of institutionalized research in the nineteenth century, the university became the nodal institution of modernity and has proved universally attractive. With such disciplines as Cultural Anthropology and the Sociology of Knowledge, culture, *Weltanschauungen*, values and science itself have now become objects of systematic knowledge; historical cultures become the message (or part of the message) of the new ecumenical culture.

The curriculum and objects of knowledge and instruction vary little from country to country in modern universities. They vary least in the physical sciences, life sciences, and mathematics. They vary most in the social sciences and humanities where the values and political, ideological, cultural and religious commitments of nations and sponsoring groups receive expression and even sponsorship. But even in these disciplines the consensually-accepted critical approaches and methodologies are largely those developed in the West during the past five hundred years.

In brief a loosely unified global culture has emerged, secular and scientific in orientation, whose characteristic institution is the modern university. This culture did not arise in a vacuum; political, cultural, attitudinal, technological, commercial and military factors combined over the centuries to bring about a compression and coerced interaction of nations and cultures, compelling mutual adjustive and adaptive responses. First it should be noted that this global culture rises out of the West, Europe and its cultural dependencies. It arises out of a tradition of classical, Greco-Roman civilization including technologies, arts and literature, law, war, religion, and a humanistic formation. Secondly, it has begun to come to maturity at the ending of an epoch characterized by the absolute, omnicompetent state as a quasi-divinity capable of the social construction of reality through the identification, formation and instrumentalization of its most intelligent and creative minds. Let me elaborate.

Prior to the Enlightenment political authorities were largely concerned with the material bases of state power: population, territory, institutionalized agricultural and industrial productivity, mercantilist controls designed to keep foreign trade in balance or produce an export surplus paid for in bullion. The intellectual dimension of state power was largely associated in Europe with civil law and with the national churches, Protestant or Catholic, whose parish organization (especially in rural areas) provided a convenient geographic base for local government and care for the orphan, the aged and the incompetent. Cujus regio, ejus religio assured a high degree of cultural and moral consensus in the vast bulk of the population. Elite intellectuality was focused in the universities, academies (like those of the Crusca or the Lincei) and newly formed royal academies of the Fine Arts and of the Sciences, and in technical schools (e.g. des Ponts et Chaussees) for industrial, civil and military engineering knowledge and skills that had outgrown the moribund guild-apprentice structure and had not yet been accepted into the rarefied intellectual atmosphere of the older universities.

Illuminism arose as a secular alternative to religion; the *philosophes*, basing themselves both on the new empirical science and the pseudo-scientific hermeticism and gnosticism re-emergent in the Renaissance, had a strong appeal to a literate, monied "new class" of professionals (lawyers, government administrators, etc.), successful and socially aspiring commercial farmers, bankers, merchants and manufacturers (and their wives), as well as survivors of the older feudal aristocracy in their new roles as leisured military officers, higher clergy and rentiers/courtiers. The Enlightenment appeal to an ethic of cosmopolitan compassion and openness, the repudiation of tyranny and injustice, of superstition and bigotry, of vulgar piety, and any religious or secular interference with freedom of expression produced the political tidal wave of the French Revolution and the modern national state as the ultimate arbiter of good and evil, truth and falsity, the well-being or misery, the life and death of its citizens. It has been suggested

that even professors and the content of higher studies in Philosophy and
Religion were often given preference in state universities (e.g. in Prussia)
as instruments of state policy and a national *Kultur*.

Based universally on classical studies, a shared foundation in the classical canon, nineteenth-century European and Anglo-American institutions of
higher learning possessed a compatible *forma mentalis* as the foundation of
literary and critical research, the study of history and the fine arts and the
elaboration of philosophical issues. By the end of the nineteenth century
the physical and life sciences had evolved their basic emphases and institutional structures, including an open-endedness and willingness to accept
revolutionary scientific paradigm shifts. In part the modern sciences grew
out of the speculative natural philosophy of the late Middle Ages, seeking
descriptive concepts and models that might be related to real-world observations. Late medieval builders found their pre-scientific empirical approaches to structural design inadequate to the complexities of buildings
like the Milan cathedral. University trained scholars like Alberti learned to
work with artists and artisans who, in turn, came to feel comfortable with
the contributions of geometry and natural philosophy. Research facilities
and laboratories on the Italian, English and German models were coupled
with the German university seminar system institutionalizing the mono-
graphic original research contribution prepared under a master's tutelage
and critically reviewed to become the professional foundation of a higher
scientific and university career.

Global consensus at the university level on the models, interpretations
and methods of the sciences raises the issue of those disciplines less
amenable to consensus based on quantification, empirical observation and
logical demonstration. What of philosophy and theology, literature and the
arts, the learned and serving professions in such areas as medicine, law, engineering and architecture? To the extent that these rest in "hard science"
there is a consensus in such areas as medicine and engineering. Much of the
world has relied on English or continental European precedents for their
legal codes while the Universal Declaration of Human Rights continues to
reflect some degree of global consensus.

In some sense the philosophic enterprise parallels the scientific. It, too,
is directed at modeling reality, identifying modes of being, entities, elements, categories and relations in the universe as knowing and known. The
level of abstraction in these models is less proximate; the terms normally
do not have an immediate, direct and measurable existential correlate, and
proof is largely tested by coherence, existential consequences for men
(singly, in groups, as a species and as one of an actual or possible family of

moral entities that can know and choose in self-awareness and other-awareness), and not least by their compatibility with the truth of individual and culturally-shared experiences and the findings of the empirical sciences. One area of contact between the empirical sciences and philosophy can be found in contemporary General Systems Theory and Cybernetics with their emphases on analogy, hierarchy and order, decision making, and information. Often the overall philosophic enterprise seems kaleidoscopic as individual thinkers and schools represent diverse patterns of perceived significance and relevance, frequently complementary, always less than comprehensive. It is a truism that philosophers are more likely to be correct in what they affirm than in what they deny.

In this view there is, perhaps, a *philosophia perennis* that is cumulative and like the sciences grows by accretion and correction. Its method is critical; its counters conceptual; its correlates the realities of mind and experience viewed as objects to be known and when in correspondence with perceived externality, correspondent to that objectively apprehended (or, for internal experience, consciously apprehended as object). Owing to the development of the natural, mathematical, and social (positive) sciences what were once unresolved (perhaps irresoluble) philosophical issues are now the subjects of consensual accord. The revolution of the earth and its circuit around the sun were finally demonstrated in the last century. Aristotle's hylomorphic universe is the contemporary universe of matter-energy and information made measurable by the insight of Shannon. Philosophically irresoluble issues about the eternity of the material universe are at least partially answered by the "big bang" with which time, space and matter-energy as we know it began.

In many respects theology, too, is amenable to consideration in terms of "model building," the selection of significant concepts representing entities, events and relationships that form a logically coherent and reasonable symmetrical system that purports to reflect "reality" in certain humanly significant, indeed, existentially crucial dimensions needed by most men to make sense of the human experience, to motivate, to govern moral decision-making, to account for the reality and experience of evil and malice, the sense of sin and also of experienced transcendence, creativity, altruism, beauty, goodness and grace in all of its many meanings. Constructs are created that would give meaning to life, promise immortality, assure a supernal order of justice, motivate, inspire, give meaning to human life and history.

Clearly the figurative arts model the world; representative painting and sculpture abstract, reflect, idealize what is seen by men—reproduce the form and semblance of what is. The surreal associates forms disassociated in reality yet meaningfully related and so creates another order of perception while the abstract arts like music, architecture, expressionist painting, sculpture and cinema make an appeal in depth to some "sense of order" deeply imbedded in the neural structure of the percipient creative artist and percipient subject mutually attuned. To create is to make new patterns of order. To know is to apprehend patterns of order in the circumambient universe. Art and science are our truly human activities and intimately associated with appreciation, affective response and a shared mutuality reflecting a culture and broadly human solidarity.

As one looks at the universe of knowledge beyond the properly scientific as categorized by the National Science Foundation, one is struck by the range of skills taught in our universities: knowledge and practice in the making of things, art as the *recta ratio factibilium*. Beyond that the curriculum is dedicated to the truly human activities implied in the terms loving, serving, appreciating. Educators, nurses, physicians, counsellors, vocational guides obviously require a formation designed to maximize their skills and opportunities for professional service. So do foresters and peace officers, agronomists and engineers—and all engaged in constructive human activity.

Although inherently an elite institution where cognitive skills (unequally distributed) are valued, nurtured and constructively focused, all benefit from the university as the principal institutional conserver, promulgator, developer and critic of the cumulative scientific and cultural heritage of mankind in all its manifestations. It is appropriate that within this emerging noösphere various nations and peoples, institutions and interests, civilizations and cultures find a special reflection in their own university-level institutions, open to and in dialogue with the global intellectual community. The core intellectual values of critical objectivity, dedication to truth, and a correlative act of faith in the "givenness," persistence in existence, coherence, integrity and identity of the real reflected in cognition would appear to underly this enterprise.

Commercially or politically inspired distortions of fact or of canonical texts or works of art pose real and continuing challenges to the conscience and consciousness of civilization. Only by having multiple loci and foci of that consciousness in an institutionally plural ecumenical community can we be reasonably assured that we shall not revert to a "dark ages," or worse, a malevolent deconstruction into permanent intellectual and cultural chaos—but rather continue in the incremental construction of a *cultura perennis* that encompasses and enhances the sum of human achievement in art and science, mutuality and appreciation.

The development of the university as the characteristic institution of the emerging global culture has been very much advanced and hastened by the ever increasing ease and speed of communications.Books and learned journals, conferences, symposia and professional meetings—all in a forum of intellectual transparency, subject to critical review, have created a noösphere with a definable but ever changing (in detail) canonical structure of consensually-accepted sources, methods and conclusions. The paradigmatic structure of each discipline and subdiscipline is subject at every level of generality to critical review and modification as evidence accumulates, anomalies are apprehended, logical flaws are discovered, predictions are verified or proven false.

It must be recognized that this intellectual universe is amazingly strong yet possessed of certain limitations and some fragility. Its universality results, in part, not only from an assent to the truths and truth-values affirmed but from its origin (now to some degree transcended) in the Western European university tradition and its principal expression in the great culture languages: Italian, Spanish, French, German, Russian, and especially English—all possessed of analogous structures and inter-translatable meanings.

Political power in any given country or locality may assert itself in educational curricula, ideological emphases, selection of "relevant" facts, models and interpretations—to the extent such "power" controls cultural, scientific and educational institutions and resources. The relativization of the "canon," deconstruction of texts, the introduction of ascriptive critical norms based on ethnicity, revisionist views of social history and cultural institutions—all of these leave the humanities and social sciences a global battleground. Every modern state since the eighteenth century has viewed education as the catalyst of social control; in France the Ecole Normale Superieure was viewed as the very soul of a new consciousness. Totalitarian mass cultures of the twentieth century tried to create "new men" altruistically dedicated to the community whether defined by national, racial or class/functional categories; American liberals dedicate themselves to an ideology of equality and its enforced institutionalization.

In literature, the humanities and the fine arts state subsidies, direct and indirect, interact with a market-oriented *Zeitgeist* pushed by critics, galleries and connoisseurs, hype and media attention in a high stakes game of prestige, public and private funding, tax deductions, jobs and influence.

It is in the "soft" disciplines that the modern university plays a particular role as critic and sifter of orthodoxies. In Italy in the 1930s, courses were taught in Mistica Fascista—and laid aside in 1944–45. What has become of Dialectical Materialism in Eastern Europe? In American secular universities religious studies, once taught by professors profoundly committed to their faith, have become objects of study by "detached" scholars. The university itself becomes the meeting ground and fighting platform of religious, political, cultural and ideological currents—some of which make an exclusive, proprietary claim to legitimacy. This is clearly the case now with "political correctness" in the United States, reflecting a secular humanist orientation alert to minority claims, environmental issues, and characterized by moral relativism and an emphasis on the omnicompetent welfare state.

A certain ethnocentricity may be expected and is appropriate to the various national universities and university systems while institutions under private group and/or religious sponsorship may be expected to sustain or at least not overtly counter the commitments and institutional interests of their sponsors. The critical climate, openness to the historical success or failure of policies and institutions, and continuing dialogue between and among intellectuals and institutions globally provide the conditions for an emerging global debate and developing commitments (individual and institutional) to visions of the good and true.

But even in the "hard," empirically-based sciences it would be naive to ignore the role of the modern state in determining the research emphases, focus, consequences and applications of scientific knowledge—in mathematics and the physical sciences, in the life sciences, the social and behavioral sciences, in communications and applied science. World War II brought "big science" to all the major belligerents, especially the United States, Britain and Germany: the Manhattan Project to make nuclear weapons, M.I.T.'s Radiation Laboratory for radar, institutional research on gas turbines and reactor engines, supersonic aircraft and rockets, advanced computing machinery both digital and analog, and many other fields. Chemistry was organized to create new materials ranging from synthetic rubber to a vast array of new plastics, silicones, coatings and lubricants. The social and behavioral sciences were mobilized in laboratories for military human factors research to help identify perceptual and motor skills, select and train aircrews and ground personnel, for intelligence research and the conduct of special operations by OSS, to track domestic and foreign opinion and identify psychological and cultural strengths and vulnerabilities whose exploitation by artfully designed communications, tactical and strategic, might speed victory. Part of the competitive advantage possessed by the "free world" both before and after World War II lay in the synergic relation between government and private-industry-exploitable science and engineering, the social and behavioral sciences, the commercial exploitation of art through such methods as Motivational Research.

This confidence in science, the momentum of its wartime successes and institutions, the domestic employment possibilities inherent in the Promethean vision of "Science the Endless Frontier," the emergence of the "cold war" and a global adversarial system, the vast enlargement of the university-trained population in America through the GI Bill of Rights—all in some way contributed to the emerging global intellectual community. Greater ease of communication and transport, tourism, and increasing homogenization of global popular culture based on movies, syndicated American TV and popular music, the rise of English as *the* dominant culture language in part as a result of the conscious cultural proselytization through U.S. military and developmental assistance, educational and cultural exchange programs, increasingly dense international business relations, American sponsored international and transnational corporate and associational groupings—all contributed to and helped define the focus and content of the emergent ecumenical culture.

In the Socialist/Communist societies emerging from more or less violent class-based revolutions or from Soviet takeover, a conscious effort was made to deprive the offspring of former elite elements of the university formation producing the communications and symbol-management skills characteristic of modern social and political leadership. Even cognitively-gifted youth of incorrect class provenance were relegated to the acquisition of productive technical skills while the increasingly university- trained "New Class" identified by Djilas assumed the managerial and symbol-manipulative elite status of their Anglo-American and Western European "bourgeois" counterparts.

For both Marxist and liberal intellectuals the state is the preferred instrument of self-formation-and-affirmation, for the realization of the will to power: directly through control of ministries, planning agencies, state corporations, public media, education, regulatory agencies—particularly in the all-encompassing realm of environmental controls. Secondly, even when private capital predominates, control of that capital is largely relegated to a new stratum of professionals: money managers, mutual fund directors, pension fund controllers, union investors, insurance and annuity fund trustees, all university trained and, as A. A. Berle put it, exercising "power without property." Members of this new class are often capable of protecting themselves and their interest by externalizing the costs of their errors of judgment (to put the matter in the best light) both tactical and strategic. American Savings and Loan organizations unload some $500 billion in bad loans on to the U.S. Treasury and ultimately the taxpayer; Mexican money managers cover the losses resulting from overvaluation of the peso by arbitrarily dropping the exchange rate and persuading U.S. and international banking authorities to underwrite their treasury bonds. Few countries can resist the populist appeal of massive redistribution to be covered by devalued currency printed by some future government.

In practice clever symbolic load-shifting to those who are productive but weak, to future generations, or to other social groups seems to assure these elite elements privileged access to wealth, power and well-being indefinitely. So-called "neocolonialism" in the "free world" was but a reflection of the symbol games played by Gosplan, the Communist party elites and the entrenched bureaucracies of the socialist world.

The failure of Peronism, the collapse of the Axis Powers in World War II, the implosion of Communism in Eastern Europe all suggest that reality will have the last word. If the cynical manipulation of symbols by a cognitive elite is crucial to modern politics, the persistent and free expression of the university-based "culture of critical discourse" is necessary to restore contact with reality, from within or from outside any given political system.

The principal challenges to the emerging global culture lie in the intellectuals' capacity to define social situations, create crises, and propose solutions. In theory, at least, out of the infinitude of events characterizing any social process any set may be extracted and mentally associated to produce a "model" of the social process or historical period. This is the *jeu d'esprit* of Umberto Eco's *Foucault's Pendulum*. And precisely this lies at the basis of historical revisionism, the rewriting of the past by each generation, each group, each interest to reflect the outlook and values of the author/scholar/critic. Since only the literate, the cognitively capable and trained, can perform this task, history must inevitably reflect not so much an economic elite as a cognitive elite. These have often been combined. To some degree winners (or their flacks) write history.

Increasingly the liquidation or impairment of an adversary's capacity for effective decision-making has become characteristic of intergroup conflict. Tampering with or sabotage of databases and critical communications, disinformation, selective deletion or impairment (temporary or permanent) of decision-makers or their critical support structures, selective impairment or destruction of command and control facilities—become instruments of intergroup conflict. And these critical elements in cultural, educational and scientific institutions are also subject to interference, control or sabotage. One recalls the battle for control of the Newspaper Guild in the late 1940's.

Every one in academia has witnessed discrediting operations aimed at academic administrators or faculty members with the "wrong ideas." And who has not been "victimized" (or perhaps "helped") on occasion by the "down" computer, the delayed mail delivery or the misplaced memo?

To my mind a real danger lies in the widespread, increasingly universal early identification of very high ability persons and the possibility of their "acquisition" and formation (or perversion) by those having resources and access—a situation envisaged by John Hersey in his book *The Child Buyer*. Cognitive data is now often combined with psychometric data on personality, interests and aptitude. Centralized talent databases such as that of the Educational Testing Service in Princeton, coupled with a recognition of talent as a strategic resource and the will and ability to use it for cultural, scientific, and political ends must present a great temptation to public authorities and/or those having privileged access to such information. Only self-conscious communities, benevolent with a sense of the common good, aware of their ethnic and cultural identities will be able to cope with this challenge. They must remain mindful of the unspoken contractual responsibilities linking the generations, be willing to accept relative deprivation, and intent to preserve some degree of moral autonomy through appropriate system boundary controls including even military defense when required.

The principal challenges to the emerging global culture are essentially political. The intellectual and institutional commitment to truth may be subordinated to interest or the will to power. In practice this may range from the selection or preferment of intellectual incompetents to avoid competition to the increasingly costly academico-political rationalization of failed economic and social policies for reasons of party and ideology. Limited cultural, religious or ethnic loyalties may affirm an unwarranted universality. The localized and ever-changing deconstruction and reconstruction of the symbolic universe could bring about a Babel of idiosyncratic "meanings" that partition the emerging, ecumenical culture of increasingly shared meanings, paradigmatic structures, empirically verifiable models describing or explaining aspects of the physical, social and mental universes. This emerging shared vision, in turn, enhances the capacity for synergetic intellectual effort at the global level extending human knowledge, understanding and capacity to cope through constructive action possibilities ranging from improved housing and nutrition for the bulk of men to the ever more profound investigation of the cosmos.

This suggests that a multiplication of institutionally independent centers of scientific and cultural achievement is desirable. In multiplicity there is an enhanced capacity for survival and exercising the critical function essential to both the sciences and humanistic studies. As supranational political and economic communities emerge there is increasing emphasis on the principle of subsidiarity, relegating to smaller communities and functional, specialized groupings (whether economic or cultural) a decision-making autonomy within the realm of their own competencies. In this context the ideal of the free university takes on ever greater significance.

In a period of superpower confrontation backed by weapons of mass destruction, cataclysmic threats gave substance to the vision of moral and intellectual nihilism, a wiping clean of the cultural slate presumably reflecting millennia of human oppression. In the 1950's I recommended USIA's providing a copy of the contents of the Library of Congress in microform to each country of the world; not only to make that cultural and intellectual resource more generally available but to preclude what seemed the imminent cultural tragedy prefigured by the destruction of the Library of Alexandria, nuclear destruction of the world's major libraries and museums.

While avoiding the pseudo-universalization of the parochial, it behooves identifiable groups, nations and localities, functional groupings, religious and cultural bodies to study and analyze themselves, their characteristics, and their past to the degree possible and in context. The conservation and affirmation of all that is valid and constructive in human experience is to advance civilization, the essential unity and integrity of the species as a manifestation of this creature's creative consciousness in this little corner of the universe.

Inevitably conflicting visions emerge and seek to affirm themselves. Among the basic values of the university are certain core elements that can help assure a reasonably serene future to the emerging ecumenical culture. First, a concern for truth—in terms not only of the instrumental effectiveness and coherence of models of reality, but also their adequacy to the objective situation they would portray. Second, a continued critical review and reassessment of the content, interpretation and evaluation of the body of human knowledge. Third, a desire for and systematic expansion of the range of knowing and valuing. Last, an atmosphere of civility in which both moral and physical violence are eschewed, where the *disinterested* pursuit of truth is encouraged by providing an assured tenor of life to those engaged in it. Perhaps the greatest threat to this emerging global culture is its politicization as a source of power, and the use of force, fraud, moral coercion, blackmail and deprivation—all the forms of persecution—to assure intellectual and moral conformity to whatever is deemed true and good this year in this place by this particular authority.

Contributors

BENEDICT M. ASHLEY, O.P. is Professor Emeritus at the Aquinas Institute of Theology, St. Louis, Missouri. He is a member of the American Catholic Philosophical Association, the Catholic Theological Society, and the American Maritain Association. He has published *Theologies of the Body: Humanist and Christian* (1985), *Spiritual Direction in the Dominican Tradition* (1995), *Justice in the Church: Gender and Participation* (1996), and with Kevin O'Rourke, *Ethics of Health Care* (2nd ed., 1994).

JOHN M. PALMS has served as president of the University of South Carolina since March 1991. He has authored more than one hundred scholarly publications, focusing his scientific work on low-energy basic atomic and nuclear physics and the effects of radiation on humans and the environment. For twenty-three years he served as the Charles Howard Chandler Professor of Physics and as an administrator at Emory University. While there he received Emory's highest award for leadership and service, the Thomas Jefferson Award.

HERBERT I. LONDON is John M. Olin Professor of Humanities at New York University, President of the Hudson Institute, and fomer Dean of the Gallatin Division of New York University. He is a prolific author, internationally recognized scholar, nationally syndicated columnist, radio and television personality, and a leading political force in New York State, where he previously ran for governor.

ALICE RAMOS holds a Ph.D. in French literature from New York University and a Ph.D. in Philosophy from the University of Navarre in Pamplona, Spain. She has published in the areas of semiotics, Thomistic metaphysics, Kantian ethical theology, MacIntyre's ethical inquiry, and Karol Wojtyla-John Paul II's Christian anthropology. She is presently working on a project in Aquinas and the transcendentals, and she is also editing the vol-

271

ume of papers presented at the 1997 Maritain conference on "Maritain and the Arts."

FRANCIS SLADE is Emeritus Professor of Philosophy at St. Francis College, Brooklyn, New York, where he was chairman of the department for many years.

DONALD DEMARCO is Professor of Philosophy at the University of St. Jerome's College in Waterloo, Ontario. He is the author of twelve books, including *Biotechnology and the Assault on Parenthood* and *The Heart of Virtue*. He is an Associate Editor of *Child and Family Quarterly* and an advisor editor for *Social Justice Review*. An extensive lecturer, he also has numerous publications in a variety of scholarly journals.

CURTIS L. HANCOCK is Professor of Philosophy at Rockhurst College, Kansas City, Missouri. He is co-author of *How Should I Live?*, a book on ethics, and co-editor of *Freedom, Virtue, and the Common Good*, a book on political philosophy also produced by the American Maritain Association. He is currently president of that association. He has published articles on Plotinus and Maritain and on topics pertaining to political philosophy and ethics.

GREGORY J. KERR is Assistant Professor of Philosophy at Allentown College of St. Francis de Sales in Center Valley, Pennsylvania. He is editor of *The Maritain Notebook*, the newsletter of the American Maritain Association, and has written chronicles of past meetings of the AMA for both *Notes et Documents* and *Vera Lex*.

ROBERT J. MCLAUGHLIN, Ph.D. Toronto, is currently Emeritus Professor of Philosophy at St. John Fisher College, Rochester, New York. He has written before on Jacques Maritain's philosophy as well as on various topics connected with ancient and medieval philosophy.

FR. ROBERT LAUDER is Professor of Philosophy at St. John's University in New York. He is the author of ten books. His articles on film and theater have appeared in the *Times*, *Commonweal* and *America*.

JAMES V. SCHALL, S.J. is Professor of Government at Georgetown University. He has taught in the Gregorian University in Rome and at the University of San Francisco. He has written over sixteen books, among which are *Another Sort of Learning, Reason, Revolution and the Foundations of Political Philosophy*, and *Redeeming the Time*.

GREGORY M. REICHBERG has taught at The Catholic University of America and Fordham University. where he is presently Associate Professor of Philosophy. After predoctoral studies in France at the Université de Toulouse and The Centre Indépendent de Recherche Philosophique, he received his Ph.D. in Philosophy from Emory University in 1990. He has published articles in the ethics of knowing, philosophical issues in theology, and the philosophy of science.

JOSEPH W. KOTERSKI, S.J. is Associate Professor of Philosophy at Fordham University. He also serves as editor-in-chief of *International Philosophical Quarterly* and Director of the M.A. Program in Philosophical Resources for Jesuits at Fordham.

FATHER ROMANUS CESSARIO, a Dominican priest of the New York Province, is currently Professor of Systematic Theology at St. John's Seminary in Brighton, Massachusetts. After studies in philosophy and theology within the Dominican Order, he taught at Providence College in Rhode Island, and later completed his doctoral studies at the University of Fribourg in Switzerland. In addition to that degree he holds the M.A. and STL. For more than fifteen years he taught at the Dominican House of Studies in Washington, D.C. He is the author of ten books and many articles, which include special studies in Thomism. Father Cessario lectures widely in the United States and Europe. He presently serves as general editor of a five-volume series in moral theology at The Catholic University of America.

PETER A. REDPATH is Professor of Philosophy at St. John's University. He is editor of the Studies in the History of Western Philosophy and deputy executive editor of the Value Inquiry Book Series for Editions Rodopi, B.V. He is also author of seven books, the most recent of which is entitled *Masquerade of the Dream Walkers: Prophetic Theology from the Cartesians to Hegel*. He is former Vice President of the American Maritain Association.

DANIEL MCINERNY is Assistant Professor of Philosophy at the University of St. Thomas/Center for Thomistic Studies in Houston, Texas. He received his Ph.D. in 1994 from The Catholic University of America. He works primarily in ethics, with a concentration on themes Aristotelian and Thomistic. He has also published on Aristotle's psychology and scientific method.

ERNEST S. PIERUCCI practices corporate law in San Francisco, California. He is a member of the Board of Visitors of the Columbus School of Law of The Catholic University of America and has served on the Board of Trustee of St. Mary's College of California. Mr. Pierucci has taught business law, philosophy of law and the Collegiate Seminar (Great Books Program) at St. Mary's College of California. He has lectured and published internationally on the relationship among liberal arts, business education, and Catholic social thought.

MICHAEL W. STRASSER received his Ph.D. from Toronto in 1963, where he wrote on St. Thomas's critique of Platonism in the *Liber de Causis*. He is Emeritus Professor of Philosophy at Duquense University. He was chairman of that department during the 1982-83 academic year. In 1984 he was Visiting Professor of Philosophy at the University of Nigeria. He has published several articles concerning themes at the intersection of metaphysics and the liberal arts.

WALTER RAUBICHECK is Professor of English at Pace University in New York. He has published a number of articles on film, detective fiction, and American literature. He has also written about Jacques Maritain's aesthetics.

HENK E.S. WOLDRING studied sociology and philosophy at the state university in Groningen, the Free University in Amsterdam, and the Goethe University in Frankfurt, Germany. He is Professor of Political Philosophy at the Free University in Amsterdam. In 1990-91 he was Visiting Professor at the University of Notre Dame. He has published several books in Dutch on the political philosophy of the Christian Democratic movement in Europe. In 1987 he published *Karl Mannheim: The Development of His Thought* (St. Martin's Press).

JEROME MERIC PESSAGNO received his Ph.D. from Yale in Islamic Studies and Arabic Language, specializing in philosophy and theology. He has lectured widely throughout Europe, including the Sorbonne. He has published numerous articles in philosophy and Islam.

MARIO RAMOS-REYES is Assistant Professor in the School of Law and Philosophy at the Catholic University of Asuncion, Paraguay. He received his J.D. from the same institution in 1981 and his M.A. and Ph.D. from the University of Kansas in 1996. Since 1990 he has worked on the history of

Christian political thought and Latin American philosophy. His latest book is *Filosofia y Pensamiento Democratico* (Catholic University of Asuncion Press, 1998). He has also published on Thomism and liberation theology and John Paul II's social thought. Currently, Professor Ramos-Reyes is Consul General of the Republic of Paraguay to the State of Kansas.

CHARLES DECHERT received his doctorate from The Catholic University of America in 1952 with a dissertation on the social and political thought of Thomas More. After work in the social and behavioral sciences within the defense establishment he taught at the International University of Social Studies, Rome, 1957-1959, Purdue University 1959-1967, and The Catholic University of America 1967-present. He has published *Ente Nazionale Idrocarburi: Profile of a State Corporation*, *The Social Impact of Cybernetics*, *Sistemi-Paradigmi-Societa*, plus numerous book chapters and articles in such journals as *International Philosophical Quarterly*, *La Civiltà Cattolica*, *Orbis*, and *Contemporary Philosophy*.

Index